World Cup '70

World Cup '70

written and edited by
HUGH McILVANNEY
and
ARTHUR HOPCRAFT

With contributions also from
JOHN RAFFERTY AND RONALD ATKIN

EYRE & SPOTTISWOODE · LONDON

First published 1970
© *1970 Eyre & Spottiswoode (Publishers) Ltd*
Printed in Great Britain
for Eyre & Spottiswoode (Publishers) Ltd
11 New Fetter Lane, London EC4
by Billing & Sons Limited, Guildford and London

SBN 413 27720 8

Contents

Illustrations

A map showing the position of the five centres where Group matches were played, and the groupings, is to be found on page 38

Preface

This book bears certain obvious similarities to its predecessor, *World Cup '66*, not least the fact that it is the work of *The Observer*'s team of reporters. Four years ago the World Cup was played in England in a context that was immediately familiar to most of the people who were likely to read our account. We did not feel any need to spill a great many words in efforts to evoke the atmosphere of Liverpool or Sunderland (though no one can deny that they have pretty remarkable atmospheres). Equally, in 1966 the principal theme of the tournament was bound to be England's challenge and naturally we concentrated on following it through to its successful conclusion.

In 1970 the situation was vastly different, and not merely because the smell in the nostrils was tortillas rather than fish and chips. Mexico's problems of heat and altitude were widely appreciated. It is far more difficult to convey how the sheer exoticism of the place built up a physical pressure. Yet an attempt to do so had to be one of our first priorities. And in Mexico England could not possibly start as favourites, could not reasonably be expected to be the central figures who would carry us through the book. Other teams, notably Brazil, demanded at least as much attention.

We decided to stick to reporting the World Cup as a chronological narrative, stage by stage from the qualifying series to the climax of the final. This approach seems to offer the best hope of capturing the mounting excitement, the psychological currents and fluctuations of form that shape the most popular of all sports events. The football dominates the story, of course, but we have written much more about people and places than we did in 1966.

9

There is not space to list the people who should be thanked for their generous interest in our efforts to make the book as accurate as possible. A number of our colleagues in the British sporting Press have been particularly helpful by reading some of our proofs. They are aware of our gratitude and, in any case, they have already demanded payment in champagne. From what we have seen of some of them in action, it would be cheaper to hand over our royalties here and now.

A last and special word of thanks is due to the Brazilian friends who have so willingly increased our knowledge of the best footballers in the world. An outstanding ally among the journalists is José Inacio Werneck, of *Jornal do Brasil*, and within the game itself João Saldanha, that wild and marvellous man, gave us the benefit of an interesting mind and a warm spirit.

The World Cup makes a good story. We only hope we have got it right.

September 1970   HUGH McILVANNEY
                                                   ARTHUR HOPCRAFT

World Cup '70

1 The Preliminary Competition

The World Cup in 1970, like others before it, had to overcome the handicap of being disfigured at birth; for its indefensible system of qualification put El Salvador, Israel and Morocco into the finals while excluding nations who could beat them seven days a week and twice on Sunday. Even Dr Andrew Stephen, chairman of the Football Association and a member of FIFA's eight-man inner bureau on the World Cup, admitted before the competition started that the situation represented 'democracy gone mad' and would have to be changed. He said that the growth of the Federation to embrace 142 countries had produced alarming anomalies, not least the fact that such as Upper Volta and Bahrain have the same voting rights as England and Brazil. Each member nation has one vote, whether it has a million registered players or a few dozen. Theoretically, countries with no standing in the game could, if they acted in concert, revolutionise its laws or its administration.

There was nothing theoretical about the illogicalities imposed on the qualifying process. Based on an arbitrary arrangement of geographical groups, this left El Salvador to compete with the might of Honduras and Haiti while all Belgium had to do was get the better of Yugoslavia and Spain. Those two powerful European nations were expelled in good company: Argentina, Hungary, Poland, Scotland, Austria, Portugal and Chile, to mention a few. They were the victims of grouping that seemed designed to cosset the weak and set the strong at one another's throats. There is something to be said for encouraging the spread of football, but the last sixteen places of the world championship are too important to be proffered as incentives.

13

That great evangelist Sir Stanley Rous would admit that
conversions should not be made at the expense of those who
have fostered the faith for decades. Rous and Stephen are two
administrators who will be working to rationalise the means
of qualifying. There is little justification in the jet age for
taking geography into account. The economic argument (that
poor national associations should not be burdened with heavy
travelling expenses) has been totally exposed. Israel's route to
Mexico was by way of New Zealand and Australia. The Scots
or the Irish, or the Argentines for that matter, would rather
go to the other side of the globe to face easy opposition than
make short and more hazardous trips.

Northern Ireland, as it happened, had the worst possible
combination: exhausting flights to Istanbul and Moscow with
the prospect of hard matches at the end of them. In the
event, Turkey were less menacing than they might have been
and Ireland made an exhilarating start in their group by
thrashing them home and away. George Best was hardly
missed in the 3–0 win in Istanbul, but his absence from the
match in Moscow may well have been crucial. Injured when
playing for Manchester United in a League Cup match two
days before the international, he did not fly out to join the
rest of the team. Dzodzuashvili had marked him out of the
goalless game at Windsor Park but Moscow might have been
more inspiring than a Belfast rent by religious bigotry. Even
the sight of Best coming through the door of their hotel on
crutches must have lifted Irish morale. As it was, they tried
bravely and might have had a happier result than the 2–0
against them. The bitter reaction voiced on behalf of the Irish
F.A. by Mr Harry Cavan was understandable. English
league clubs, which owe so much to the nurseries of Scotland,
Ireland and Wales, have mean records in the matter of assisting
these countries by releasing players. In this instance, however,
Best had to accept a major share of the responsibility. If he had
declared an overwhelming commitment to Ireland's cause it is
difficult to believe that Sir Matt Busby or Wilf McGuinness

would have stood immovably in his way. He would surely have been spared the risks of that marginally significant League Cup match. What is beyond argument is that the World Cup was the poorer by the absence of a forward who, on his day, has more to offer than any other in Europe.

On the evening when Russia were dousing Ireland's challenge, Bobby Brown and his players were living through the quintessential Scottish World Cup experience in Hamburg. Their complex psychology – in which the style, the way of doing things, is in a vital sense more important than what has been done at the end of the day – has prevented them from coming to terms with the conditions of the tournament. This and the more mundane limitations of the insular men who run their game leaves them in the position of millionaires in an alien currency. 'We are,' says one Scottish journalist, 'up to the neck in great players and we couldn't win a raffle.'

Group Seven was always likely to lie between the Scots and the West Germans, with their contrasting capacity for extracting maximum effectiveness from the talents at their disposal. That capacity took a long time to manifest itself in Cyprus where the only goal was delayed until injury time. The Cypriots, a motley collection of clerks and garage hands, did not long sustain the illusions encouraged by this achievement on their own peculiar pitch. Their final goal figures were two for and thirty-five against, Scotland claiming thirteen from them and Germany equalling that aggregate by scoring a dozen at home. German optimism was swollen by a brilliant performance at Hampden Park. Only a spectacular late goal from Murdoch gave Scotland a 1–1 draw. Against Austria in Nuremberg, however, eighty-eight minutes had been played before Muller settled the outcome. The Germans, not for the first or the last time in the World Cup, seemed to enjoy a lot of good fortune but they are a side whose efficient application tends to make their own luck. In Hamburg their luck was made mainly by Scotland. The generosity was evident in the selection of the Scottish team. Gemmell, who is really an attacker in a full-back's shirt, was chosen to face Libuda, a notably fast, orthodox winger. This task might sensibly have been allocated to Greig, a vigorously stubborn defender. With Haller, the nominal outside-left, withdrawn as usual into midfield, Greig was given the luxury of overlapping space that would have been far more rewardingly exploited by Gemmell. Instead, it was Gemmell who was exploited. The Scots, inspired by the marvellous example of Bremner, Cormack and Gray in the middle of the team, outplayed the Germans for nearly all of the ninety minutes, yet lost their early lead and fell 2–1 behind. Gilzean rectified the injustice temporarily with an equaliser but calamitous positioning by Gemmell allowed Libuda to break for the winning goal. Mr Bobby Brown, the Scotland manager, must surely reproach himself for failing to switch Greig on to Libuda and perhaps also for neglecting the opportunity to substitute Cooke for Johnstone in the last minutes when some of the Germans could hardly stand. The Chelsea forward's disrupting runs might have broken them. Scotland's match in Austria was now meaningless and defeat merely a footnote to their disappointment.

Wales, suffering badly from the restricted availability of players and the restricted vision of their officials, were sunk without trace in Group Three. Italy and East Germany used them for target practice and the Welsh emerged pointless with only three goals scored for the loss of ten. Italy's figures were exactly the reverse and seven of their goals were taken by Luigi Riva, the tall, muscular striker whose consistent deadliness would help Cagliari to the Italian championship just before Mexico. His countrymen, in search of atonement for the *débâcle* of 1966, saw Riva in a messianic light, looking to him to erase their reputation for submissiveness when removed too far from home and mother. Riva's legend was nourished by the scoring feats in the qualifying series and the happy result of the conclusive match with the East Germans in Naples. The countries had gone into the game level on points but by the interval Italy had three goals and firm reservations for Mexico.

Some of their players crossed the Atlantic with revived memories of 1966 when they were eliminated by North Korea and pelted on their return home by angry crowds who had waited through the night at Genoa airport. The coach of that side, Edmondo Fabbri, was abruptly replaced by Feruccio Valcareggi, a fifty-year-old who limits himself to fifteen cigarettes during a game. Valcareggi approached the rebuilding job quietly; one of his first decisions was to concentrate on forming a 'real' national team, with no regrets over the loss of the Argentines and Brazilians who had previously been welcomed as the sons of transplanted Italian families. Of the first twenty matches after he took over Italy won twelve, drew seven and lost one (3–2 to Bulgaria in the European Nations Cup) and scored forty goals against fourteen. They went on to win the Nations Cup in a replayed final with Yugoslavia, who had, almost literally, kicked England out at the semi-final stage. Just as the Italians were beginning to dream of repeating the World Cup victories of 1934 and 1938 they reverted to character early in 1970 against Spain in Madrid. A two-goal lead was wiped out when their sweeper Salvadore put through his own goal twice. All the old self-destructive uncertainties had reappeared and the team's prospects in Mexico again seemed problematical.

Elsewhere in the European Groups there was the expected ration of the unexpected. Portugal, semi-finalists at Wembley four years before, experienced cumulative humiliation in Group One. The Greeks, greatly improved since the importation of Yugoslav coaches, started Portugal's slide by beating them 4–2 in Athens. Next there was a 2–0 defeat at home by Switzerland and a struggling draw with Greece in the return at Oporto. Ironically, Portugal's only victory in the six matches was a fine 3–0 win over Rumania, the qualifiers. Rumania, profiting from the two years of intensive work by their coach Angelo Nicolescu, were reaching the World Cup finals for the first time since the war.

Belgium became the first nation to qualify for Mexico by

B

surviving a confusion of contradictory results in Group Six, where Spain and Yugoslavia proved expert at inflicting mutual damage. The unlikeliness of Belgium's achievement was emphasised when they lost their last Group match 4–0 to Yugoslavia and then went down 3–1 to England on a sleet-chilled night in Brussels. Belgium's neighbours, Holland, found hostility less intermittent in Group Eight. The Dutch, whose club football has improved out of recognition in recent seasons, finished one point behind Poland and two behind Bulgaria. This was the third time in succession that Bulgaria had made it to the World Cup finals but their previous record there was not intimidating: one point from a goalless draw with England in 1962, no points from their three matches in Liverpool in 1966.

Any surprise over the inclusion of Sweden in the Mexico sixteen did not last beyond a glance at their two rivals in Group Five. The old troubles over the release of players from their various European clubs weakened the Swedes sufficiently to give France a 3–0 victory at home. But the French, whose domestic game is in tatters, were readily beaten in Sweden and permitted the feeble Norwegians to leave with two points. All this made subsequent suggestions that Sweden would be lively outsiders in the finals seem extravagant. Group Two was predictably close. Czechoslovakia, finalists in 1962, and Hungary, finalists in 1954, should have found Denmark and the Republic of Ireland no more than minor distractions from their straight fight. But it was a 3–2 defeat in Denmark that undermined Hungary's position and even taking three points from the Czechs did not spare them a play-off. This early form was stunningly refuted in Marseilles where Czechoslovakia shattered the Hungarians 4–1.

The shock from South America was the emergence of Peru at the expense of Argentina. It was a development that could not be expected to sadden many people in Britain. Apart from the self-destructive cynicism shown by Argentina in their quarter-final with England in 1966, when Rattin's dismissal crippled them as they appeared to be taking control, there had been the souring experiences of Glasgow Celtic and Manchester United against Racing and Estudiantes in the World Club Championship. The same inclination to allow violence to supplant, or at least obscure, their traditional skills weakened the Argentinians in their qualifying series with Peru and Bolivia, although political manoeuvring among the administrators of their game had already combined with the selfishness of their leading clubs to create major handicaps. They changed managers late in the day, Adolfo Pedernera replacing Humberto Maschio, and so abbreviated their time of acclimatisation in La Paz, which is 5,000 feet higher then Mexico City's 7,500. All they had to offer in the first match in the Bolivian capital was physical brutality. They lost 3–1 and were warned by the Argentine dictator, General Ongania, that they had better behave more respectably in the future. Their moral conduct improved but their football remained inadequate. Losing in Lima to Peru, they recovered partially by beating Bolivia 1–0 in Buenos Aires and entered the return game with the Peruvians needing victory to force a three-way play-off. But Peru, inspired by the managership of Didi, twice a World Cup medallist with Brazil, had been playing with spirit and flair from the start of the series and now they refused to be budged. Ramírez, one of their two fast wingers, scored the two goals that gave them a draw. He would stay on the fringe of their side in Mexico but could be satisfied that he had already done the state some service.

Uruguay, another of the 1966 quarter-finalists and winners of the championship in 1930 and 1950, qualified readily over Chile and Ecuador but the performance was marred by the ruthlessness of their methods. They did not concede a goal in their four matches and dropped only one point, away to Chile. Many of the familiar faces disappeared from the Uruguayan side as a result of Juan Eduardo Hohberg's enthusiasm for youth. (Perhaps he felt that young limbs could better inflict the savage fouls that were Uruguay's speciality.) But the coach had the good sense to retain the great goalkeeper Mazurkiewicz, and Rocha, one of the two or three best all-round inside-forwards in South America. Rocha's World Cup would be blighted by injury, but Cubilla, the small, portly outside-right, would be one of its most impressive players.

For Brazil, the matches with Paraguay, Colombia and Venezuela were not so much a qualifying series as a triumphal procession. They alone among all the nations in the tournament finished their Group games with a perfect record, claiming twelve points and twenty-three goals (against two). Their closest match was 1–0 at home over Paraguay, the group runners-up. Nine of Brazil's goals were scored by Tostão, who thus equalled the total of West Germany's Muller in these preliminary rounds, but one of the matches brought the beginnings of the eye injury that would put Tostão's whole future in jeopardy. This apart, these six games gave João Saldanha much cause for satisfaction. He had been summoned to the job of managing the Brazilian squad at the beginning of 1969, apparently on the principle that the severest critic of the fiasco of 1966 and after should be asked to sort out the mess. Saldanha, despite the wildness of his personality and the extremity of some of his views, introduced consistency to the selection of players and set a confident, thoughtful course for Mexico. He did not complete the journey as manager. The animosity he had aroused and contemptuously ignored in C.B.D., the governing body of Brazilian football, was given a far more damaging edge when Pelé became one of his most determined critics. Saldanha, who had begun to talk of medical problems affecting Pelé, particularly a deficiency in his eyesight, showed a willingness to drop the great forward, and to question his capacity to do himself justice in Mexico. This may have been as much an attempt to goad or discipline Pelé as a genuine misgiving, but it had the effect of alienating the player. When Saldanha went armed in search of an old enemy, Yustrich, the large and loud manager of the Flamengo team, he provided the opening for C.B.D. His own instability complemented the intrigues of those intent on bringing him down and he was told that the technical committee in charge of the World Cup challenge was being dissolved. 'I am not an ice cube to be dissolved,' Saldanha told them. 'If you are firing me you had better say so. Don't hide behind words.' He was fired, a decision that must have brought relief to the military government of Emilio Garrastazu Médici. Neither the the dictator nor his underlings could feel comfortable about having a man with a long record of liberal thinking and left-wing activity as their ambassador at the World Cup. Their choice as successor was much less controversial. Mário Zagalo, whose intelligent running between the midfield and the outside-left position in Brazil's winning teams of 1958 and 1962 earned him the nickname of The Ant. Zagalo is a strong-minded man but his opinions tend to be firmly related to football.

Mexico's automatic entry into the finals as the host nation opened the way for a battle of the pygmies in the Central American section. Twelve nations in four sub-groups competed for the place habitually occupied by the Mexicans. Honduras, Haiti, the United States and El Salvador survived to the semi-finals, in which Haiti beat the United States home and away (stirring humiliating echoes of what the U.S. had done to England back in 1950). The Honduras–El Salvador confrontation produced no such clean-cut execution. El Salvador were beaten 1–0 in Honduras but when they won their home leg 3–0 a shooting war broke out. The patriotic rioting that attended the two matches detonated a situation that had been explosive for years. El Salvador is the most densely populated of the Central American countries with three million people. Honduras has five times the area but a million fewer inhabitants. Some 300,000 land-hungry Salvadoreans migrated across the 860-mile border between the two countries, setting out to farm unoccupied land. But land reform laws moved many of them off recently, following Honduran claims that the immigrants were troublesome and constituted a potential fifth column.

After the patriotic violence at the two matches, the countries broke off diplomatic relations on June 26, 1969, and there followed claims and counter-claims of provocation, of airliners being fired on, burnings and bombings. Before peace was restored 3,000 deaths had been reported. In the meantime, on June 27, a decider had been played in Mexico City. El Salvador won it and went on to meet Haiti, who had organised a thorough preparation that involved removing their national squad from the league championship. When the Salvadoreans won 2–1 in Port au Prince the return at home appeared to be a formality. Instead, it brought them an astonishing 3–0 defeat and yet another play-off, this time in Kingston, Jamaica. A goal in extra time by Ramon Martínez, who had also scored in the play-off with Honduras, put El Salvador through at last. Their journey to the World Cup finals, by way of twelve matches and a little war, established some kind of record.

Mexico, whose status as hosts had given El Salvador the opportunity to mix with their betters in football, had their own worries. Their European tour in 1969 was disastrous. They won only one game, against Norway, and were beaten by such lowly rated countries as Luxembourg and Denmark, though they did manage goalless draws in Portugal and Spain. Lack of goal scorers has been their most glaring defect for some time. They took only four goals in the seven matches of their tour, three more than they totalled in the three games they played during the 1966 World Cup. To add to Mexico's difficulties, Ernesto Cisneros and Gabriel Nuñez, both of whom were in the 1966 team, were suspended from the 1970 finals because they slipped away for a night out while the squad were training in Acapulco. Outsiders could not help reflecting that Acapulco is less than an ideal setting for the monastic life.

Group 15, the Asian section, was confused to the very edge of comprehensibility by political differences. First North Korea, the natural favourites after their execution of Italy in 1966, refused to play their eliminating matches in Israel and withdrew. In the other half of the draw, Rhodesia, whose inclusion stretched the already strained criteria used to define the Asian section, found their rivals unwilling to visit or entertain them. The issue was side-stepped by a decision to exempt the Rhodesians, who were at least fielding black players, from the early rounds. They were given a bye into a play-off with Australia, who had finished two points ahead of South Korea and four ahead of Japan in the opening series of games in Seoul. After two draws with Rhodesia in Mozambique, Australia beat them 3–1 at the third attempt to continue their extraordinary travels in search of a qualifying place. They had to face Israel, easy victors in two matches against New Zealand, whose resignation showed in their agreement to play twice in Tel Aviv. Australia might have been overrun by a much superior Israeli team in Tel Aviv but the inspired brilliance of their goalkeeper, Ron Corry, kept the score to 1–0. However, the optimism the Australians carried into the second match in Sydney was unjustified. They could do no better than draw, and were left with nothing to show for a succession of expeditions that made the wanderings of Marco Polo look like a day-trip to the seaside.

Morocco were the luckiest of the qualifiers for the Mexico finals. In the first sub-group in the African section, which contained eleven nations, they beat Senegal in a play-off in Las Palmas, then went on to two goalless games with Tunisia. This time the play-off produced another draw, but Morocco moved forward on the toss of a coin. In the last stage they faced Nigeria and the Sudan, both of whom were strongly fancied. Although beaten in Nigeria, Morocco profited from the two draws played out by Nigeria and the Sudan and made their own position secure by beating the Sudanese 3–0 in their last match.

While all these tense skirmishes were taking place around the world, England were striving to find the men, the collective physical condition and the psychological and tactical approach that would keep possession of the Jules Rimet Trophy they had won without leaving Wembley in 1966. Understandably, Sir

Alf Ramsey kept faith with as many of his winning team as
kept their edge. When his party left for Mexico more than a
month before the Finals, it included eight of the men who had
made that euphoric lap of honour with the Cup four years
before: Banks, Stiles, Jack Charlton, Moore, Ball, Bobby
Charlton, Hurst and Peters. Of the other three, Cohen had
been taken from the game prematurely by injury and Wilson
and Hunt had begun the natural decline towards the end of
their careers. Hunt, whose modesty and infallible friendliness
would make the World Cup a more enjoyable experience for
those who shared his company in Mexico, still looked hard and
fit enough to let his new opponents in the Second Division
know he was around. But the ungraceful art of snatching or
scrambling goals, which at best had made him a controversial
member of the England side, was too little in evidence to
justify any thought of a trans-Atlantic journey.

   Indeed, Hunt had given way long before to such as Lee,
the Manchester City forward, who is similarly blond but
different in almost all other respects. Whereas Hunt's strength
often made him appear cumbersome, the muscular power of
the much shorter Lee gives him an explosive flexibility. Fast,
brave and skilful, with a two-footed variety in his violent
shooting, his one noticeable deficiency as a striker is in his
heading, and England would expect Hurst and Peters to
compensate for that. Hurst had continued to develop his game
since 1966 with the honesty of purpose that is his hallmark on
the field. The best judges in British football, with Sir Matt
Busby prominent among them, overflow with admiration for
the forthright courage, athletic resilience and technical
excellence that enable him to battle through the relentless
maltreatment inflicted on the aggressive front runner. Hurst's
West Ham partnership with Peters had been broken by a
transfer that took Peters to Tottenham Hotspur. And their
alliance in the England team was more fundamentally undermined by Peters's form, which was more often bad than good
as Mexico drew near. There was never any likelihood that

Ramsey would lose confidence in a player he once praised as 'ten years ahead of his time' and most objective critics agreed that the challenge facing England was one that called for Peters at his most effective. But the deep doubts about him were not allayed by his all but invisible performance against Scotland at Hampden Park, the team's last match prior to their departure. The result, a goalless draw, did little to obscure the fact that England were almost run into the Clyde. Obviously there was general fear of an injury that could cost the victim his place on the plane for Mexico, just as the breaking of a leg in a League match at West Ham shortly before had deprived Paul Reaney, the brilliant Leeds United full-back, of his. But even that legitimate apprehension did not entirely excuse the scurrying defensiveness of England, whose sole intention seemed to be to suffocate the game in midfield. Even in sparring, world champions should look something out of the ordinary.

Two men who did meet that requirement were Moore and Banks. Both had been fully matured players in 1966, the world's best in their positions. All that had changed since then was that they had become better. Stiles and Jack Charlton in contrast, the one because of injury, the other because of injury *and* age, had lost ground. Charlton's replacement, Labone of Everton, had also suffered an enforced absence and struggled to regain his form when he returned. But he was a clear favourite to play in the Finals, as was Mullery, who used his prodigious physical resources and workmanlike skills to hold on to the defensive midfield position he had taken from Stiles.

Until Reaney's sad accident, Ramsey was entitled to feel that he had solved the alarming problem created by the loss of Cohen and Wilson, who served him so marvellously at full-back in the Wembley World Cup. Leeds had provided obvious successors in Reaney and Cooper, a converted winger with the speed and firmness to be a formidable obstacle in defence and the intricate control to be a frightening menace on his frequent surges forward. With Reaney temporarily crippled, Newton and Wright, two experienced internationalists, would compete for the privilege of partnering Cooper. Hughes, a hard young Liverpool player equally at home in the back line or the middle of the team, would be the cover for the Leeds man.

The probable absence of Stiles would be the only change in England's midfield. Bobby Charlton, surviving several periods of mediocre form and many premature obituaries, found his appetite for football sharpening again in the early summer of 1970 and was good enough to withstand the competition from Bell, an inside-forward whose lung power and comprehensive talent have done much to restore Manchester City's fortunes. Alongside Charlton in the middle would be Ball, the best living argument for Ramsey's creed. In the early days Ball's most noticeable quality was his selfless industry, his refusal to be out of the game, whether his side were attacking or defending. But to this foundation he added the techniques and perceptions of a great constructive player, translating his passion for the game into a hunger for improvement. Undoubtedly his growth was shaped and accelerated by his association with Ramsey's England. By May 1970, as the party prepared to leave, it was apparent that Ball would be a vital influence not only in Mexico but, barring misfortune, in Munich four years later.

They left behind a record between the World Cups that could be considered good or moderate, according to the point of view. What had to be admitted on all sides was that those who had seen that record built up, step by step, had rarely been in danger of having a heart attack from the excitement of it all. On the basis of results alone, it was difficult to fault Ramsey. His men lost only four of the thirty-four full internationals played in the four years between the winning of the Jules Rimet Trophy and the take-off for Mexico City. But football, despite the incessant parroting on the virtues of 'professionalism,' is not merely about results. It is also about style, about the way results are achieved, about pride. It is,

or should be, at the highest levels about making the hair rise
on the back of the spectator's neck, making him thrilled and
glad to be there watching. Such a situation was a rarity with
England in the late 1960s. In the main their policy was to
concentrate the game in midfield, even if it meant committing
half-a-dozen men to that area. They seemed to prefer to nibble
at the opposition like ants, rather than try to devour them like
lions. Of course, that is an excessively derogatory analogy.
The unquestionable class of their players was always liable to
break out of the system (which was generally 4–4–2 rather than
4–3–3) and did so spectacularly in a superb 4–1 slaughter of
Scotland in 1969 and matching performances in the Latin
American tour that followed. Nevertheless, the total lack of
outright specialists in wing play often robbed England of
vital width in attack – until Cooper established himself, the
overlapping full-backs were almost always feeble imitations of
wingers – and their assaults sometimes had the trundling
predictability of a weary rush with a battering ram. Thus
their scoring average was well under two goals a game in those
thirty-four matches, though sixteen of them were at home and
twelve of them were against Scotland, Ireland or Wales. It
must be said that the case for restoring wingers to the side was
weakened by a dearth of potent members of the species in the
English League. Winning the World Cup without them probably
discouraged their use. At any rate, by the beginning of 1970
the only two undeniably great wingers in Britain were an
Irishman, Best, and a Scot, Johnstone. The best of those
available to England was Thompson, of Liverpool, a man with
a gift for transmuting the wonders of his ball control into a
dross of negative finishing. Thompson is the sort of player who
might beat all eleven opponents then lose the ball to the referee.
Yet his skills towered over those of the other moderate footballers specialising in wing play in an England that had for the
moment abandoned the traditions of Matthews, Finney and
Bastin. So Thompson was one of twenty-eight players taken
to Mexico by Ramsey, who was not obliged to name his

official squad of twenty-two until a week before the start of
the tournament. But many people suspected that the Liverpool
outside-left had little chance of figuring in the final choice.
If Ramsey decided to end his partial but significant neglect
of the wings, and it was clearly advisable that he should, it
seemed more likely that he would do so by using players
capable of switching to the job rather than one devoted to it
exclusively. This theory brought to mind immediately Coates,
the driving force of a young Burnley team. Small and balding,
Coates now deploys his wide range of abilities from midfield
but he has considerable experience of operating on the wing
and the extreme speed and elusiveness to do damage there at
any time.

In the event neither Thompson nor Coates survived the
trimming of the party on the brief tour of Colombia and
Ecuador that was undertaken with the idea of assisting acclimatisation to altitude. England had spent two quiet weeks in
Mexico City, wisely allowing the players to catch their breath
(which can be a problem at 7,500 feet) after the rigours of
their club programmes. Then they flew, with a long sweaty
delay in Panama, to Bogotá to begin a week that should have
been a simple part of their preparation but proved instead to
be one of the strangest any touring English footballers have
ever known. The football itself was encouraging enough. On a
field left sodden by furious rain, the team Ramsey saw as his
first eleven played with splendid confidence to rout Colombia
4–0, with Ball at his best and Peters suggesting that he was
rediscovering his phenomenal mobility and his sharpness near
goal. Helped by cool temperatures, most of the players found
they had no need to impose restraints on their game once they
had forced themselves through the distress of the first five or
ten minutes (Moore indicated, with engaging pedantry, that
his uneasiness had lasted three). The stumbling 1–0 victory in
the "B" match that preceded the full international did confirm
that the gap between the battle-hardened core of the squad
and the ambitious recruits had narrowed hardly at all. How-

ever, there was no need to draw despondent conclusions. Although Kidd and Osgood were sadly ineffectual and Clarke and Coates (when he was substituted after injury had removed Stiles) were less than inspired, the extentuating fact was that these reserves were at a crippling disadvantage in never previously having played as a unit. They could not possibly approach the spontaneous understanding and cohesion of the senior side. Certainly Ramsey was not disenchanted with Osgood, the tall, infinitely graceful and intermittently deadly Chelsea centre-forward, or Clarke, the leaner, more economical striker of Leeds United. Both were to be retained in the twenty-two.

In the meantime, however, the manager was profoundly, if privately, disturbed by moves to bring a charge of theft against his captain, Moore. As the party took off for Quito, the charmingly unmetropolitan capital of Ecuador, where they would face the same schedule of two matches on the one day – and with the altitude increased by nearly a thousand feet – those journalists who were aware of the sinister developments could identify a pervasive tension. But perhaps only Ramsey, with his senses primed to detect the faintest rustle of hostility, saw from the beginning the full nightmarish potential of the accusations made against Bobby Moore in Bogotá.

'This is the worst thing that has happened in my seven years as England manager,' he said at a stage when those few of us who had early knowledge of the incident that had occurred in a jeweller's shop were satisfied that it would peter out as a minor local embarrassment. In the days that followed Ramsey's definition proved so grimly accurate that problems which would have been considered crises at any other time were accepted as petty additional irritants, like specks of dust in an eye already splashed with acid. When the six players were discarded to reduce his pool to the permitted maximum of twenty-two, a series of entirely avoidable misunderstandings on the part of some newspapers caused the six (Shilton, McNab, Sadler, Coates, Kidd and Thompson) to be haphazardly

informed before Ramsey had a chance to take them aside in
Quito. He was faced with bitter and unusually forthright
complaints from men who felt, as he certainly did, that one of
the most disappointing days of their careers need not have
been one of the least dignified. Normally his resentment of the
Press, whose request for consideration of deadlines created the
risk of confusion, would have been spectacular and prolonged.
But, coming as it did in the anxious interlude between two
phases of the Moore case, this row with a few journalists soon
became part of the memorable trivia of the tour. Similarly,
when the main party arrived back in Mexico City and Jeff
Astle lurched heavy-eyed from a plane on which he had drunk
several whiskies to subdue his terror of flying, Ramsey could
have been expected to react drastically. However, though his
anger was fierce enough, it never seriously disturbed his
preoccupation with the fate of the team captain he had been
forced to leave under arrest 2,000 miles to the south.

The England party had left Bogotá for Mexico without
Moore, assigning Dr Andrew Stephen and Denis Follows, the
chairman and the secretary of the Football Association, to
support Embassy efforts to gain his release. (Understandably,
there was a cool response from Ramsey to an offer by Bobby
Charlton, who had been with Moore in the jeweller's shop,
to stay behind as an ally or a fellow victim.) But, to an extent
that the least sentimental of us found affecting, the party's
spirit remained with Moore in Colombia. In his absence the
momentum of their previously confident progress towards the
World Cup diminished visibly. It was not that this literally
incredible episode, or the lurid exaggerations that flourished
in the Mexican Press after Astle's sad little aberration, came
near to unnerving them. They simply could not devote themselves exuberantly to football while a friend they are happy to
accept as their leader on the field was exposed to attempts to
discredit him in the eyes of the world.

Anyone who thinks this suggests a melodramatic view of the
situation should look closely at the implications for Moore if

the accusations had been given legel credence. Or, better still, anyone who feels that way might study the immediate effect of his arrest on Sir Alf Ramsey. There have been times in the last few years when Ramsey and his captain, for all their huge mutual respect, have appeared to be less than bosom pals, but the warmth of the manager's concern throughout Moore's detention in Bogotá was unmistakable. 'You won't see a smile on my face until I see Bobby Moore,' he said, with no trace of portentousness. 'And I won't feel happy until I have found out how he is. This feeling has nothing to do with England or the World Cup. How can I drive the players in these circumstances?'

When Moore rejoined England eventually in Guadalajara – having sustained the other-worldly flavour of the affair with statements about being happy 'to be a free man once again' and glad the accusations had 'been shown to be unfounded' – fellow players lined the entrance to the Hilton Hotel to applaud him in. It was an unashamedly emotional moment and even Moore, whose personality incorporates an ice-making machine, was obviously moved.

Fortunately, the ice was available when required during the previous five days. Moore's prominence in the England party made his experience all the more painfully significant, more likely to do deep and widespread damage to morale, but of the footballers travelling under Ramsey he was perhaps best equipped to withstand the strain of an ordeal that had sufficient echoes of Graham Greene (if not Kafka) to push an ordinary man towards hysteria. Moore is rather less hysterical than a computer. One of the precious few amusing ironies in what happened in Colombia was the thought of him on the answering end of an endless succession of questions. The night before he was detained, during a talk that had nothing to do with the case, journalists reproached him lightly about his habit of reducing conversation to an interrogation. João Saldanha, the former manager of Brazil, who backed Moore vehemently in the Mexican Press throughout his difficulties, once said: 'That

Bobby is a wonderful conversationalist. He asks me one hundred questions and when I ask one in return, he replies with the hundred-and-first question of his own.' Reminded of such exchanges, Moore smiles slowly, lets his eyelids droop, then looks at you with mischievous frankness: 'Well, you've got to try to learn something as you go through life'. Clarity and firmness of purpose, carefully understated, is the essence of his nature on and off the field. Just how much that particular strength meant to him and his manager while his participation in the World Cup was in doubt can only be properly understood if the events are recalled in order and in detail.

The trouble began on the evening of Monday, May 18, within hours of England's arrival in the Tequendama Hotel, which rises new and comparatively opulent at a wide junction on a road that soon afterwards merges with the shabby commercial centre of Bogotá. English players, on their first visit to Colombia, were on a leisurely reconnaissance of gift counters and Moore and Bobby Charlton were in Fuego Verde, one of four jewellery shops in the hotel. Precisely what happened in the small (four yards by four yards) shop on the ground floor is still obscure, submerged in contradiction, but by the following morning, as the squad trained in thundery sunshine at a military school, some of us learned that police had been called in to investigate an alleged theft. The handful of us who knew were informed by a photographer colleague who had happened to witness the stir in Fuego Verde. Subsequent raucous assertions in some Fleet Street offices that news of the case was suppressed by chauvinistic journalists were touchingly romantic. Those reporters not excused by total ignorance of the incident, and the uninformed were the great majority, realised that there was nothing solid to be printed at that stage, that any attempt to make a story of it would involve jeopardising Moore's reputation on the strength of a complaint the police had still to decide to pursue.

So when we reached Quito we felt able to concentrate on football. After England's 'B' team beat the Ecuadorean club

1   Belgian players leave no doubt about their feelings after the award of a
highly questionable penalty to Mexico

2   Peña scores the penalty for Mexico against Belgium

3 Russian goalkeeper Kavazashvili, with added support from Serebrianikov,
punches the ball away to thwart a Belgian attack

4 Luigi Riva is embraced by an Italian photographer after putting in his
first 'goal' of the tournament in the match against Israel. The euphoria was
short-lived, however, for a few moments later the referee disallowed the goal

5 A Mexican fan, fat and
friendly towards Brazil

champions, Liga Deportiva Universitaria, 4–1 and the first
team beat the Ecuador national side 2–0 (Astle scoring three
altogether and sharing a fourth in the secondary match),
any questions put to Moore were about the difficulties of
playing at 9,300 feet. These had been severe as Alan Ball,
probably the most vivid personality in the group, emphasised
afterwards. 'I knew we were in bother when I spoke to Tommy
Wright as he came in after the first match. I asked him if it
were hard out there. He tried to speak but all he could do were
keep swallowin'. There was all white flecks round his mouth
and his eyes was rollin.' After about fifteen or twenty seconds
he said, "F—g hard." And it were. You know Alan Mullery
always shouts at us. Go here, go there. He's a great worker
and he drives you on. Well when he tried that out there all
that came out was this sort of gurgle. Nobody had enough
breath to run, let alone shout. I thought the talk about altitude
were crap, me. I thought I could run for a week. But I found
out different today. When did you ever see our lads when
they didn't want to know the ball? Well it were like that today.
Like that.' He dropped his chin on his chest and made a
gesture with his right hand, halfway between dismissal and
resignation.

Yet almost before he had his breath back Ball was enthusing
about the privilege of playing in the World Cup. He said he
could not understand the four players (Shilton, McNab,
Coates and Kidd) who, having failed to make the final twenty-
two, had opted to fly home as soon as possible. 'It's the lads'
own business and I know they are choked but I couldn't do
what they did. This is going to be a great tournament and even
if I could only watch I'd want to be here. My old man said,
"You've got all your life after thirty-five to smoke, drink or go
with women." That's what I believe. I love football. If I am
lucky enough to play against Brazil my old man will cry.
And maybe I won't be far behind him. Me out there with
Pelé and those fellas. I'll say "This is the big time, Ballie. This
is it, man, this is it".'

C

Less than twenty-four hours later Bobby Moore was finding that the big-time, especially in Latin America, brings unexpected complications. There had been muted apprehension that on the way back through Bogotá to Mexico City his freedom might be menaced by the claims that he had stolen a piece of jewellery, now identified as an eighteen-carat gold bracelet encrusted with diamonds and emeralds. The fears were justified. As the England men sat down in the Tequendama to watch the film *Shenandoah*, Moore was approached quietly and escorted out of the friendly insularity of the darkened room into a week of isolation as an accused man. Dr Andrew Stephen was to say later: 'Until this happened I did not know Bobby Moore really well but I am now enormously impressed with him as a man. He never lost his nerve or his dignity through all this.'

From the start, the evidence presented to the examining magistrate, Pedro Dorado, did nothing to undermine Moore's serenity. The three principals ranged against him were Danilo Rojas, a mild-looking man in glasses who was asking £6,000 in moral and material damages resulting from the theft of the bracelet, which he valued at just over £600; Clara Padilla, the blonde, attractive shop assistant who suggested initially that Moore took the bracelet from a cabinet fixed to a wall while his 'wide shoulders' were obscuring her view; and Alvaro Suarez, a slight man in his twenties who entered the case after he testified that he had been walking past the shop when he looked through the glass door and saw Moore in the act of committing the crime. Almost as soon as Dorado began his private examination in his cramped, functional office on the ground floor of Bogotá's central court building, major discrepancies appeared. Padilla admitted that she had not actually seen Moore put the bracelet in a pocket or elsewhere on his person. Rojas pointed out that he had never said he was quite certain it was in the cabinet when Moore and Charlton went into his shop. Contradictions in Suarez's evidence were even more serious. He had said that he saw Moore take the jewellery and reported the theft immediately to a member of the Tourist Police in the hotel. But the policeman's testimony was that he was not notified until an hour-and-a-half later.

By this time Colombian public opinion was firmly behind Moore and the shop was a target for critical telephone calls, some mentioning blackmail. In the Mexican sports paper *Esto* João Saldanha said that Moore was being victimised as footballers of the Brazilian clubs Santos and Portuguesa had been in comparable circumstances in Bogotá. When he and four Botafogo players had been questioned about stealing a jewel in a shop on Curaçao, Saldanha, his article added, had forced the policeman to lock the door and search the place until 'the shit' was found in a back room accessible only to the employees. 'Canallas [bastards]!' wrote Saldanha. 'Bobby Moore is an honourable man.'

Meanwhile, Ramsey had been almost literally cornered by reporters at Mexico City airport. From the moment it was announced that England would bring nearly all their supplies from home, importing everything from fish fingers to a bus, the Mexicans had been unsympathetic. (There were, of course, more complex reasons for their antagonism and these will be discussed later.) Now at this disorderly Press conference a Mexican said he wanted to welcome England anew. Ramsey said he must be joking. The newspapers were not joking the next day. A picture strip showed Astle in another part of the same airport lounge with his head lolling, his eyes closed, then slumped drowsily on a couch. The stories alleged wholesale drunkenness. It was all the most vicious nonsense. Only poor, nervous Astle had drunk anything worth the name. And a player who was sitting near him said he did not have enough to knock him out. 'I reckon he had taken a sleeping pill and it was the double effect that did him.' The same companion was asked why he did not prevent the big forward from overdoing the liquid tranquilliser. 'I said, "Look at the size of him. He's thirteen stone. He would have given me a right hiding." '

The disproportionate fuss made about Astle's condition reflected the inter-racial animosities that are endemic in the World Cup and make many people suspect its ultimate validity. Would a few calming whiskies have a disastrous effect on his physical or moral well-being? The only immorality in the incident was on the part of the papers that inflated it so preposterously.

Luckily, the word from Bogotá was more pleasing. At a reconstruction of the scene in the jewellery shop the versions offered by Padilla and Suarez were so at variance as to seem descriptions of quite different occurrences. Suarez, who had been assumed to be merely a passer-by unknown to Rojas, now emerged as a jewel salesman. By Thursday, May 28, it only remained for Moore to make a ten-minute appearance before Dorado and hear the magistrate rule that so far he had no evidence of substance nor any credible witness to incriminate the England captain. But the case would remain open and Moore would have to report to a Colombian consulate if required. Moore said goodbye to the two detectives who had become his friends while guarding him at the home of a Colombian football official (occasionally joining him in a kick-around with a ball in a courtyard behind the magistrate's office) and headed for a frenzied reception from reporters and television crews at Mexico City.

That squalid, drizzle-soaked turmoil he endured with the inviolable composure he had shown all week. 'The blond figure staying absolutely cool in the middle of that crazy mob – Jesus, he looked almost noble,' an awed Englishman said afterwards. Moore made respectful references to the conditions of his release: that he must be available to the Colombian authorities any time within the next thirty days to assist with their inquiries. But British Embassy officials insisted that there was no need for further concern, that if he were required at all it would be as a witness. Their confidence remained unshaken through the tiresome reverberations that were to continue long after the World Cup was over. All the alarmist stories that came out of Bogotá – suggestions that new evidence had strengthened the case against Moore, that he might even have to return to Colombia – were calmly contradicted by the Embassy's reassurances. They said all along that the England captain was in the clear and in the end even the tortuous Colombian judicial system, and the eager stringers of British newspapers, had to acknowledge the fact. Suspicion turned eventually on his accusers who were alleged to have rigged a plot to incriminate him, presumably with simple financial motives.

But that was part of an unknown future when Moore spent his first night of freedom having a drink with his friend and West Ham club-mate Jimmy Greaves, who had just driven into sixth place in the World Cup car rally. Next morning he took the short flight to Guadalajara and the business from which he had been kept too long. Regardless of his innocence, he had already served a sentence by being deprived of adequate training for five days. But no one doubted that he had the will to make himself fit in the two days before England's opening match with Rumania – least of all the Colombians.

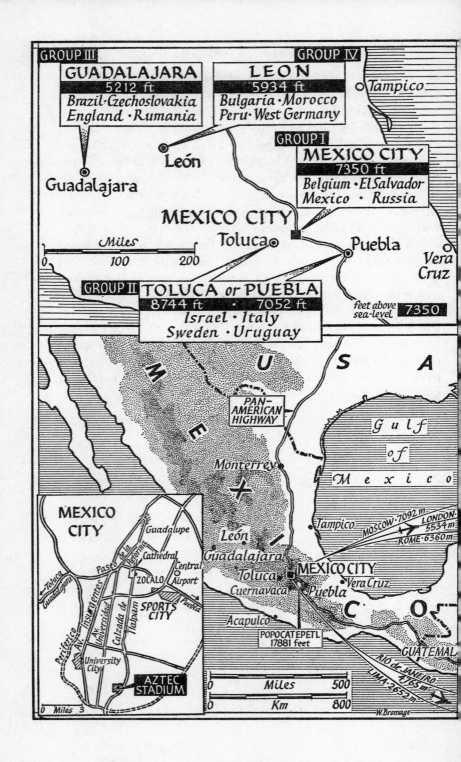

GROUP III

GUADALAJARA
5212 ft
Brazil·Czechoslovakia
England · Rumania

GROUP IV

LEON
5934 ft
Bulgaria·Morocco
Peru· West Germany

GROUP I

MEXICO CITY
7350 ft
Belgium ·El Salvador
Mexico · Russia

León

Guadalajara

Tampico

MEXICO CITY

Miles

0   100   200

Toluca

Puebla

Vera
Cruz

GROUP II

TOLUCA or PUEBLA
8744 ft   ·   7052 ft
Israel · Italy
Sweden · Uruguay

feet above
sea-level   7350

M E X I C O

U S A

PAN-
AMERICAN
HIGHWAY

Gulf

of

Mexico

Monterrey

Tampico   MOSCOW·7092 m.   LONDON·5534 m.
ROME·6360 m.

León

Guadalajara   MEXICO CITY

Toluca   Vera Cruz

Cuernavaca   Puebla

Acapulco   RIO de JANEIRO·4765 m.

POPOCATEPETL
17881 feet   GUATEMAL

LIMA·2652 m.

MEXICO
CITY

Guadalupe

Paseo de la Reforma

Cathedral   Central
Airport

ZOCALO

Toluca
Guadalajara

SPORTS
CITY   Puebla

Periferico   Av. Insurgentes   Av. Universidad   Calzada de Tlalpan

University
City

0   Miles   3

AZTEC
STADIUM

0   Miles   500

0   Km   800

W.Bromage

2 Group One

Belgium, El Salvador, Mexico, U.S.S.R.

MEXICO v. U.S.S.R.

Aztec Stadium, Mexico City, May 31

By 10.30am. on Sunday, May 31, an hour and half before the opening match of the tournament, the Aztec stadium was already thunderous with drums and chants; and the packed, restless crowd gleamed red, white and green as they waved their flags and rose repeatedly in their clothing of national colours to scream their expectation at the sun. There were 112,000 people in this vast, circular bowl, and they were building a fierce tension out of their impelled cacophony. Later in the competition the visitors from countries where emotional response is not so readily released would have reason to look back on this brilliant Sunday as one of the less alarming experiences of Mexican instant delirium. But at the time it seemed such an extreme of mindless exuberance that the whole point of our presence, the football, was going to be lost in the carnival.

Yet in the corners of one's senses, as the noise and vivid movement briefly and occasionally subsided, there were sombre intrusions into the near-trance the crowd was inducing. Down on the rich green pitch, just inside one right-angle of the surrounding flower beds, an Army band played in khaki and battle order, steel helmeted and with rifles slung at the shoulder, to nudge at the memory of the indiscriminate killings of demonstrating students in this same city only two years before during the Olympic Games. And the euphoria itself,

39

once the mind could be jerked aside from it, roared the reminder that this World Cup had been repetitively considered in terms of its likely violence.

So much had been written of the South American hostility towards European football; of the desire for 'revenge' for South American 'ill-treatment' in 1966; of the inevitable explosions when conflicting temperaments collided over the interpretation of 'fair' and 'foul' on the field; of the impossibility of referees' controlling players fired with such insistent national ambition. Now, after the marching bandsmen, the parade of small boys wearing the playing colours of the sixteen teams – the England colours loudly booed and jeered without consideration for the Mexican children wearing them – the formal speeches from the Presidential box and the massing of the FIFA flags, these predictions were to be put to the first test. Pessimism could not be avoided amid the marvelling, as the opening ceremony reached its end in a spectacular prettiness: 50,000 multi-coloured balloons rising gently from the pitch in huge clusters, like chandeliers against the ceiling of an ice-blue sky.

Even in retrospect one feels no sense of churlishness in having resisted the embrace of Mexican exultancy in those fevered moments of relish. Twenty-four hours earlier FIFA's deep concern at the probable nature of this tournament had been given unequivocal expression by the president, Sir Stanley Rous. When managers and officials respresenting most of the sixteen finalists were brought together on Saturday, ostensibly to iron out any lingering administrative problems, Sir Stanley made an emphatic appeal for 'a genuine, sporting approach' to the coming football.

There was no question of this being merely a little formal, avuncular finger-wagging. The words were solemn, and the manner deliberately urgent. He said: 'We ask . . . that you warn your players that any violent or brutal play will result in their dismissal from the field. So too will any retaliation, and particularly any show of dissent from referees' decisions.'

This was Rous's final warning after months of nagging at both referees and national football authorities. It was nearly nine months since he had delivered an uncompromising speech of complaint and remonstration at a FIFA referees' conference in Florence, in which he was specific about most of the failings in top class refereeing which contribute so much to the evils in modern football.

He asked then: 'How many referees will give a penalty against a home team early in a match, when play is often most fierce?' And he told the conference: 'We have all seen indirect free kicks given inside the penalty area instead of penalty kicks. We have all seen referees whistle for penalty offences inside the area, and then place the ball a foot or so outside it.' He was bitter about 'referees who are tired, overweight, unfit or just plain lazy', and who often left vital decisions to their linesmen. 'These men ought to retire,' he said.

Rous was still pursuing this aggressive line of outspoken thought when he arrived in Mexico. As a former referee who handled thirty-four international matches he has always had a fully developed regard for the importance in football of the man with the whistle. If it can fairly be complained that it has taken Rous too many years to carry the message to the referees, it is equally true that no other voice in FIFA has ever remotely approached this degree of boldness, however belated, in acknowledging one of the most dangerous areas of deficiency in the sport.

A few days before the tournament opened, standing in the sun at a British Embassy reception for the English team, Rous reasserted all his previous dissatisfaction with much international refereeing. He had seen a recent example of cowardice which appalled him: a referee changing two vital decisions, each one affecting the score in a game, on the intervention of a linesman who was 35–40 yards away from the incident. He said: 'I've been telling the referees here that if I see one of them change a decision like that because of a linesman he's dead as far as I am concerned. These referees have got to accept responsibility. They know the laws of the game better than I do. It's courage they need.'

The preliminary matches which Rous had been watching had given him no comfort at all. 'The players are still losing their tempers, arguing with the referee, even in the warm-up matches,' he said. 'Things don't look very hopeful with some of these teams.'

Observations of that kind were being reported from numerous corners of the competition. If not all of them had quite the stamp of respectability that went with Rous's carefully weighed words they still added up to a considerable aggregate of alarm. There could have been few journalists or football officials in Mexico in the week before the opening match who did not seriously fear that the tournament would be intolerably disfigured by violent play and inept refereeing, or even that it might be ended prematurely for those reasons.

When Rous faced his first Press conference of the tournament, on May 23 in the grand-American setting of the Maria Isabel Hotel in Mexico City, the questioning returned again and again to these fears:

Was the whole future of the World Cup in danger?

No, but the future participation of individual countries could be, if they ignored FIFA's appeals and warnings.

Was it true, as a report from Brazil suggested, that there was 'a plot' involving English officials, particularly Sir Stanley and Ken Aston (the English representative on the Referees' Committee), to establish a refereeing system which would unjustly penalise non-European players?

The accusation was entirely false.

If a player was sent off the field, would he be automatically suspended?

In general, yes.

How was the language difficulty to be overcome?

The three officials for each match would have a common language; but it was not necessary for referees to be able to talk to players. 'It is better if they can't sometimes.'

So how would the referee communicate?

With his whistle.

That last riposte was typically Rous. At seventy-five years of age this former secretary of the English F.A. was still capable of combative quick thinking on his feet (and later the political in-fighting of the tournament would give him further opportunities to show his talent for it). But while the answer dealt with the questioner it did not dispose of the problem. We all had clearly in our minds the ugly memory of that exercise in miscommunication in London in 1966, when it took the West German referee, Herr Kreitlein, eight minutes to send off Rattin, the Argentine captain, and restart the quarter-final against England. It was unimaginable that if a similar situation were to arise in a European–South American game in Mexico the match could possibly be finished.

So a few days before the 1970 World Cup began a very black question-mark hung over the capabilities of the thirty chosen referees, and over FIFA's ability to prepare them. Their selection alone was dubious. A glance at the list was sufficient to show beyond any doubt that they were not the thirty best referees in the world. The referee from the United Arab Republic, Mr Aly Hussein Kandil, was aged fifty; there were men from the United States, Ethiopia and Bermuda, whose experience of handling football at the highest level could not be adequate, however fit and honest they were. There were two particularly notable absentees, Italy's Lo Bello and Brazil's Marques, who were both regarded in their own countries without serious challenge as referees at the top of the ratings.

But political compromise has a busy hand in every aspect of the World Cup. Referees arrived in Mexico in much the same way that some of the teams did, not because they were excellent but because lobbying and block voting decided who should be pitted against whom. The diplomatic explanations for some of these odd choices were more creditable for their dexterity than for their conviction. Rous said that since FIFA spent a

great deal of money on training referees in countries where
football was weak 'it would be an insult to the referees if they
were not taken into consideration for the World Championship'. Ken Aston argued that it was right and proper to use
the World Cup to extend the level of a country's refereeing.
Rous said that the most popular of the leading countries'
referees were not necessarily the best; Aston thought it fair to
'give someone else a chance' since Lo Bello and Marques had
already officiated at a previous World Cup. (So, it might be
added, had the elderly Mr Kandil.)

None of these arguments answered the complaint that, on the
face of the matter, some of the world's best and most vulnerable
footballers were going to be exposed to considerable physical
abuse without the protection of the referees most accustomed
to spotting it. But FIFA, for the first time in its history, could
claim that it had taken some firmly practical steps to correct
the deficiencies inherent in the eccentric choice of referees that
politics imposes. For the first time FIFA had devised a training
scheme for the referees specifically for a World Cup.

It is astonishing to note, in Aston's words, that: 'The
maximum preparation we ever had before was a pre-tournament conference of about one hour, with a general pep-talk.'
Nothing could show more starkly how far behind the development of football the whole philosophy of refereeing had fallen.
While the game had grown to the most intense physical
competitiveness the referees were still expected to be able to
control it by some form of magical exercise of assumed understanding: the inspired outsider, supposedly armed with an
integrity that would silence any protest at inefficiency. It was
one of the grimmest jokes in football.

In Mexico, at last, some of the modern principles of coaching
footballers were applied to the referees as well. For the first
time they were brought together a full week before the tournament began; previously they merely had to report forty-eight
hours before. Also they were all accommodated, like a team,
in the same hotel. They had a daily schedule of training and

group talks. At their conferences they studied a film which had
been put together from sixty different incidents, mostly in
international football, involving tackling and controversial
aspects such as the goalkeeper's four-step rule.

They were grouped for discussions according to their
command of one of four languages: English, French, German
and Spanish. This afforded some petty political point-scoring,
as when the Egyptian and the Israeli, both with English, took
opportunities to snub each other, but at least it made it possible
for the referees to argue the application of the laws at length.
When the thirty were all together each man received simultaneous translation through headphones.

(It is an instructive sidelight on the effectiveness of this
attempt at unification that the referees at least managed a
little collective bargaining of a mildly aggressive kind: they
won themselves an increase in their daily allowance for living
in one of the world's most expensive cities, from £8 to £10, and
they persuaded the reluctant management of their hotel to
provide them with set meals at a cut price. England's referee,
Jack Taylor, arguing with the special knowledge of a master
butcher, was credited with a particular stubbornness in the
latter dispute.)

By the middle of the pre-tournament week the referees had
achieved a fair impersonation of, say, a school old boys football
club, subduing old resentments and present jealousies as they
settled into the arduous task of getting fit for matches in
defiance of age and burdening flesh. Every morning a bus took
them out to a sports club in one of Mexico City's most affluent
suburbs, where they trained under the little West German
FIFA coach, Dettmar Cramer. He was shrewd at his job. The
referees said they were impressed by the way he adapted his
demands on them, according to their ages and the differing
conditions in which they arrived.

One could see readily enough that he had his problems: there
were some grey faces and some wobbling paunches as the
referees lapped their training pitch. The city's altitude, at

7,500 feet, was clearly a severe distraction to some of them. Yet there was an appreciable boisterousness among the more robust. Nearly all the referees were in their mid-forties; they were kicking into goal and dribbling the ball with noisy pleasure.

Aston, with a towel over his head and shoulders against the burn of the sun, was garrulous in his gratification at what he plainly regarded already as a success story. He said: 'Look at them, the sweat's pouring out of them, isn't it? Do you know what's just happened? At the end of his session Dettmar said, "Thank you, gentlemen," and they broke into spontaneous applause.'

He pointed out other members of the Referees' Committee, two of them stretched out drenched on the touchline. 'It's really a gimmick, I suppose – you know, the officers joining in with the troops,' he said. 'But it's working. The boys are saying, "Even the old crabs on the committee are having a go".'

Aston was emphatic that the referees had established 'a tremendous *esprit de corps*'. He said: 'It has exceeded my wildest expectations. . . . Honestly, there's no problem at all here.'

Aston's enthusiasm was difficult to resist. But the thought persisted that vigorous amiability among the World Cup referees still did not guarantee any courage or uniformity in quelling violent football. Aston smothered the doubt like a goalkeeper at the feet of a centre-forward. 'On interpretation of the laws there is no division between the South American and European referees at all,' he said. 'That division has always been much smaller than the Press and the television commentators have made it. Look, I've seen the same kind of tackling in South American football as you get in the English League and in Italy. It's only when you get it in a match against Europeans that the South American players make use of it.'

But in spite of this fulsome assurance it was evident that the critical controversy over the familiar European defender's tackle from behind remained a nagging concern for many of the referees. This tackle, in which, as the defender's foot hooks from behind, the man in possession is almost certain to be tripped, even if the tackler goes for the ball, had provided a focus for most of the heated South American complaints about European criminality on the football field.

While Aston talked about 'unanimity' and, as a slight reservation, about the need for 'a litte give and take', the French-speaking group came hurrying to him. Dispensing with words, and with agitated gestures, they went into an energetic demonstration of variants on the tackle from behind. After each lunge and stumble they turned to face Aston with palms held upwards and eyebrows raised in puzzled dumb-show. Aston said: 'See what I mean?' The comment was unintentionally as ambiguous as the referees' verdict on their simulated 'incidents'.

As a rider to his confidence Aston, who had an eventful career as a referee, made one unanswerable point about the conduct of the games to come. He said: 'We think we've got unanimity. But unless the teams know exactly what inter-pretation to expect there will be problems. You can't start teaching players lessons on the laws in the middle of a World Cup match.'

Reinforcing this view, the Referees' Committee issued on the eve of the tournament a guide to discipline on the field. It went to all the team managers, who were asked to instruct their players to pay attention to it. Inevitably the document had to lose some persuasive strength because it contained the qualifying line: 'The decision in many cases is a matter of the referee's opinion.' Even so the detail in the guide was admirably clear and its publication underlined FIFA's declared intention that the World Cup referees should be strict and the players well aware of it. The guide included these points:

A tackle with a foot lifted off the ground was 'permissible unless it is seen to be dangerous to the opponent';
A sliding tackle which tripped the opponent without

making contact with the ball would be punished by a direct free kick;

A tackle from behind would be permitted, as long as the ball was played without contact with the legs of the man in possession; but an indirect free kick would be given if the tackler kicked his opponent before the ball, and a direct free kick if the tackler first charged his man;

A man who used an arm to hold off an opponent would be punished by a direct free kick, as would a player who jumped at another under the pretext of attempting to head the ball;

Running across an opponent's path (the form of obstruction most used by South American players) would incur an indirect free kick;

Arguing with the referee would bring a caution;

Any 'deliberate physical foul' might cause a player to be sent off the field without previous caution.

None of this advice added anything new to the standard conduct of football; but issuing the guide was important, because it showed that FIFA had recognised the special problems of World Cup football, and had been bold enough to alert everyone to them and then invite players, coaches and referees to vindicate the tournament. No player or official could now easily plead innocent ignorance or honest misunderstanding.

But FIFA's president, a day before the first match, was in a sceptical mood. Rous said: 'I suppose there will still be managers who will just say casually to their players, "Oh, by the way, don't argue with the referee".' It was pessimism grown out of disillusioning experience.

In selecting the referee for the inaugural match authority had plainly gone for a man to hammer in the nails of their message. The choice – some people would argue that the man's nationality made him unrivalled – was of the West German, Kurt Tschenscher, aged forty-two and one of the World Cup

6   Half-time marching display at Puebla

7   Sweden's Bo Larsson flies through the air after being tripped. The two
    Uruguayan players are Atilio Ancheta (*left*) and Luis Ubiñas

8   Geoff Hurst's header is saved by the Rumanian goalkeeper Adamache

9   English 'mascot' Ken Bailey and a Brazilian supporter in Guadalajara

referees in 1966. His linesmen were Taylor, the Englishman,
and Keith Dunstan, Bermuda. The three were among the
fittest of the officials in training. No one doubted that they
would need calm pulses at noon on May 31.

The pre-match excitement had gathered with a galloping
momentum. Mexico City, that mass of contradictions in which
splendour and vulgarity, misery and exquisiteness entwine
amid a prevailing sense of combustible raffishness, had lit up
its metropolitan streets overnight with a characteristically
disarming touch. All along the Reforma, the tree-lined dual-
carriageway which is the city's Piccadilly and Mall and Golden
Mile, fairy-light footballs bounced in the air from the heads
and feet of fairy-light Juanitos, replicas of the figure of the
little boy in a sombrero used by Mexico as the World Cup
emblem. And overnight there was a tentative prelude to the
rhythmic sounding of car horns which was to be so memorable
an accompaniment to later scenes of chaotic revelry.

Inside the stadium, after a noisy and impatient drive to join
the acres of vehicles parked, so it seemed, to the horizon, we
were taut on our ledge among those roaring tiers, ready for the
first kick of the tournament. The chanting of 'Me-hee-co' was
like punches in the ear; the balloons, detached from their
clumps, drifted on the still air like blossom; there was a hard
heat.

In less frenetic circumstances during the past few days there
had been reason to doubt whether this opening match would
be much distinguished either by the thrill or the elegance of its
football. Russia had to be regarded as much the strongest side
in Group One since Belgium seemed to have skills but a lack
of power; Mexico appeared still a 'developing nation' in
footballing terms and El Salvador an improbable presence.

But the Russians had looked sullen and pale in their shabby,
bare hotel, with its prison-like railings and general air of
suspicion, and what information came out of the camp consistently suggested boredom and subdued dissension. More

D

materially, Mexico had suffered the serious loss of their midfield player, Alberto Onofre, who broke a leg during training.
(He was replaced by Marcos Rivas, the organising committee
setting aside the rule on the deadline for final listing of players
so as to accommodate him.) The prospect was not exactly
golden.

In the first minute of play in this World Cup we were shown
one of the problems which the thin air of high altitude created
for players unaccustomed to it. Evriuzhikhin ran cleanly away
from the Mexican cover on the left and crossed hard to the far
post, where Nodia was perfectly positioned for the shot but was
completely deceived by the unexpected pace of the ball.

Quickly afterwards came the first foul of the tournament, a
harassing tackle from behind by Bishovets on Vantolra, as
the Mexican defender shielded the ball from him. Within
seconds the West German referee had awarded fouls against
Nodia, for dangerous play, and against Shesternev, the Russian
captain, for his heavy contact with Valdivia. It was already
apparent that Tschenscher was performing exactly the role of
implacable disciplinarian that FIFA had implied, if not
declared, they wanted of him.

The early play was tentative in attack, nervily wary in
defence. Both sides maintained careful 4–3–3 formations, with
Mexico soon suggesting they would be much the more ready
to hurry forward from the middle, and the Russian defence
hinting at a frailty out of proportion to the threatening abilities
of the Mexican forwards. The first quarter of an hour was
certainly more notable for its diffident football than for any
enterprise.

But after twenty minutes Shesternev betrayed his own reputation as one of football's most secure defenders by misjudging
the flight of a high through ball, and López sprinted forward
with instant opportunism to head at the goal as the ball
bounced in front of him, close to the six-yard line. Kavazashvili
made a remarkable save, punching out with both fists.

The crowd responded to this near-miss, the game's first

startling activity in attack, with a series of roars that seemed to make the concrete move. The noise had barely lessened when Herr Tschenscher pounced, over-zealously one felt, on what looked like a trivial error of nervousness by the Russian goal-keeper; Kavazashvili was penalised for taking too many steps with the ball in his hands. Guzmán's free kick, taken no more than twelve yards from the goal, thumped into the wall of defenders, then went careering out for a corner. Again it was pushed out, but was immediately returned to ricochet off a Russian body. López leapt forward to half-volley over the bar.

Now half an hour had passed; the players had run into an urgent, aggressive pace. But the tone of the match remained watchful and stern; it was never to take off into optimism. Rapidly in the closing section of the first half two Russians, Bishovets and Lovchev, prompted elaborate gestures of dis-approval from Herr Tschenscher. The crowd bayed while the Press stand argued whether Tschenscher was showing the players the yellow card, to denote official cautioning, or merely re-packing his breast pocket. (It transpired that Lovchev was booked, but not Bishovets. In Tschenscher's case Rous proved right about the greater certainty of the language of the whistle; the man produced the card like a magician with too many rabbits.)

For twenty minutes after the interval the Russians took control of the match. With Puzach substituting for Serebriani-kov on the right of the midfield there was a more certain touch in the side's build-up. Soon Bishovets produced a confident, flowing run, and after taking a return pass from Muntian he put in a fierce shot just wide of a post, a moment before he sank under a tackle.

Bishovets' fleetness and his elusive swerves during this period made him easily the most exciting forward of the match. But he was harshly treated by the Mexican defenders, Peña and Pérez bringing him down dangerously close to the penalty area with particular callousness. A free kick by him, hit short and low across the area, was beyond the Mexicans' anticipation; but Puzach, unimpeded, put the ball high over the bar.

Behind the Russian front runners Asatiani, Muntian and Puzach were darting into the debris of broken Mexican attacks to carry the ball swiftly forward. It seemed that Mexico, the lighter and less studied side, were now to be overwhelmed. But abruptly the game shifted in character; Mexico increased the weight of their tackles, lifted the pace; Russia, with Bishovets looking bruised and dejected, having headed wide from within touching distance of Calderón, regressed into a half-ordered defensiveness.

The game ended much as it had begun, in a flurry of body-checking against a general uneasiness. There had been no goals, no great invention, no extreme violence. The crowd's final applause was a slight noise compared with their welcoming of the event. But there was a sense of relief more than disappointment. Such had been the fear that had accompanied the suppositions about this World Cup that its opening game seemed to have been a return to a mundane sanity rather than a betrayal of hopes. It had been simply a tough, mediocre football match. It could have been worse.

Herr Tschenscher's busy use of the yellow card was eventually given official translation as cautions for Logofet, Asatiani, Nodia, as well as Lovchev, of Russia, and for Peña, of Mexico. Ken Aston had some fluent words afterwards, and surely they were apt. He said:

'I bet that German referee gets a tremendous slating. But what is he to do? Everyone's been saying that there's going to be terrible violence in Mexico. Well, do you want that, or do you want the kind of refereeing we had today? I know what I'd rather have.'

Mexico o   U.S.S.R. o

BELGIUM *v.* EL SALVADOR

Aztec Stadium, June 3

Twelve games and a war that kills 3,000 people make an exhausting path to the World Cup finals, even by the flamboyant standards of Latin American football. So El Salvador's appearance in the last sixteen was regarded with a great deal of curiosity, if not much expectation. After all, they had struggled to eliminate footballing nonentities like Curaçao and Trinidad, had been taken to a play-off by Honduras – followed by that murderous 72-hour punitive expedition – and had needed another play-off against Haiti to qualify for Mexico.

Despite the efforts of several hundred El Salvador followers to arouse enthusiasm with their blue flags and spirited chants, this second Group One game at the Aztec Stadium was a grey anticlimax to the colour and fervour of the opening ceremony and inaugural game. The stadium was less than half full and the sun shone sporadically and weakly. As the players lined up for the national anthems the white-shirted El Salvadoreans were, with a couple of exceptions, dwarfed by the Belgians. There was an immediate temptation to compare them with the North Koreans of 1966, but the resemblance was little more than physical, as we were to see quickly.

The first ordeal of the afternoon turned out to be the playing of the El Salvador anthem. After several verses the band paused for breath and the Belgian players broke away gratefully, only to be halted sheepishly in their tracks by another rousing chorus. Cheered on by the Mexicans, who were hoping for an upset to help their own team towards the quarter-finals, El Salvador began brightly, winning a share of the ball but hardly ever penetrating the Belgian penalty area. El Salvador's back four were drawn up rigidly across the field as the Belgians, pushed by the industrious Van Moer, began to probe for weaknesses. They found plenty. El Salvador were disastrously vulnerable to the quickly played through-ball.

In the first minute Lambert, tall and rugged and an

enthusiastic chaser of half chances, almost caught a weak back pass by the captain, Mariona. But the goalkeeper, Magaña, dressed in black and wearing a large floppy cap, saved the situation with a dive at Lambert's boots. It was the start of a busy afternoon for this eccentric but able goalkeeper. His saves during the match included a sliding tackle on Lambert, who was so astonished that he failed to score; and on one occasion Magaña raced off his line to head clear a high back pass, still wearing his cap. Unfortunately, he was also fond of taking occasional goal kicks side-footed, which several times plunged his defence into trouble.

The Belgians, through Van Moer and Puis, won instant control of midfield and it was Van Moer, his socks round his ankles, who struck the first blow after thirteen minutes. He let fly from thirty yards and Magaña, late going for the ball, was completely deceived by its speed through the thin air. Next Puis, palpably left-footed, was given room to set up two more long shots, but this time Magaña was ready.

The Belgian back line, mainly from the Standard Liège club, showed their teamwork the first time El Salvador really threatened. Rodríguez put Martínez, his country's leading goalscorer, in possession near the penalty area but before he could manoeuvre a shooting position Martínez was swamped by three red shirts. Soon afterwards Martínez unveiled his power and set the tom-toms beating in the stands when, taking a free kick for hands against Thissen, he struck a tremendous shot just too high. Apart from these isolated thrusts, Belgium dominated. But they rarely threatened; the game was free of rough play and almost equally devoid of excitement. Belgium, and in particular their captain Van Himst, seemed unable to adjust to the combination of the ball's slowness over the thick, tough grass and its bullet-like velocity through the air.

Five minutes into the second half Belgium deserved to score again. Lambert, whose prodigious throws almost equal those of Chelsea's Hutchinson, lobbed the ball deep into the penalty area and it fell to Van Moer, who smashed in a tremendous shot. But Magaña threw himself high to his right to turn it over the bar as Van Moer gaped in sheer disbelief. However, after fifty-five minutes it was 2–0, and again the persistent Van Moer was the scorer. Semmeling, whose darting runs were a source of increasing embarrassment to the El Salvador backs, broke down the right and crossed the ball head high. Van Himst lunged and missed, typically on this miserable afternoon for him, but his challenge was enough to distract Magaña. The goalkeeper could only fingertip the ball to Van Moer who ran it home joyfully, finishing in the net himself.

The game was now effectively ended as a contest, and the biggest roars, which must have puzzled the players, came from large groups of spectators huddled round tiny portable TV sets watching the Brazilian goals going in against Czechoslovakia. After an hour El Salvador brought on Cortes Méndez in defence for Mendoza. He arrived just in time to see Van Himst miss an open goal, nudging the ball wide of Magaña but past the post.

El Salvador's only real chance came when Belgium lost possession with too many men upfield and a long clearance found Aparicio. He raced down the middle clear of all defenders but Piot was off his line like an Olympic sprinter and dived at Aparicio's feet to smother the shot. Poor Aparicio lay on the ground for several seconds in despair as the crowd whistled and jeered, but he got a commiserating pat on the head from Piot. Belgium broke away immediately and a superb backheel from Devrindt put Van Himst in on goal. Again he shot feebly wide, rousing the bored crowd to a chorus of 'Mexico, Mexico'.

El Salvador, who had never looked imaginative, now also ran out of enthusiasm. But Belgium were able to manage only one more goal, from a penalty. Devrindt's chip sent Semmeling careering into the penalty area, where he was chopped down by Mariona. As soon as the injured Semmeling had been treated Lambert took the kick, scoring emphatically to Magaña's left and then limping off to be replaced by Polleunis.

The game proved one thing. El Salvador, as they had admitted, were in Mexico to gain experience and very little else. Magaña, though, felt this defeat needed his analytical explanation. He said at the Press conference afterwards: 'Our forwards lack experience. I am the most experienced player in the team, and if I had been in the forward line the result would have been different.'

Belgium 3   El Salvador 0

U.S.S.R. *v.* BELGIUM

Aztec Stadium, June 6

After the sterility of their opening game against Mexico, the familiar arguments were levelled against Russia. They were too stereotyped, too predictable, lacking flair and flexibility said the newspapers, both in England and Mexico. The ponderous bear would be baited by the quicksilver Belgians, some thought. They had clearly not watched Belgium's distressingly un-convincing display against El Salvador three days previously.

The Russian team manager Gavril Katchalin dropped three players from the side which had drawn with Mexico – Lovchev, Serebrianikov and Nodia – and replaced them with Dzodzua-shvili in defence, Khurtsilava (who had played so well against England at Wembley in 1968) in midfield and Khmelnitski in attack. Belgium, well aware they would be unable to indulge in the 4–2–4 they had employed with impunity against El Salvador, replaced the injured striker Devrindt with Standard Liège's tough defender Jeck.

Russia again had to face some of the heat they had endured on the opening day of the tournament but this time the four o'clock kick-off ensured that half the pitch lay in the shade of the Aztec Stadium's vast tiers, and by the interval the field was completely free of the bright sunshine.

Belgium went off like a Panzer division operating in good tank country, thrusting forward swiftly and confidently and pressing the Russians into distinctly un-Soviet haste and harassment. In the first minute Khurtsilava's wild back pass cost a corner, and soon the Russian defence was leaning heavily on the familiar figure of Shesternev, who was striding around in the manner of an overworked but composed fireman attempting to stamp out a prairie blaze without the assistance of water. Van Moer, again playing superbly in the middle for Belgium, was Russia's principal tormentor, and was getting fine support from Dockx.

The turning-point came after only a quarter of an hour. First Belgium should have scored. Afonin felled Semmeling out on the right and the Belgian floated the free kick beautifully into Van Moer's well-timed run. Kavazashvili could only parry the header and the ball came back to Van Moer, who from inside the six-yard line struck the bar. Van Moer was still shaking his head in disbelief when Russia scored, dramatically and unexpectedly. Bishovets took a short pass from Khmelnitski, moved forward a stride and pounded a thirty-yard shot past Piot, who dived late. It was a replica of Belgium's own first goal against El Salvador. Two minutes later Belgium almost conceded a second, when Khmelnitski's lunge at an inswinging corner by Muntian from the left was blocked on the line by Piot.

This success instantly dispelled Russia's hesitancy and introversion. In midfield the tall, strong Asatiani found the confidence to match his physique and Muntian's peripatetic industry gained a sharp, cutting edge. The front three – Bishovets, Khmelnitski and Evriuzhikhin – now getting the service they had been denied, started running full tilt at the Belgian back line and opening breaches which even the hardworking Jeck could not plug. Belgian confidence was further undermined by Piot's penchant for punching balls he could have comfortably caught; but after nervily scrambling away Evriuzhikhin's dipping corner kick the blond goalkeeper redeemed himself with a magnificent save from Muntian.

Ill-fortune struck Russia when, with half an hour gone, Kaplichni gashed his head in a collision with Lambert and had to go off. His place was taken by Lovchev who, with Van Himst again strangely ineffective, was given time and space to settle into the centre of the Russian defence; and we were even treated to the rare sight of the massive Shesternev forsaking his defensive patrolling to surge upfield and release a fine through-ball which enabled Muntian to put Piot through his acrobatic paces. Seconds later the elusive Muntian scurried forward again, wheeling around the rubble of Belgium's defensive wall and forcing Piot to concede a corner.

At the start of the second half one looked in vain for a resurgence of Belgian spirit. Instead, as the game flowed steadily away from them the players indulged in bouts of bickering and recrimination which gave some support to the rumours circulating in Mexico City that some of the team were homesick and others were unhappy over a differential pay scale.

Then, after an hour, Russia scored twice in six minutes. The first of these came, fittingly, from Asatiani, their most accomplished player. Penned in on the left-hand edge of the penalty area, Asatiani worked his way smoothly inside two Belgians and drove the ball past Piot. The third goal fell to Bishovets, who burst through the centre and finished with a massive shot.

With fifteen minutes left, Russia brought on Kiselev for Dzodzuashvili and quickly went four up with one of the best goals so far in the tournament. When Khmelnitski's progress from left wing towards goal was barred he squared the ball across the width of the penalty area to Evriuzhikhin. It was promptly chipped back towards the penalty spot and Khmelnitski, diving full length past Dewalque's tackle, headed just inside Piot's right-hand post. Even the Mexicans had to cheer that one.

Bishovets, with a double taste of success, almost had a hat-trick when he turned Kiselev's cross just under the angle of post and bar – but Piot clawed it clear. Five minutes from time, however, Belgium got a goal which was to have unexpected consequences in the Group One table. Van Moer's long-distance pot shot evaded Kavazashvili's dive, slapped against an upright and rolled out to Lambert who kicked it high into the net.

So those who had been saying that Russia couldn't score were proved wrong, four times. Katchalin understandably expressed satisfaction with the result afterwards, but Belgium's manager, Raymond Goethals, did not attend the Press conference. There was much urgent patching to be done before the vital match with Mexico.

U.S.S.R. 4   Belgium 1

MEXICO *v.* EL SALVADOR

Aztec Stadium, June 7

The combination of a cloudless Sunday morning and the prospect of Mexico's first World Cup win for eight years clogged the roads to the Aztec Stadium hours before the noon starting time. Cars, lorries, buses and trams were festooned with flags and crammed with people happily anticipating some good old-fashioned slaughter in the sun. El Salvador were clearly regarded as sacrificial offerings on the Aztec altar, and well before the kick-off the stadium was filled with fans giving a brilliantly coloured overture of their flag-waving, chanting and whistling routines.

The Mexican manager, Raul Cárdenas, was understandably satisfied with the performance of his back line against Russia, but he made two changes in the middle and two more in attack. Cárdenas bowed to a week-long campaign in the local Press by recalling his experienced striker Enrique Borja, a nephew of Gustavo Díaz Ordaz, Mexico's president and the man who officially declared the World Cup open. As the teams lined up Borja knelt in prayer. His supplications, echoed by the capacity crowd, looked like earning swift response when Mexico won three corners in the first five minutes, each greeted by a roar worthy of a goal.

But El Salvador were not to be intimidated. They held on coolly through the early hurricane and Martínez had the stadium shrieking in apprehension when he back-headed a free kick just over Calderón's crossbar. In the next minute the shriek became a wail when Rodríguez outpaced the Mexican captain Peña to a through-ball, only to see his snap shot hit an upright.

It was not long before the referee, the Egyptian brigadier-general Aly Kandil, imposed his presence. When Cortes Méndez walked away with the ball after Mexico had been awarded a throw-in Kandil booked him, a reaction more in keeping with the suppression of military insubordination than with controlling a football match. El Salvador captain Mariona was next to be booked. His offence: wasting time over the taking of a free kick.

Mexico's clumsiness was exceeded only by their mounting hysteria as they failed to break through. Once four players tried to head in a free kick and succeeded only in colliding with each other. Then when Padilla, endlessly inventive and energetic on the left, combined with González to work an opening, his cross was chested down by Fragoso to Borja, who mis-hit the ball wildly. Valdivia was next to fire over after González's shot had bounced off Magaña's chest. With Cortes Méndez, Quintanilla and Flamenco Cabezas winning a surprising number of balls in midfield, El Salvador looked more assured and more dangerous than the agitated Mexicans. Once Calderón had to plunge desperately to stop Aparicio scoring.

Then came the first ugly incident in the conduct of the tournament. The electric scoreboard had been indicating half-time for fully a minute, with the English linesman, Jack Taylor, vainly trying to draw Kandil's attention to the fact, when the ball went out of play inside Mexico's half. The other linesman,

Keith Dunstan of Bermuda, signalled a throw to El Salvador, but as they moved forward to take the ball, Kandil overruled Dunstan and awarded a free kick to Mexico. The perceptive Peña pushed it quickly down the left to Padilla. Padilla's cross, swift, low and accurate, ran to Borja who, alone in front of the net, completely missed his kick. But Valdivia was also there and he scored easily. As Kandil pointed to the centre spot El Salvador went berserk, milling round the referee and yelling at him to talk to Dunstan. Kandil pushed them away and held up his yellow warning disc, which prompted several Salvadoreans to turn their backs on him, offering their numbers. He obliged by booking Flamenco Cabezas and Magaña. They refused to restart the game and Kandil had to fetch the ball from the net and carry it to the centre circle. Ordered to kick off, El Salvador booted the ball into the crowd, whereupon the referee blew for half-time at last and prudently waited for the players to leave the field before following them down the tunnel.

After the interval Mexico fielded López for Borja, who had been in wretched form, and inside a minute they had scored again through Valdivia. Taking a pass from Fragoso he moved into the right corner of the penalty area, shook off two tackles and shot across Magaña's body into the far wall. They were soon three in front when Munguía lobbed the ball forward to López, who headed it down for Fragoso to score. By now El Salvador's admirably disciplined play of the first half seemed to have belonged to a different team. They were kicking aimlessly and their tight marking was a mere memory.

With fifteen minutes left Mexico pulled off López and brought on Basaguren, who shot their fourth goal – a ludicrous gift – seven minutes from the end. Mariona dispossessed Valdivia but tried to walk the ball clear. With Valdivia nagging at him, Mariona tried a back pass to his goalkeeper which failed to roll into the penalty area. As Magaña desperately tried to kick it away Valdivia reached the ball first and cut it back to Basaguren, who angled his shot into an empty goal.

The victory, combined with the news of Brazil's defeat of England in Guadalajara, brought an exultant demonstration of national fervour, the noisiest and most colourful Mexico City had ever witnessed. By late afternoon thousands of people had massed on and around the steps of the Independence Monument on the city's main boulevard, Paseo de la Reforma, endlessly chanting 'Mexico, Brazil'.

Traffic was soon brought to a halt along Reforma's three miles, and within two hours the whole city centre was paralysed. Drums throbbed, rattles whirred and bugles sounded cavalry charges as groups of young people raced through the streets, doing conga lines in and out of smart restaurants in the sophisticated Zona Rosa district. Cars with shrieking people perched on roofs and bonnets lent their horns to the caco-phony until batteries went flat or radiators boiled, when the vehicles were abandoned, adding to the chaos. The red, white and green of Mexico was everywhere. Clothing was outrage-ously improvised. One youth doing the samba on the roof of a stranded car was wearing a red sweater, white shorts and green plastic bags wrapped round his legs. Statues sprouted sombreros and flags, and the whoop-up went on almost until dawn, culminating in a raid on the FIFA headquarters at the Maria Isabel Hotel, where a ten-foot fibreglass football was wrenched from the roof of the entrance lobby and dribbled away into the night, never to be seen again. Next day shopkeepers checked on their goods, tested their shutters and wondered what would happen if Mexico won their next game.

Mexico 4   El Salvador 0

U.S.S.R. *v.* EL SALVADOR

Aztec Stadium, June 10

The David and Goliath aspect of a match between the world's biggest country and the World Cup's most improbable qualifier failed to stir much interest in Mexico City. Russia were already certain of a quarter-final place and El Salvador's capacity to absorb punishment seemed the only point at issue. The Mexicans, saving their lungs for the next day's key clash with Belgium and obviously convinced that the only way El Salvador could stop the Russians was by planting mines and laying barbed wire, stayed away in such large numbers that at one stage it looked as though the crowd might be out-numbered by the massed vendors of cushions, souvenirs, beer, hot dogs, sweets, cigarettes, ice cream and soft drinks. That good old English phrase 'end of season atmosphere' applied to this match, and the weather added a grey cloak of its own. There was a heavy overcast and thunder rumbled around the mountains, announcing the arrival of the Valley of Mexico's rainy season.

The Russians left out out their key midfield man Asatiani and also felt secure enough to do without the speed and pene-tration of Evriuzhikhin. They were replaced by Serebrianikov and Puzach, while the fair-haired Kiselev came in for Kaplichni, whose head wound sustained against Belgium was still not healed. El Salvador, in the sort of carefree mood that sometimes goes with elimination, gave a gallop to four of their reserves.

Russia soaked up the Salvadoreans' familiar flurry of enthusiasm from the kick-off and suffered no deeper indignity than seeing Kavazashvili make a confident stop from Portillo. After Rodríguez had achieved the distinction of beating Shesternev, only to lose control as he set himself for the shot, Russia flicked into overdrive and the expected one-way assault was on. The ball was being won with the minimum of fuss, moved forward with loving care and then used as an instrument to intimidate the crowd behind El Salvador's goal. Sere-

brianikov was the first to scatter the sparse terraces, followed
by Puzach, whose sense of direction with a diving header from
Khmelnitski's centre was much better, but still not good enough.
The Soviet monopoly was so absolute that even Shesternev
once found himself in El Salvador's penalty area. Obviously
enjoying the novelty, the Russian captain next produced an
incredibly delicate dribble, capped by a cunning centre
which curved out of Magaña's reach as he moved to take it.
The ball dropped on Khemelnitski's head by the far post; he
put it firmly into the crowd.

For a while after this Russia experimented with deep
floating crosses, but the project was abandoned when they saw
that Magaña had curbed his habitual flamboyance in deference
to such distinguished opposition. Still the Russians ran the
game with precise, controlled play which could have kept a
cricket scoreboard busy if it had contained the extra ingredient
of accurate finishing. One typical movement drew on the talents
of practically every Russian and, typically, ended with Puzach
shooting too high. Significantly, Bishovets again looked the
one player who might get a goal. After a marvellous penetrating burst had been wasted because nobody moved quickly
enough to collect the pass into Magaña's goal area, Bishovets
angrily went alone the next time and put a fierce cross drive
narrowly past.

But by half-time El Salvador, like Texans who had never
heard of the Alamo, were still holding out and perhaps hoping
for an act of God to rescue them. At one stage it looked as if
they might get it. Clouds hung over the Aztec's top tier, the
thunder was angry and insistent, and to complete the comparison with a murky English November afternoon the floodlights were switched on.

The first hint of Russia's apprehension came with the substitution of Evriuzhikhin for Puzach on the resumption, and his
busyness took quick toll against a team who seemed to regard
the second half of all their games as entirely unconnected with
the first forty-five minutes. Only five minutes had gone when

Bishovets, scuttling after a knifing through-ball from Serebrianikov, steered his shot just inside Magaña's right hand post.

With still no sign of a Russian deluge, the elements provided one of their own, sweeping the thin crowd from the
exposed sections and eroding El Salvador's resolve even further.
But as so often happens in such a one-sided affair, El Salvador
were suddenly given a equalising chance. After a throw on the
right Portillo hit a hard, dipping centre into the heart of the
area. For once Shesternev was absent and Kavazashvili
seemed to have taken root on his line; but Rodríguez, within
touching distance of the goalkeeper, looked this particular gift
horse in the tonsils, lunging with his head and missing. The
opportunity was not likely to come again.

Russia's second goal, seventeen minutes from the end, was
engineered and, inevitably, scored by Bishovets. Taking a pass
from Serebrianikov, Muntian eluded three defenders in a
dribble, and Bishovets survived a crash tackle to score firmly.
But Russia needed more goals to ensure the prize of a quarter-
final in the Aztec Stadium instead of the thin air of shabby
Toluca, and Asatiani's appearance for Kiselev after eighty
minutes was a measure of their anxiety.

Talking to the Press afterwards Gavril Katchalin managed to
avoid wincing when someone asked if he was satisfied with his
team's performance. 'We thought we would have a better
result,' he replied, his face a passing imitation of a Mexican
stone idol. When the inevitable question came about the non-
appearance of Lev Yashin in goal (the Mexican Press had
confidently predicted before every match that he would play),
Katchalin agreed with his questioner that Yashin, in his
fourth World Cup, was a good goalkeeper, 'but there was no
reason to change our best goalkeeper for a good one'.

El Salvador's disappearance from the competition without
scoring did not appear to have upset their coach, the stocky
verbose Hernan Carrasco. 'We have been getting better and
better each game,' he maintained. 'Our achievements have
been great.' And Rodríguez, who had earlier missed their best

E

chance against Russia, supported Carrasco. Goals didn't matter. 'We came to a very great school to learn.' Understandably, Russia did not share his feelings about goals. Their failure to fill the net meant an anxious wait to see what Mexico would do against Belgium.

U.S.S.R. 2   *El Salvador 0*

MEXICO *v.* BELGIUM

Aztec Stadium, June 11

Mexico had built a new national training centre for the World Cup, and installed their team among its still-uncompleted splendours a month before the tournament began. Hacked out of the harsh black volcanic rock of the Pedregal area, the centre lay about equidistant from the Aztec Stadium and the Olympic Village and in clear sight of both. Behind a high wall and a grille gate guarded by armed police the Mexican players relaxed three to a room in an elegantly simple hacienda-style building of rosewood and wrought iron, surrounded by rose gardens and practice pitches and overlooked only by the volcanic peaks which isolate the Valley of Mexico.

Like loyal boxing managers, both team chiefs told the newspapers that their boys would be O.K. on the day. Belgium's Raymond Goethals, small, slim, and with a cigarette dangling permanently from his lips, said Belgium would join Russia in the quarter-finals. Raul Cárdenas of Mexico, tall and ruggedly handsome, showed no sign of the crushing responsibility of steering his nation to their first-ever quarter-final. He talked readily and quietly to the trickle of journalists who managed to get past the guns on the gate. Yes, he said, he expected to win.

And all Mexico massed riotously behind him. Bands blared from the stands and cheer leaders bounded up and down exhorting the massed sections dressed in red, white or green uniforms to even more exhausting efforts; the baying babble was so evocative of a Hollywood Colosseum set that one English journalist asked 'Where's Nero sitting?' Above the large welcoming placard which announced that Mexico Opens Its Arms a fat man in a sombrero teetered on the retaining wall above the deep trench dividing the people from the players, his back to the pitch and manipulating a massive Mexican flag. He kept it up right through the game with utter contempt for his safety and unswerving disregard of what was actually happening behind him. Jungle drums beat out the Me-hee-co Ra-ra-ra rhythm as the teams appeared, walking with the measured step of bullfighters and dressed in unfamiliar colours in surrender to the dictates of the TV cameras. Mexico, almost hidden by a flock of photographers and even an artist doing rapid sketches, wore plum shirts instead of their green, and Belgium were in white.

After his dismal forty-five minutes against El Salvador, the Bring Back Borja campaign had been abandoned, and his place in Mexico's attack went to Pulido. Belgium, minus the injured Lambert, surprisingly picked Polleunis and kept the dangerous Devrindt on the substitutes' bench.

The mathematics of the match were that Belgium needed victory to stay in the Cup, while Mexico could qualify by drawing. But a draw seemed to be the last thing on their minds. The first shrieks were for Guzmán's narrow miss from Munguía's short free kick, awarded when Valdivia was fouled by Thissen. Belgium obviously considered that Valdivia was the man to mark, and proceeded to make their mark on him. He was hacked and harassed whenever he got the ball, the heaviest boot being Thissen's. Eventually a crunching collision put Valdivia off the field for brief treatment and Thissen was glared at, spoken to and booked by the Argentinian referee, Norberto Angel Coerezza.

Piot's proven vulnerability to the long shot had not been overlooked by Mexico, and Pulido, after hammering a superb crossfield ball to Fragoso, ran full tilt on to the return to shoot fractionally high from outside the area. The heavily pressed Belgians had hardly sampled the grass in their opponents' half when, in the sixteenth minute, Mexico were given the goal they had been chasing so energetically. Van Moer, deep in defence, miskicked a hasty clearance high into the air and as it fell near the penalty spot Jeck and Valdivia went for it. Jeck swept it away a split second before Valdivia could get there, and the Mexican fell over Jeck's outstretched leg with the ball well out of danger. But Mr Coerezza pointed for a penalty and Valdivia, who had been about to get up, did a bit of agonised rolling.

The Belgians' astonishment gave way quickly to fury and they surrounded the referee, who backed up against a goalpost for protection, waved them away and even threw a counter-punch as the players jostled him. The ball was booted high into the crowd; when it was retrieved Mexico's captain Peña moved up and shot a competent goal to the left of Piot's clawing dive.

Belgium, fragile enough before this, were in tatters and as Valdivia ran for Fragoso's pass near the penalty line Polleunis, acting on some suicidal impulse, moved away from the striker. With space and time to take aim Valdivia hit Piot's left-hand upright and the ball rebounded clear across the penalty area. Back came Valdivia to beat Piot to a weak back pass; he ran the ball to the bye-line but angled it just too strongly for Munguía's lunge.

Suddenly and incredibly the Mexicans eased their pressure, and Belgium, pushed by Jeck, Dockx, Semmeling and Van Moer, began to put their game together, and gave us the first glimpse of Calderón's frailty in goal when a gentle shot by Van Himst slid under his body for a corner.

As he blew for half time Mr Coerezza underwent another angry assault from the Belgians, particularly Piot, who paced off the pitch behind the referee making blatant money-count-ing signs and was booked for it.

The officials and the Belgian players were on the field and waiting two minutes before the Mexicans, looking strangely drained, straggled up the tunnel from the dressing rooms, to the announcement that Basaguren had replaced the mauled Valdivia. After a further minute's wait Mr Coerezza blew for the restart with still only eight Mexicans lined up. Among the temporarily missing trio was their captain, Peña. Nervous, edgy and apparently unable to credit that they were so close to qualifying, Mexico had completely lost their urgency of the first half hour. Vantolra gave away a corner unnecessarily and when Calderón flapped feebly at the kick it fell to Semmeling, whose shot was kicked off the line by Peña. Next Polleunis wasted a fine chance and was so disgusted that he provoked a clash with Peña and was booked.

With just under half an hour left Polleunis was replaced by Devrindt and straightaway Belgium almost equalised. Devrindt, unmarked, set himself firmly for Semmeling's floating centre and headed hard past Calderón towards the top corner. But Guzmán, standing on the line, kicked it acrobatically over the bar, finishing in the back of the net himself. From the corner Van Moer's header was clutched just in time by Calderón, and Belgium's resolution began to melt. They threatened only once more, Devrindt's shot flying wide to apprehensive squeals.

Time ran out with the Mexicans playing tip-tap possession football and the ecstatic crowd roaring chorus after chorus of *Cielito Lindo* and lighting paper torches to salute a memorable day for their country.

Afterwards, in the interviewing area underneath the stadium Cárdenas, chewing gum and wearing sunglasses against the glare of television floodlights, said he thought Coerezza's penalty award 'perfectly fair'. Then, in a style of which Sir Alf Ramsey would have approved, he dismissed questions about Mexico's 'negative play' in the second half. 'In the end what counts is a victory, and this was a victory.' He pointed out that Mexico had taken five points from three games, scored five goals and conceded none.

Waiting for Goethals turned out to be a waste of time. The angry Belgian manager stalked past the interview platform, but stopped in the exit tunnel to answer the questions of some British journalists, who were threatened by armed police called by a stadium official. Eventually the large and amiable Roland Petit, head of the Belgian delegation, ambled on to the interview platform, to be asked at once what he thought of the referee. 'I think that he might be an excellent referee, though his marking of the penalty was too strict,' he smiled. M. Petit's smile evaporated when a Mexican asked him 'You said that El Salvador and Israel should not be in the world championships. Now that you will be going home with these teams, has your opinion changed?' He snapped back, 'I could ask if you think that Mexico is strong enough to be here'.

At that very moment thousands of Mexicans were giving a jubilant affirmation to M. Petit's counter-question. Within minutes of the result on this Thursday afternoon, people abandoned their work, swarmed from offices, shops and building sites and on to the streets. They didn't need to be told by the football editions of the evening papers, which had used the size of type normally reserved for wars and miracles, 'WE QUALIFY'. Oil drums, dustbins, petrol cans and kitchen implements banged out the joyful message. One barefoot old woman, wrapped in a black shawl, tapped out the Me-hee-co rhythm almost reverently on a saucepan lid with a spoon. Rampant mobs of young people surged through the city, uprooting traffic signs, tearing saplings and branches from the parks and paralysing traffic even more swiftly than on the previous Sunday. Some of the more daring ones leapt on passing trams, dragged the poles from the overhead wires and danced on the roofs of the vehicles as they lay immobilised all over the city like beached whales.

On the Paseo de la Reforma strolling clumps of celebrants clogged the roadway; cars rolled along the wide pavements and through the shrubbery, and the vastly-outnumbered police wisely affected not to notice.

Saucer-eyed infants were paraded up and down by beaming couples to witness the memorable night, and under the glittering fairy lights the conga lines were winding up and down; one bunch of revellers paused to jeer mindlessly at the Union Jacks outside a restaurant called The Piccadilly Pub. As darkness fell the celebrations became more vigorous. Large gangs collected at every road junction, effectively sabotaging what little traffic progress there had been. The Press buses, which had set out for the city like a team of cautious covered wagons, were cheerfully assaulted by children who beat out the Me-hee-co rhythm, yanked open the rear doors and rocked the buses from side to side. After more than three hours the Press was still marooned in this ocean of dancing, screaming people. Plainly the night belonged to them. The buses were abandoned and the burdened photographers launched themselves, sweating and swearing, on to the pavements and into the swarming madness of this dazzling night.

Mexico 1   Belgium 0

GROUP ONE

	P	W	D	L	F	A	Pts
Russia	3	2	1	0	6	1	5
Mexico	3	2	1	0	5	0	5
Belgium	3	1	0	2	4	5	2
El Salvador	3	0	0	3	0	9	0

3 Group Two

Israel, Italy, Sweden, Uruguay

The drama in the topography alone added piquancy to watching the football in Group Two. The matches were shared between the cities of Puebla, eighty-five miles to the south-east of Mexico City, and Toluca, forty miles to the capital's south-west, and the journey to each stadium was by a road climbing high to a spectacular proximity with Mexico's volcanoes. The route to Puebla took us close to the snow peaks of Popocatepétl, 17,872 feet, and the giant's 'sleeping lady', Ixtaccíhuatl, 400 feet smaller. The extraordinary sunsets on this route, like huge daggers of lightning in the subtlest merging of pastel colours, fixed themselves unforgettably in the mind.

But while the similar magnificence of Toluca's setting was such a memorable pleasure the town had little to justify it as a place where sea-level footballers should compete for the World Cup. Toluca stands at 8,800 feet, reached by a drive from Mexico City which has one's ears popping much of the way – the road mounts to about 10,000 feet before it dips towards the town – and the place has a capricious June climate, mixing fire with wind and drizzle.

Toluca was included as a World Cup venue very late in the arrangements, and the explanation appeared to lie in the twisting lanes of Mexican politics, not in those of international football. The city is the capital of the State of Mexico; it had a young, ambitious governor, with a reputation as a coming force in the PRI, the country's ruling party; local popularity and national status were in jeopardy for a politician unable to deliver the vital goods in World Cup and Election year.

Except for its height, which had immediately noticeable effects on breathing and even, one suspected, on mental concentration, Toluca looked an oddly familiar town to an English football follower. Small (population just under 100,000), with narrow streets of squat, terrace houses linking shops, offices and factories, it had the insular atmosphere of a Northampton or a West Hartlepool, with a big bus station as a centre-piece, a huge street market of cheap goods for low incomes and a permanent air of sighing afternoon.

Toluca's football ground put the similarity beyond doubt: a rectangle of outer walling, stained and topped by broken glass and straggling barbed wire; cramped offices, too few lavatories, a damp chill in the stands. The ground held 30,400 spectators, and for only one of the four matches it staged was it to be filled.

Puebla was an altogether different proposition. Because of its sixty churches, many of them with an arresting architecture characterised by coloured tiling, it has won a loosely applied description as the Rome of Mexico. But to match the English comparisons with Toluca it is much better to bracket the city with Bath. At just over 7,000 feet Puebla is like a huge rock garden, the residential streets undulating through its shrubs so that every other corner is a vantage point.

Its stadium, built in 1968, is a miniature Aztec, circular and tiered, with a capacity of 35,500. Where Toluca was grim, Puebla's ground was roomy and unusually pleasant. The abundant Mexican talent for vivid decoration had given the main entrance a striking mural in which an Aztec battle scene and a football match converged in a tangle of limbs.

The city had prepared for the World Cup with flair and generosity; the pre-match and half-time entertainments, with bands and marching girls and dancers, grew more elaborate with each game. For one match the Press room was hung with water-colours by local children of football scenes: players in blues, reds and yellows, with popping eyes and immense arms stretching out in extremes of anguish, under titles such as 'La Protesta', 'Faul!' and 'Gol de Mexico!' Whatever football we were to see here Puebla and its people were never to disappoint us.

Group Two gave every prospect of high skill and tense confrontation. Both Uruguay and Italy were previous twice-winners of the Jules Rimet trophy, and both were indisputably equipped with fine talents. The question mark against both sides was whether their ingrained habit of obdurate defensiveness would prove too inhibiting to allow them to show the best of themselves.

Uruguay were living and training in Puebla, sharing an attractive ranch-style hotel with the Belgian party (in Group One), and as they sat around their garden pool in the afternoons they looked a thick-muscled, confident unit. The Italians lived in Mexico City, moving to Toluca to train from time to time, their every hint of injury or dissent inducing, as always, a shrill babble of excitement from the circus of Italian journalists like the effect of snapped elastic in a girls' school bus.

The Swedes stayed in Toluca, patiently trying to make a cohesive side out of their imbalance of home part-professionals and star players reclaimed for the tournament from Scotland, Belgium, Germany, Holland, Switzerland. But Israel, well aware that they were the weakest side in the Group and one of the least equipped in the competition, found it hard to settle. They left their first Toluca hotel, because its position in one of the main streets prevented them from escaping the hordes of curious children, and the ever-present pop music kept them awake at nights; they moved to a motel, and had cameras and watches stolen; they transferred to Puebla, and suffered a mini-epidemic of stomach trouble.

Yet Emanual Sheffer, the tiny Israeli coach, with a skin like a splitting chestnut and the impatient manner of a man loving trouble, said on the eve of the Group's first match that he was ready to surprise the world. 'We've shown what Israel can do in building a nation, and in war,' he said. 'Now we want to show what we can do in football'. That sounded like the spirit of the World Cup.

ISRAEL *v.* URUGUAY

Puebla, June 2

Puebla's thick, green turf shone from recent rain, and its surface must have contributed to one of the critical injuries of the tournament. Just short of the tenth minute of Group Two's opening match Pedro Rocha, the Uruguayan captain, rose easily to a high free kick in the Israeli penalty area, failed to make contact with the ball and then crumpled awkwardly as he landed. Within a few seconds he was being carried from the field on a stretcher. His damaged leg ligaments were to ensure that he would not play again in the competition.

The loss of an attacking midfield player of Rocha's quality could be expected to depress any team. It says a good deal for Uruguay that they were never to reveal any serious disruption because of Rocha's abrupt exit. They replaced him with Julio Cortés, dark and sinuous, although in a more deliberate, less deceptive way than Rocha, and Cortés was seldom less than efficient. That might stand as a fair collective description of the whole side; one can only speculate on whether Rocha might have made a more appreciative one possible.

Uruguay looked as physically intimidating as any side one has ever seen. Their back four were individually big, and as a group around their penalty area suggested a tag match in a professional wrestling ring: Ubiñas, the most thickly built, Ancheta, straight and hard, Matosas, pale-featured under thinning hair, Mújica, a heavy mover but deceptively quick. Montero Castillo and Maneiro, nominally linkmen, were usually extra defenders; both Cortés and Espárrago played most of the time well behind Cubilla and Losada.

But even though this expected, withdrawn approach from Uruguay struck us as needlessly cautious against Israel's part-timers it was always plain that the South American team was of a special order. The massed defensive cover fell into place the moment it was needed like a close-fitting door. And when the

concerted attacks were begun from Mazurkiewicz's goal area
the movements had a swift economy.

It was an attack of that kind which brought a scoring chance
two minutes after Rocha had left the field. The ball was pushed
quickly from the right diagonally to Losada, running fluently
in from his touchline. The curling shot had Wissoker, the
Israeli goalkeeper, stretching for contact.

Israel's clerks, bus drivers, students and mechanics sustained
a scurrying conscientiousness, the players with true basic
talent among them quickly standing out from the general
inadequacy. Primo, athletic and fast with a respectable imitation of the George Best hair, tackled firmly and showed an
astute eye for an overlap from his position on the extreme
left of five defenders; Shpiegler had a lightweight cunning in
his through passes from midfield; Faygenbaum was twice too
quick on the turn for Ancheta, first forcing Mazurkiewicz to
punch intuitively away, then putting the ball over the bar.

But Uruguay always had a calm, darkly watchful control of
the game. Cubilla alone was permitted the improvisations of a
soloist. Plump and round to a comic degree, he showed that he
could dribble the ball to most serious effect.

Yet the real damage was done by Uruguay's defence.
Mújica intervened in one of Israel's puzzled-looking passing
movements on the left, then hit a long cross to the Israeli goal
area. Maneiro was balanced in position for the header into
goal.

Puebla's young bandsmen and girl marchers captivated the
crowd at half-time with a swaggering performance of the St
Louis Blues March, straw hats and staves of flowers shimmering in the bright light, and afterwards the football seemed all
the more stern. Israel brought in Wallach for Talbi in the
midfield, then Bar for Rom in the rear. Uruguay remained
solemnly secure.

Six minutes after the re-start Mújica, the maker of the first
goal, put in another. Maneiro, once again stealing through
the Israeli defence into a menacing position, had a shot beaten

out in an uncertain, slapping reflex action by Wissoker. The ball ran loose to Mújica, who immediately struck it hard inside the far post.

Uruguay's general pace was now reduced so that the players' use of the ball had an exaggerated exactness. Even Cubilla, when he found the Israelis prepared to harass him belligerently as he swayed in deliberation over the ball, was now collecting and releasing passes from static positions, the chubby figure the more amusing for its earnestness.

But still Uruguay were not prepared to let an opportunity for professional persuasion slip by. Losada, brought down on the edge of the Israeli penalty area, lay writhing as if skewered: Bob Davidson, the Scottish referee, gestured impatiently to him to get up, and the cure was immediate and complete. Losada promptly sped to his touchline.

The crowd, who had selected Cubilla as their favourite, shrieked then groaned as the ball dropped at his feet six yards from the Israeli goal and he hit it heavily against the bar. And just before the end they moaned for him again, when he directed a gentle free kick through a great arc, and Wissoker got his right hand to the ball just as it arrived in the far, top angle. The fat man was really no joke.

Israel 0   *Uruguay* 2

ITALY *v.* SWEDEN

Toluca, June 3

On paper Sweden's pool of players looked as strong as any they had ever put into a World Cup. Their manager, Orvar Bergmark, who played ninety-four times for his country at right back, had the use of one of Europe's sharpest goal-takers in Ove Kindvall, borrowed from the Dutch club, Feyenoord; and with the other retrieved migrants, Grahn (Grasshoppers, Switzerland), Axelsson and Turesson (Bruges, Belgium), Persson (Glasgow Rangers), Olsson (Stuttgart, Germany) and

Nordahl (Anderlecht, Belgium), he had no reason to suspect the range of professional skills behind that striking power.

But his team selection for Sweden's first match in Mexico was plainly made much more with the Italians' forward strength in mind than his own. There was no Persson, no Nordahl, no Turesson to support Kindvall and Leif Eriksson in the front. Sweden's concentration of defensive and midfield players looked like an attempt to frustrate Italy at the Italians' own game. The question was whether this approach would turn out to be sensible or presumptuous.

There was a marked similarity in the Italian and Swedish performances in the qualifying rounds: each was indebted heavily for goals to one forward. Of the ten goals scored by Italy seven had come from Luigi Riva, the coldly brilliant Cagliari striker. Kindvall had scored six of Sweden's twelve. How would these two now compare in direct opposition?

Toluca's early afternoon was lit with heat, as the spectators brightened the drab concrete with their pennants and banners. The Italian supporters invalidated the smallness of their number by the flourish and noise of their trappings: huge sombreros, bells, bugles. But the sun withdrew as the 4pm. kick-off was reached; the match was played under cloud.

For three of the Italian team this new beginning in the World Cup in shabby and chill surroundings must have had a special cautionary note. The last World Cup finals match that Albertosi, the goalkeeper, Facchetti, the captain, and Mazzola had played was the one in which North Korea put them out of the 1966 tournament in Middlesbrough. Gianni Rivera, then aged twenty-two, also played in that humiliating game; but now he was among the list of substitutes, with the usual aura of winsome petulance separating him from his coach, Feruccio Valcareggi. The Italian camp was divided on whether this lyrically stylish midfield forward was vital to the side or would merely decorate it.

Quickly once the ball was moving the Italian formation was in its battened-down position: a back four, with Burgnich and Facchetti flanking Cera and Niccolai, Bertini a little in front of them, Domenghini and Mazzola and De Sisti within short-passing distance of him, and Riva and Boninsegna a long way in front.

But if the disposition looked over-wary there was soon evidence that it did not prohibit fluency. Mazzola dropped the ball into Domenghini's stealthy stride, a quick cross found Boninsegna wide of the penalty area, and Boninsegna's delicate chip bounced at Riva's feet two yards from the goal. Riva was facing the wrong way, but with one of those inventive movements which denote the true virtuoso he twisted into the ball to send it off his body against a post.

This was the first instance of Riva's capacity for turning the look of a situation from the unlikely to the unfortunate; the crowd's response showed that they had spotted a very special player.

Within twelve minutes Italy scored, helped by a wretched nerviness from Sweden's goalkeeper, Ronnie Hellström. Boninsegna hit a careful corner kick on the left to Domenghini, waiting just outside the penalty box. Domenghini shot quickly, but not hard. Hellström went down on one knee at the near post, and seemed to be well behind the ball in good time. Astonishingly the ball passed under his body as he leaned to take it.

The Swedish marking and tackling was understandably more close and more harsh after that. Now Axelsson joined Olsson at Riva's shoulders, and the three were so close, even when Riva was merely pacing restlessly in wait for the ball, that they kept colliding in a confusion of apologetic gestures and irritable head-shaking. Boninsegna was Cronqvist's responsibility; and, as it turned out, his undoing.

For Sweden the compact, busy Bo Larsson was gradually distinguishing himself as the side's most effective player outside the defence. Always moving, a hungry tackler and a deft user of the short pass, he reminded one of Alan Ball, although without possessing quite that player's telling bite.

10   The Brazilian team that played against England (without Gérson).
Left to right top: Carlos Alberto, Brito, Piazza, Félix, Clodoaldo, Everaldo.
Left to right bottom: Jairzinho, Rivelino, Tostão, Pelé, Paulo Cézar

11   Banks gets to Pelé's header to make the save Bobby Charlton said was
the best he had ever seen

12 Pelé sprawls alongside Mullery in the Eng
area, but Moore and Peters gesture that he di
Cooper gets on with the game

13 Pelé is tripped by Lupescu in Brazil's gan
against Rumania

14 – and the aftermath

Elsewhere the Swedes looked stretched beyond their capacities. Svensson, trying to act as the central hinge of the side, looked stolid against the smooth mobility of De Sisti. The intent exchanges between Domenghini and Mazzola might have slight impact on the Swedish defence, and might leave the crowd with nothing to thrill to; but in midfield the Swedes could make little positive intervention. Italy seemed to be tying up the game.

But there was also a sense of self-testing about the Italians' play. This altitude needed to be understood and, if possible, its effects made harmless. Riva amazed with some of his bursts of acceleration, waiting flat-footed and deceptively slump-shouldered for his favourite long, swift ball from deep behind him, and then hurtling out of the reach of his markers' lunges. He had a header saved, saw Boninsegna brought down after sending him away with a remarkable feint and flick, all in one movement, was body-checked on the edge of the penalty area, and one of his shots was blocked to one side of Hellström.

It seemed that Riva, Boninsegna and the altitude were the key factors in the match. Shortly before the end of the first half both these Italians were showing signs of unusual fatigue, both leaning over, hands on their knees, heads sunk low. At the interval both took a long time to get off the field.

Neither was as frequently to be seen hurrying away from the Swedish defenders in the second half. Italy, with Rosato now calmly confident in place of Niccolai, who had suffered an ankle injury after thirty-five minutes, were avid for the ball but less and less ready to be adventurous with it.

This conservation gave little help to Sweden. Their attack barely existed. Kindvall, looking so thin and pale a personality against Riva's proud menace, was simply not an influence in the match.

The excitements were well spaced by Italy's patient diligence. Cronqvist was cautioned by the English referee, Jack Taylor, after felling Boninsegna with a charge that dumped the light Italian on the grass like a dropped jacket. De Sisti hit a long

F

ball like a hawk's flight for Boninsegna poised at the left
corner of the Swedish penalty area, and Olsson's body took
the full force of the shot. Mazzola shot from twenty-five yards,
and Hellström could only watch the ball past the post.

Sweden took off Eriksson, which seemed to matter little,
and then Larsson, whose justified exhaustion had left them
without recognisable tenacity in the middle of the field. Seven
minutes before the end Kindvall pounced from the centre of
the penalty area to put an invitingly unaccompanied ball into
the net, and was ruled off-side. The Italian supporters, who
had by now built up a screaming volume of abuse for Jack
Taylor, who did not see as much assault on their players as
they did, approved shrilly.

Riva managed a last sprint and a shot past Hellström's right
post, and the game's closing half-minute was accorded an
unbroken chanting of 'Ee-tal-ya'. Afterwards both managers
confessed their players damaged by the thin air of Toluca to a
degree beyond their fears before the match. Remembering the
game, we were not surprised.

Italy 1   Sweden 0

URUGUAY *v.* ITALY

Puebla, June 6

The aggregate of skills available to these two countries invited
us to hope that this would be the showpiece match of the
group. Both teams had already shown, if against unimpressive
opponents, that they had individual players of particular
quality and that they could lift the level of their collective play
as the need arose. Now perhaps each would demand from the
other a sustained account of the full range of abilities.

The circumstances were encouraging: the late afternoon was
warm and bright, the comfortable stadium nearly full, the
crowd agreeably excitable. As if pointedly to nudge the teams
into their most attractive form, Puebla sent on to the pitch

before the kick-off sixteen engagingly clever small boys who
juggled with footballs, from instep to knee, to a challenging roll
of drums from the band. A tiny Juanito, in white shorts and
green shirt and enormous straw sombrero, stood on the touchline with one foot on a ball, facing the main stand. The mood
was refreshingly cheerful.

Uruguay made one change from the side which had beaten
Israel, bringing in Bareño for the forward, Losada. Italy had
not disturbed the team which had won against Sweden, Rosato
holding his place for Niccolai, who was not to play again
after his injury in the first match. But this time Rivera was
not even among the substitutes. Reports were still snarling
out of the Italian camp about his disaffection and its disrupt-
ive effects.

Play began in a gay chorus of enthusiasm from the crowd,
and ten minutes later only a crushing tackle by Maneiro on
De Sisti reminded us that the game was under way at all. It
was one of those extraordinary periods of football when two
sides are so cautious of each other that they contrive to avoid
even the appearance of playing. There was simply nothing to
watch.

Maneiro's foul did not put an end to the non-football. The
free kick was taken, the spectators' shocked grumbling was
spent and there followed another five minutes of reciprocal
inactivity. The ball was seen to be moving, but its flight
communicated no purpose. Then Bertini broke into the tor-
por with a sudden shot from twenty yards, and a surprised
Mazurkiewicz just got an arm to the ball to turn it away.

Five minutes afterwards De Sisti was brought down heavily
again, this time by Ubiñas. It was clear that De Sisti had been
picked out by Uruguay as the one Italian midfield man they
had to suppress. He was watched at least as closely as was Riva.
But it was a midfield men's battle, if one can permit the absurd
inaccuracy of that word in the context of so flaccid a match;
the forwards' presence was rarely noticed.

What pattern the game possessed led us inescapably to the

conclusion that Italy were mostly to blame for the invincible tedium of the game. They were known, by reputation and recent evidence, to have the more flexible side, to be capable of the more varied enterprise. They had the midfield qualities of readily adaptable pace and guile to insist on a match of cut and counter-thrust. Italy could surely have forced a full-blooded response from Uruguay; they elected not to. Uruguay, for their part, were content in their compliance.

Both camps must have been confident that they could reach the quarter-finals at the expense of Israel and Sweden, as long as one of them did not fall to the other. The realities of the strange swing of fortune in football would make it highly dangerous for two sides to count on such an outcome; but in this instance it looked very much as if the teams accepted the opportunity of a valuable draw with progressive gratitude.

From time to time there were excellent little bits of play. Cortés judged his long, looping ball perfectly for the pace of Ubiñas, overlapping on the wing, and Albertosi had to punch the ball away from Espárrago's head, when Ubiñas made the cross. (Cortés was cautioned soon afterwards for a foul on poor De Sisti, who must have regretted his obtrusive busyness; he was severely battered for it, in no good cause.)

The exasperated crowd began the slow-handclapping and whistling which were to punctuate the remainder of the match. Then abruptly the noise changed to acclaim. Boninsegna hit exactly the kind of pass Riva most relishes, long and hard and low, so that he can exploit its pace and his own acceleration behind it. He was clear of Ancheta in an instant. Then he paused, shifted to the right and hit a fierce shot into the side-netting.

That piece of work came five minutes before half-time, and it seemed like a day since the match had started. Four minutes later Mazzola used his more sinewy strength to push through two attempted tackles in a run directly down the middle into the Uruguayan penalty area. But when he released the ball Boninsegna responded sluggishly, and the chance was lost.

At half-time Puebla's prancing boys and girls added a little more cheek to their St Louis Blues March, and the pitch was toured by a huge replica of a football carrying a dozen infants, in brilliant silk and satin, who blew kisses at us. The crowd cheered the show, then booed the reappearance of the players. Domenghini was spared this embarrassment, since he was replaced by Furino.

Soon Riva was in aggressive action, turning away from Ancheta and Matosas as they converged on him and shooting hard against Mazurkiewicz's body. But, as in the first half, this was an isolated instance of the man's quality. He was not to threaten Uruguay's goal again.

Cubilla only once gave the crowd the fun they expected from him, after seventy minutes. Feinting and shimmying with the round body balanced above the ball, he tried to urge Facchetti into a tackle. Facchetti was implacably still. Cubilla went skipping round him, to a roar of delight from the stadium, and ran smack into Bertini who promptly thumped the ball into touch. The applause died in the throat, as if Bertini had put his foot down it.

For a few minutes Uruguay seemed to want more pace, more combat out of the game. But it was too late for that. Italy absorbed the running and the inter-passing in their deliberate passivity. The booing and whistling were bitter at the end.

Uruguay 0   *Italy* 0

SWEDEN *v.* ISRAEL

Toluca, June 7

In the bright warmth Toluca had that yawning, belly-scratching character which is universal to working-class towns on Sunday mornings, the front doors open in the long rows of terrace houses, people contemplative on their steps. The surrounding hills were firmly etched, green and brown, against the pale

blue sky. The brass band at the stadium could have been the
Stockton-on-Tees Salvation Army; and the analogy was the
closer for the sad fervour in the singing of the broad-vowelled
Israeli national anthem. The Star of David flags were thickly
grouped among the Jewish supporters, perhaps 500 in a crowd
of around 5,000. But the football destroyed this lulling air.

The Swedes' attacking intentions were explicit in their
substantial team changes from the line-up against Italy. Persson
and Turesson, both fleet runners, came into the forward line
to flank Kindvall; Nordahl, who is always eager to go forward,
was placed in the middle three. Grahn, Cronqvist, Nordqvist
and Eriksson, so limp a forward line against Italy, were left out,
and Hellström, whose performance in that earlier match had
been marked by a callow nervousness, was replaced in goal by
the older Sven-Gunnar Larsson. Israel held to the side which
had completed their first game, with Bar and Wallach retaining their places against Rom and Talbi, for whom they
had substituted.

It was soon evident that this would be a game in much different mood from that of previous matches in Group Two. From
the start there was a ready optimism in the forward play on
both sides; plainly both coaches saw the need for pace and
enterprise – if only, perhaps, to dismiss from mind that persist-
ing fear of Toluca's altitude.

After nine minutes Israel emerged from the flurry of rapid
probing with the game's first clean-cut attack. Shpiegel saw the
opportunity presented by a sudden mis-positioning of the
Swedes' defence, and began a run with the ball from close to
the half-way line. He was allowed to penetrate to the edge of the
penalty area, but delayed his shot fractionally too long. The
bodies were massing in front of him as he hit the ball, and the
shot was blocked.

Quickly Olsson spotted a similar chance, as the Israelis
hurried to close a huge gap in the middle of the field, and he
was usefully positioned twenty yards from goal for Kindvall's
deft return pass. But Olsson's shot was wide.

A key factor was already established: both teams, in their willingness to run forward with the ball, were leaving themselves vulnerable to the quick counter. So when an Israeli attack ended in a shot from Faigenbaum, a parry from Sven-Gunnar Larsson and a big clearance from Axelsson, the Swedish front men were free to use the ball as it came looping through the empty midfield. Kindvall, looking immeasurably more swift and bold than he had against the Italians' tackling, received it just inside the penalty area, shot without hesitation and brought a firm save from the goalkeeper.

The little crowd was delighted with all this dash and aggression. But it was increasingly apparent that the manner of the football was putting great strain on the teams' already limited capacities for tactical organisation. The middle of the field was scarcely contested; communication between attack and defence was largely by the most old-fashioned of hopeful punting. It was beginning to look like the honest endeavour of college soccer.

Little Emanual Sheffer, ignoring all the stern warnings that had been issued from Mexico City, saw the dangers in this telltale amateurishness and stood taut on the touchline, screaming and gesturing to his players for closer contact and quicker movement from around their own goal. He was seen by the linesman, who flagged busily for the referee's attention. But Seyoum Terekegn, the Ethiopian referee, ignored the incident. His unconcern seemed ominous, and as things turned out we were right to worry about it.

There was a disturbing naïvety in Terekegn's work. Some of the nudging and barging was gathering in vigour and brazenness around both penalty areas, but was not being punished. Yet when Bar, Israel's combative little defender, made a spectacular dive out of his own confusion near his bye-line, when he was about to concede a corner to Nordahl, Terekegn was deceived into awarding Israel a free kick. The Swedes, and some of the spectators, were properly indignant.

Two near-misses, one in each goal area, were typical of the

perilous excitability among both defences in this half. First, Persson's dipping shot from fully thirty yards attracted Wissoker's consideration only at the last moment. Wissoker's leap was frantic in its alarm; the ball beat him utterly, and thumped against the top angle. Then, Selander miskicked wildly, going for a clearance in his penalty area; Faigenbaum's shot was stopped on the ground.

The second half was barely under way when another state of bewilderment occurred in the Israel penalty area. Wissoker, having advanced to block a shot from Turesson, was still yards from his empty goalmouth as Bo Larsson's lob dropped the wrong side of the bar.

Turesson, whose height and blond curls made him almost a caricature of the Nordic hero, was rewarded for all his generous running soon afterwards. Selander, cutting inside from the right, surprised the Israeli defenders with the suddenness of his pass well beyond Wissoker; Turesson had arrived exactly on time, to sidefoot the ball into the net.

Within two minutes Israel were level again. Shpiegel dropped the ball in front of Shpiegler twenty yards from Sweden's goal, and Shpiegler immediately drove fiercely, left-footed, past Larsson at shoulder height.

But now, in the last half-hour of the match, the teams' brave determination turned to a sour ill-temper. Terekegn, with his slow eye for all kinds of infringements, came close to losing control of the match.

Sheffer was growing increasingly indifferent to the rules. He was frequently on the touchline, yelling instructions, and as often on the field with his two trainers when an Israeli player needed attention. It was too provocative for at least one of the Swedish players: Turesson kicked the ball at the Israeli coach. Still Terekegn did not intervene.

The tackling, heavy and crude, was now overshadowing the rest of the play. There was a climax to the ugliness. Faigenbaum tripped Selander just outside the Israeli penalty area, then fell in turn; Faigenbaum was still on the ground, only a foot or so from the dead ball, as Svensson sent the free kick just over the bar. Then as Sheffer, his two trainers, the referee and one linesman argued in a bunch of players Schweger, the Israeli inside-forward, collapsed in the penalty area. Terekegn hurried to the spot, but clearly had no idea what had happened. He called both captains together for a talk, and what was left of the game was a little less bloodshot.

(That incident was eventually resolved by Ken Aston, who was the FIFA inspector at the match. He reported that he saw Orjan Persson strike Schweger. The Disciplinary Committee accordingly added Persson's name to those of Bar and Primo, cautioned by the referee.)

The last attacking thrust of the game came from Israel: Shpiegel, accelerating between Olsson and Axelsson, two excellent defenders now labouring under tiredness, was too exhausted to sustain his pace as the ball trickled away from him, and a despairing prod sent the ball wide.

Sheffer was impish with smiles afterwards. His team had won a point they well deserved, he said. Orvar Bergmark, Sweden's coach, was cold about his players. 'They could have done better,' he said. Neither would discuss the referee. The questioning look on Sheffer's face suggested he didn't know there had been one.

Sweden 1   Israel 1

URUGUAY *v.* SWEDEN

Puebla, June 10

At nine o'clock on the morning of this match the man who was scheduled to referee it, Aírton Vieira de Moraes, of Brazil, was interviewed by Sir Stanley Rous, the president of FIFA, and Ken Aston, of the Referees' Committee, in Rous's suite at the top of the Maria Isabel Hotel. De Moraes had to be asked whether he had solicited either team for money in return for favouring them in the game.

The Brazilian referee denied the accusation; the denial was accepted.

But De Moraes did not handle the match. Instead it was given to Henry Landauer, the American, and the Brazilian took Landauer's place as a linesman for the match between El Salvador and Russia. The matter could not, of course, be ended by a simple switching of games. For a few hours the World Cup seethed with the whisper and contumely of scandal.

It had developed overnight. Rous and Aston learned from some Swedish journalists that Puebla was rife with rumours of approaches by De Moraes to one of the teams, or both. The origin of the rumours was never pinpointed beyond the reference to a shadowy informant known as 'a Brazilian journalist' or, more cryptically, 'a man working with the Brazilian journalists'. Rous described the incident as 'a plot to discredit' De Moraes.

The officials with the Swedish party dismissed the rumours, and did not attempt to contact FIFA in Mexico City about them. But Rous, as he was to explain later, agreed with De Moraes that the circumstances made it impossible for the Brazilian to handle the game. But neither man was prepared for the bitter reaction from the Uruguayans when Aston arrived at Puebla shortly before the kick-off to deliver Rous's letter announcing the change of official.

Alfredo Fernández, the head of the Uruguayan delegation, immediately called a Press conference. His team would play the match under protest, he said. Rous was acting improperly in changing the referees. There was an implication against the Uruguayans, because a South American referee had been withdrawn abruptly from the game. 'We haven't seen this man; we know nothing about this,' he said. Uruguay would make a formal complaint to FIFA.

(When the complaint was lodged Rous was to reply with his formidable mixture of dignity and verbal body-punching. He was surprised, he said, by Fernández's attitude 'about something which was done for the benefit of his team'. Rous added: 'He

protests too much. No one has accused him of offering bribes.
Our experiences in such matters are that they are never done
direct.')

So there was an acridity in the savouring of this game, as
huge white bubbles of cloud gathered over the stadium and
Puebla put on another inventive little entertainment. This time,
as the band played the countries' national anthems, a bank of
five hundred children behind one goal moved coloured cards
in front of their chests to turn themselves into huge flags of the
two nations. There was charm and originality in Puebla.

For a while the football had a tense liveliness. Sweden at
last appeared to have reached the assured mobility that their
camp had been promising. Orvar Bergmark had rung more
changes in his attempt to find the most effective combination
from his pool of players, and now Leif Eriksson was reinstated in
place of Turesson, to work in the front with Kindvall and Persson; the captain, Nordqvist, was back in the defence and Goran
Nicklasson replaced Nordahl as the advanced midfield man.

With only one point and one goal from the two previous
matches Sweden had no chance of reaching the quarter-finals
unless they could win this game by two goals. Even then it
would require of Israel an emulation of North Korea's defeat
of Italy, in the last match of the group, to give Sweden a place
in the drawing of lots that would be necessary.

If it seemed a forlorn situation for the Swedes they did not
begin the game as if they shared the view. Just after half a
minute Eriksson spun to send the Uruguayan defence lurching
the wrong way and then hit hard against Mazurkiewicz's
right hand post. The goalkeeper was helplessly unprepared for
the shot. Four minutes later Bo Larsson, industrious as ever in
his running in the middle, saw a shot charged down in the goal
area. And soon afterwards it was another run by Larsson which
cut through the Uruguayan defence and gave Kindvall the
chance for a lob which floated on to the back netting.

But the best attacking movement of the first half involved
Eriksson, then Svensson, then Kindvall in a rapid progress of

passes on the left. No Uruguayan player got close to the ball
before Kindvall cut inside to shoot. Mazurkiewicz reiterated
his known ability with a one-handed save.

This first half-hour contained Sweden's best football in the
tournament. Kindvall, lissom and effortlessly quick off the
mark, at last looked like one of the world's best forwards, the
ease of his movements making Uruguay's heavier men appear
coarse-grained and dull-witted. Svensson was much more
confident, less mundane in his use of the ball than before.
Eriksson, who had appeared so frail in the diffidence of his
first game, was sufficiently restored to look physically bigger in
his increased speed and his relish for the ball.

Uruguay were not comfortable in this half. They had omitted Cubilla, which left the team stern without relief. Zubía and
Maneiro both tried shots from well outside the penalty area;
otherwise Uruguay were content to block and contain. The
crowd, liking Sweden's ambition, howled twice for penalties
against Uruguay, first when Bo Larsson careered through a
somersault after contesting the ball with Ancheta, then when
Ancheta crudely impeded Kindvall, even though the Swede
seemed to have been beaten by the pace of the ball. In the
second instance the referee equivocated distressingly by awarding Sweden an indirect free kick almost on the penalty spot.
The entire Uruguayan team grouped around their goal; the
ball flew past its right post.

Half-time gave us more dancing girls, more swank from the
marching boys with straw hats and canes, and then Uruguay
got their strangle-hold firmly round the second half. After ten
minutes of it Kindvall took a severe kick on the left knee from
Ubiñas and rolled over the touchline, while Ubiñas hurried on
to shoot into the side netting.

It was soon obvious that Kindvall's show of pain was no
sham. Four minutes after the incident he received a pass on the
right, spurted forward and immediately stumbled. He managed
to put in the shot, then was helped off the field. Turesson came on.

It was not just Kindvall's gliding pace that had by now gone from the game. Uruguay had made the weight of their tackling and the grim order of their play tell at last. As Sweden rapidly lost their eagerness Cortés, Maneiro, Montero Castillo, Matosas and Mújica assumed an increasingly arrogant jealousy for the ball, playing out the minutes, and Sweden's remaining life in the tournament, in a tantalisingly measured interchange of passes.

The crowd slow-handclapped. Uruguay were as unconcerned as a watched kettle. Except, that is, when there was an opportunity for some time-wasting. Mújica, about as delicate as a pillbox, collapsed under a collision with Eriksson as if killed outright. He lay stretched in the crucified position long enough for even this disaffected crowd to clamber back into the South American cause.

But that rediscovered sympathy could not withstand the excessive demand the Uruguayans put on it. The mass of blue shirts hung round their own penalty area was too familiar, too alienating. Back came the boos and whistles. And amid them, in the game's dying seconds, Sweden scored a consoling, winning and useless goal. Persson crossed from the right and Grahn, who had substituted for Nicklasson for the last eight minutes, stole through the line of defenders to head in at the far post.

Sweden had seen the last of this World Cup. Eduardo Hohberg, Uruguay's coach, now dealt with some aggressive questioning from the Press very much in the way his defence had entangled the Swedish forwards. Would he have fancied being a spectator at Uruguay's matches? He was a coach and could not consider spectators' requirements. Did he not think his team had been excessively defensive? The first objective in travelling from Montevideo was to reach the quarter-finals. Had Sweden's win surprised him? Anything was possible in football.

No one, so far, had got much change out of Uruguay. Even the winners here were still the losers.

Uruguay o   Sweden 1

ITALY v. ISRAEL

Toluca, June 11

There was snow on the road to Toluca, and the town was grey and bedraggled in its puddles. But the few score of Italian supporters achieved an impressive din before the match, with hooters, bells, tambourines, rattles. One could not help recalling similar noises four years before, a couple of hours before Italy disappeared from the World Cup in England under the gymnastic assault of eleven dwarfs from North Korea.

But there was a greater sense of Italian expectancy here, and with good reason. The side had not yet appeared much ruffled out of its measured expertise, its self-understanding. The Italians had so far appeared more restricted by their own conserving caution and by Toluca's height than by the interference from the opposition. They had only to draw this game to win the group; they would need to lose by two goals to be dismissed from the tournament. The chanting of 'Ee-tal-ya' was swelled by a lot of people associating themselves with success as the sun arrived to light up the kick-off.

Israel introduced a new defender, the small and neat Bellow, in place of Wallach, a six-foot midfield man, so that the team now looked biased in favour of ferreting aggression. But Italy seemed anxious for a quick goal, and the fluency of their attacking in the first twenty minutes rendered this Israeli defence near to helpless.

De Sisti strode up to Shoum to take the ball away and send it swiftly forward to Mazzola in one peremptory movement; Mazzola ran, with that thin, neck-stretching action, cleanly into the penalty area and shot hard against Wissoker's palms. Again De Sisti dismissed an Israeli challenge, then slipped a low ball forward for Riva; Riva's shot was held. Soon Riva was felled heavily by Rosen on the edge of the penalty area; Mazzola tapped the free kick to one side, and Riva shuddered the wall of defenders with his shot. Domenghini ran hard on the left, crossed low to Riva, and Riva failed with this third chance, his foot striking the turf before the ball. De Sisti took aim from twenty yards and beat Wissoker, to see the ball come back off a post.

Schweger and Rosen were trying to mark Riva, and they were finding legitimate contact next to impossible. But Riva could not quite bring together his acceleration and his accuracy with the ball. Once more he moved away from Schweger into the Israeli penalty area, and then put the ball three yards wide of the far post.

Emanual Sheffer was now on the touchline, shouting and waving instructions at his team. Airton de Moraes, the Brazilian referee, immediately ordered him away. Sheffer was to find De Moraes much less tractable than he had the Ethiopian, Terekegn, a few days before.

But there was a depressing of the Italian pace and tenacity, another instance of the sudden tiredness they had suffered before in this stadium. The Israelis found it less of a struggle to win the ball; Italy were less mobile, their tackles heavier in the need for decisiveness in static positions. So Faigenbaum suffered a severe knee injury, under Rosato's hurtling impetus. He would not play in the second half.

But there was not enough skill, not enough ascendant personality among the Israelis to press home the opportunity given them by this Italian relapse into defence. They made one scoring chance: Shpiegler, allowed in from the left unmolested as the Italians paused for an offside decision that never came, prompted an excellent save by Albertosi, who rushed from his goal to hold the ball on the ground.

The appearance of Gianni Rivera for the second half was the most significant event of the match. In substituting for Domenghini he was in the Italian midfield for the first time in the tournament. The Italian supporters greeted him in shrieking adulation, although he gave them little reason for rapture in what he did on the field. But his inclusion for half a match suggested that the Italian camp had at last resolved its dilemma over this player, whose fine touch with the ball can be so destructive of opposing defences but who seldom approaches beyond the outskirts of the vital battles for its possession.

He played unobtrusively here, and it was fair to assume he was looking for the 'feel' of the competition more than any chance for quick, dramatic impact. There was not, indeed, much more drama left to the game. Riva appeared badly ill-treated, when Schweger pulled him off the ball by his shirt and Shoum thumped bodily into him within a split second on the edge of the Israeli penalty box; but De Moraes saw no offence. The referee was far more excited by Primo's charge into Boninsegna's back, and the shower of cushions and hats it provoked from the outraged Italian supporters.

At last Riva got the ball into the net. He waved urgently for Bertini to hurry the ball to him, with a big cross from the right, and then he was away from Schweger to rise high and head past Wissoker. A photographer rushed from behind the goal to embrace and kiss him. Riva's proud delight was changed suddenly to an attitude of supplication, hands together in prayer, as he turned to see Seyoum Terekegn, the linesman, with his flag raised. The referee, who had pointed to the centre-spot, deliberated with Terekegn and then disallowed the goal.

One small thrill remained for the Italians in the crowd: a shot by Rivera from a cunningly worked position in front of goal, which Wissoker stopped near the line. If a goal from Riva was to be worth a photographer's kiss the sighs from these supporters suggested that their adored Gianni had just been denied an unthinkable reward.

The bland face and manner which Italy's coach, Feruccio Valcareggi, presented to us later bore the same devious message that had come from Uruguay's Hohberg. The quarter-finals were the target, and had been reached; so what possible complaint could there be against the team? Surely no one was suggesting that Italy hadn't been trying to score in the past three games? Sheffer was bright and blunt: 'If Italy and Uruguay play in the quarter-finals as they did against us, it will be Russia and Mexico who will win.'

Italy o   Israel o

15 Brazil's Jairzinho beats Banks
and Peters for the only goal of
the game against England

16 Bobby Moore exchanges shirts
with Pelé after England's match
against Brazil

17   In refreshing shadow, Brazil's Everaldo competes with the Rumanians
Satmareanu and Dumitru (15)

18   Moroccan goalkeeper Allal Kassou cannot stop Cubillas scoring the
first goal of the match for Peru. At the right is Sotil, who initiated the attack;
the Moroccans in the goalmouth are Lamrani and Moulay Driss

GROUP TWO

	P	W	D	L	F	A	Pts
Italy	3	1	2	0	1	0	4
Uruguay	3	1	1	1	2	1	3
Sweden	3	1	1	1	2	2	3
Israel	3	0	2	1	1	3	2

4 Group Three

Brazil, Czechoslovakia, England, Rumania

Through late May and early June the days in Guadalajara were
of an enamelled brightness and the sun drained the strength out
of fit men with the insistence of a poultice. These should have
been weeks of increasing rain in that part of western Mexico
but the beginning of the wet season was displaced by a heat-
wave. Even the local people complained that the weather was
unnaturally fierce for the time of year when spring should have
been making its last stand against the onslaught of the tropical
summer. Those of us who had been in Guadalajara with the
England party the previous May were sweatily resigned to the
heat. We had not expected anything less after that first visit,
a succession of sweltering days when anyone who put his hand
on the bonnet of a parked car was liable to find his palm
cooked medium rare. Then, England had played in the cool
of late evening and, thus encouraged, had produced some of
the most exciting football of their Latin American tour. Now
they and their rivals in Group Three, Brazil, Czechoslovakia
and Rumania, would have to endure the sun at its most
damaging, with Sunday matches due to start at noon and
weekday games at 4pm., an hour that was, if anything, more
hazardous.

   Guadalajara is built at an altitude of just over five thousand
feet (5,212 according to the more meticulous gazetteers) but it
lies well south of the Tropic of Cancer and it is only in winter
that it could be said to live up to the tourist propaganda about
its 'mild, clear, dry climate'. Clear and dry it certainly was as
the World Cup approached, but anyone who could describe it

as mild would be likely to tell you that hell is a good place for getting brown.

To build up as much resistance as possible to the enfeebling effects of the sun the assembled footballers were obliged to train in the conditions they thought they would face in competition. England's sessions at the Atlas Sporting Club, where the field was as green and almost as true as a British bowling green, were generally scheduled to begin at the same time of day as the next match to be played. Inevitably there was evidence of suffering. 'I was better off in jail,' Bobby Moore muttered to journalists on the touchline as he laboured through his first full day's work after his Colombian ordeal. In the Group matches Moore was to be one of the players who appeared most spec-tacularly punished by the temperature, his shirt invariably darkened from collar to waist by floods of sweat. But he would run through the soaking discomfort as if it were as negligible as a sunshower and his contribution to the championship was made the more memorable by our knowledge of the difficulties he was forced to overcome. Others among Sir Alf Ramsey's men were less formidably equipped to cope with the demands of the climate and watching them at the Atlas Club, sweating as freely as fat men in a Turkish bath, then propelling themselves wearily towards the cool drinks laid out for them by Dr Neil Phillips, we wondered if they could perform competitively in such heat. Phillips nodded and smiled in answer to the question. 'Yes. It will be very hard but they can do it. That's what they came for.' The answer seemed to have more of the bulldog than the scientist about it, but no one doubted that Phillips, as conscientious as he is progressive, was giving the players all the assistance and safeguards medical research and the regulations of the tournament made possible. Of special measures taken to combat dehydration he would say nothing, favouring the slightly theatrical secrecy that was fashionable with the four countries based in Guadalajara, but we learned later that one of his innovations was a pill whose refinement enabled the England men to take a higher concentration of salt than athletes had previously been able to absorb in one dose. Phillips, satisfied that he was doing everything in his power to support Ramsey's defence of the title, was impressively serene. He could not be expected to foresee that a medical crisis would have a decisive influence on England's fortunes. At least for the moment all was going smoothly. Whether because of the thoroughness of their preparation or their determined, practical spirit – or, improbably, because they were blessed with a basic physiological advantage – the English players were managing to live with problems that had already cut deep into the confidence of the Rumanians, who would be their first opponents.

Soon after reaching Mexico Mircea Lucescu, the young captain of Rumania, found his weight had dropped by ten pounds. Yet he was standing up to the heat better than many of the others. Dobrin, whose ability to combine skill in midfield with great effectiveness as a finisher earned him the vote as Rumanian Footballer of the Year in 1966–7, was virtually invalided out of the squad before a ball had been kicked in earnest. During early practices he and his team-mates had been tying their shirts round their heads and they had announced their intention of covering themselves with protective lotion when they took the field to play Group matches at the Jalisco Stadium. But Dobrin was denied the chance of playing in those matches. He developed the initial symptoms of heatstroke, was declared out of the meeting with England and, sadly, never recovered sufficiently to be recalled to the side. Lucescu, who owed his promotion to captain as much to his maturity, education and gift for languages as to the rich but erratic flair he brought to the middle or front line of his team, felt that two weeks' exposure to the Guadalajara conditions would give the Rumanians an appreciable edge in the opening game. The English reached the city a full week after the Rumanians and the unfortunate Moore arrived from South America only three days before he was due in action. Applying the findings of medical research into the effects of heat, Ramsey had his squad training for ninety-minute periods in temperatures of up to

88 degrees Fahrenheit. This, according to the best estimates, would permit adaptation up to a maximum of 88 degrees. But in their most testing match at the Jalisco they would find themselves playing in 98 degrees and no man was to lose less than ten pounds in weight. It was interesting, and a little frightening, to recall that in 1953 the American Army had issued an edict forbidding new recruits to do any training when the thermometer rose above 85 degrees.

Although he believed the discrepancy in acclimatisation would tell against England, Lucescu insisted that no amount of precaution would enable any European team to play more than an hour's football at top pressure. 'It is impossible to do more than that,' he said, his attractive, boyish face clouded by the memory of what happened when his own men had tried to go beyond this limit. 'The heat is terrible.'

Of course, the heat was not terrible for everyone. Something like three thousand supporters from Britain, rather more from Brazil and an enthusiastic sprinkling from eastern Europe had stretched their annual holidays and their budgets to descend on Guadalajara like a vast benevolent army of occupation. Many of the British were genuine, eighteen-carat fanatics, the sort of magnificent obsessionists who suspect that when Jesus performed the miracle of the walking on the waters he was bouncing a football on his instep at the time. However, at least as many balanced their interest in the World Cup with a determination to have a good holiday anyway, regardless of the results at the Jalisco Stadium. Quite a few showed a desire to drink Mexico dry of tequila but after fighting the worst of three falls with that deadly liquid, which qualifies for the old Glasgow rating of two-and-a-half somersaults to the glass, the bravest were inclined to seek out the English pubs that were established in Guadalajara during our stay. One of these was clearly meant to remain as a permanent gathering place for the lively minority of the city's one-and-a-quarter million inhabitants who are young and rich enough to see themselves as swingers. It bore about as much resemblance to the corner local as the Savoy

Grill does to a Wimpy Bar but its self-conscious sophistication was comprehensively undermined on one evening by the importation of Ye Olde Englyshe Knees-up, a beer-swilling sing-song climaxed by a muddled attempt to introduce a little action according to the Marquess of Queensberry. There is nothing like an abortive brawl for giving a pub a touch of authenticity.

The other pub was truer to the genre, a large bare room in the Fenix Hotel in which one of the tourist organisations had set up a bar complete with a blonde barmaid whose West Country accent sounded like a commercial for cider. The Fenix Hotel also accommodated the Press Centre (on the twelfth floor, reached by lifts so slow that people were tempted to make sleeper reservations) and some of the incredible force of British footballers who were in Mexico as spectators. They could have produced a team that would have been backed to beat half-a-dozen of the countries in the World Cup. In defence, Garry Sprake, Terry Hennessey and Peter Rodrigues of Wales could have been backed by John Greig of Scotland and Chris Lawler of Liverpool; in the midfield, Billy Bremner and Bobby Hope of Scotland could have worked alongside Johnny Giles of Eire; at the front the Scots Charlie Cooke and Colin Stein might have combined with Roger Hunt or Jimmy Greenhoff of England. There would have been ample reserves on hand and no trouble finding a manager to take charge. Sir Matt Busby, Don Revie, Joe Mercer, Tony Waddington, Bobby Brown, Walter McCrae, and Tommy Docherty were just a few of those to be met in hotel lobbies or around the swimming pool of the Guadalajara Country Club. Docherty, as it happened, was in a mood to compete for a playing place in the side. Burning slowly towards a tan, he was to be found most days in trunks and bare feet, volleying a large rubber ball around the swimming pool of the Gran Hotel with a fearsome vigour that had drinkers at the poolside tables crouching like men under shellfire. He remains, for all his vicissitudes, the most aggressively and likeably ebullient figure in football, a man who starts talking at two hundred words a minute when he opens his eyes in the morning and steps up the rate as the day goes on. His conversation is mainly a stream of jibes and puns and outrageous jokes. When a rather thin friend jumped into the pool: 'Who threw a pair of braces in the water? Look at him – throw a Polo mint over him and drag him out.' Or when a footballer who had been drinking Cuba Libre with marked enthusiasm emerged after a swim: 'I'm keeping my mouth closed in that water from now on. With the Bacardi that is coming out of his pores, one swallow and you'll be drunk as a lord.' Docherty, in fact, could not keep his mouth shut even when faced with the other argumentative Scots who usually gathered with him at the Gran. 'Here we are again,' one of them said wryly, 'talking a terrific World Cup. If they ever award it for chat we are odds-on.'

Those raucous middays made up a vividly pleasant memory for many of us but they may have seemed like a British plot to the Rumanians, who were using the hotel as their headquarters. They, the English and the Czechoslovakians all adopted the doubtful policy of booking into accommodation that was shared with members of the public, not only other guests but floods of casual visitors who came to pursue autographs, to stand and gawk or to force themselves into fatuous conversations with the players that would be embellished as souvenirs of Guadalajara ('Then I told Ballie that he'd have to pace himself better, y'know, save something for the second half'). The Guadalajara Hilton had been opulently restful the year before when the England players took to it strongly enough to urge Ramsey that they should stay there for the World Cup. But no great imagination was required to foresee how different it would be during the competition. It was one thing to have the odd Texan turning curious ('Ain't that Robbie Moore?') but quite another to have thousands of young Englishmen swarming through the place, whooping and jostling late into the night, now and then stumbling into the swimming pool. Throughout the World Cup the place had something of the atmosphere of a richly appointed Butlin's. And that was a secondary problem. Much more alarming was the campaign of harassment waged by a spontaneous alliance of Brazilian and Mexican supporters.

The reasons for the Mexicans' hostility towards the English were numerous, diverse and complex. Among the minor causes was probably the slight residue of the emancipated colony's ill-feeling towards people from a former centre of imperialism, even if the British Empire's connection with Mexico was somewhat tenuous. The fact is that the modern form of this resentment among Latin Americans is more likely to be aimed at Anglo-Saxon races, partly because of their natural capacity for being smug about darker skinned peoples with different cultures and even more because of the heavy paternalist hand that the United States lays on the lives of so many of them. With Mexicans, a profound touchiness about issues of national and personal pride, which are rarely differentiated, is part of the way of life. The obsession with *machismo*, the code of manliness, is so widespread that one sometimes fears that a derogatory remark about the weather in a man's home town may be seen as justification for a duel. Many of the foreign squads took pains to cope with this local phenomenon which was obviously a hazard as real, if not as important, as the climate and the altitude. But England under Ramsey made no such effort. Ramsey, indeed, was a provocative beacon who drew the fire of the Mexicans on his men. One of the most consistent elements in his behaviour is a public lack of warmth towards anyone born outside England. At best he is likely to appear indifferent towards them, at worst he can be witheringly scornful. When *machismo* collided head-on with the Little Englander there was bound to be bitterness. The criticisms that would be made of Ramsey for his tactics, his timing of substitutions and general handling of the team had infinitely less validity than complaints about his apparent attitude to people of other nationalities he encountered. This was exemplified in his Press conferences, where he gave the impression that he was speaking under duress and was about at any moment to plead the Fifth Amendment. Quite often he did, in effect. Obviously many of the questions were foolish but frequently his irritable reaction was excessive. Even the most unbiased Mexican journalists (a group which did not include the columnist who had developed a paranoia about Britain after some maltreatment, real or imagined, in 1966) swiftly concluded that Ramsey had not the remotest interest in being liked. They accepted the invitation to dislike him and, with the Press's encouragement, seemingly the whole population set out to give England a hard time. The extent of the problem was evident long before the competition got under way. On the very night of England's arrival back from their tour of Colombia and Ecuador, the night when Jeff Astle was moving unsteadily off the plane towards a viciously inflated scandal, there was that brush with a group of reporters who wanted to know his feelings on the arrest of Bobby Moore. He said, reasonably enough, that he would make a statement at a later date if he felt such a statement was necessary. Understandably, he became annoyed when he had to repeat his position, in identical terms, six or seven times. It was when the collective interview deteriorated into a debate on responsibility for the bad relations between the English and the Mexicans that he revealed his gift for aggravating a delicate situation. 'Why do you people do this to us?' he asked. The answer was another question. 'Don't you think the way you are treated is the result of the way *you* treat people?' After some profitless argument, one of the Mexican journalists, apparently anxious to end the discord and start afresh, said: 'Anyway, we welcome you now with open arms'. Ramsey let out a careful, metallic laugh. 'Surely, you must be joking,' he said. Next day one Mexico City newspaper carried a headline that read: 'England Arrive Drunk and Without Bobby Moore', and there were stories saying that players had been drinking with 'the spirit of pirates'. Possibly the same criminal distortions would have flourished whatever Ramsey's response at the airport but there is no doubt that from first to last his approach was a thorn in the rump of a people who could imagine themselves pricked by a feather. And it burdened his players with an additional pressure when that was the last thing they needed.

Having been chosen as a target, the English party were especially unfortunate to find themselves utterly exposed at the Hilton. The Brazilian supporters who toured the central streets of the city in nightly convoys, ten or a dozen clinging to one car, waving flags and singing and slapping the bonnet like a drum, could assemble outside the hotel to join with the locals in endless baiting. The Mexican police stood looking on blankly most of the time. Those of us who had witnessed their reaction to much more restrained demonstrations in another context during the summer of 1968 could only assume that their quiescence was a matter of policy. Yet the England players declined to regret their choice of accommodation. 'Before you think of anything else, you must have air-conditioned rooms and reliable food and we've got those things here,' said Bobby Charlton, composed amid the swirl of humanity in the hotel lobby. 'Even having all these people about isn't bad in every sense. There are distractions, of course, but at least you're not likely to get that killing boredom of being shut up in a training camp.' Charlton, who would rather rationalise than complain, was obviously taking the optimistic view but it does seem possible that English footballers would brood excessively if kept in the kind of isolation imposed on the Brazilians, whose experience with their clubs involves long periods of being confined to the company of other players.

The term in Brazil for the residential camp of a football team is *concentração*, or 'concentration', and some of the journalists who made futile attempts to penetrate the boundary walls of the Brazilians' suburban motel, Suites Caribe, felt the name had a sinisterly appropriate ring. Suites Caribe, with its inoffensive attempt to simulate hacienda architecture, was in effect a comfortable prison for the players. Far back from the single entrance, where high metal gates were screened with hardboard and patrolled by armed policemen, they reclined on yellow plastic sunchairs round the cement swimming pool or gossiped languidly over the railing that ran the length of the horseshoe balcony outside their rooms. All forty rooms had been taken over. Apart from training at a recreation club nearby, excursions beyond the walls were extremely rare and almost always under the eyes of a security force said by Brazilian journalists to number fifteen men flown in from their own country in addition to the guards provided by the Mexican authorities. The chief security officer was a Major Guaranys, whose wrestler's physique would have been sufficiently intimidating without the dark rumours that surrounded his name. There was one story about a political reporter being forced to leave a plane – while it was flying over the sea. It was presumably Guaranys who suggested a system of special credentials for the Press, who were instructed that their World Cup identification cards must be supported by two extra photographs if they presented themselves at the motel. Thus armed, journalists still had to restrict their visits to a few 'open mornings' during the World Cup: an hour-and-a-half of mingling and chatting with the players on the lawns around the swimming pool. For the rest of the time even those from Rio were no better off than the fans, mainly girls, who gathered under the verandah of the small, square building that fronted the motel. On most of the beautiful Guadalajara evenings, after the swift, elongated sunsets out on the rim of the plateau, there would be one or two of the footballers on the verandah, trying to catch the books or balls that were inexpertly tossed towards them for autographs. Sometimes they would crowd out there, sitting on the rail, to harmonise traditional songs. Their warmth readily broke through the atmosphere of secrecy and suspicion that had been created by the representatives of the Brazilian military régime who controlled all administrative aspects of the World Cup challenge. The delegation was in the charge of a Brigadier, then there was the heavyweight major, and the leading figure among the three men looking after the squad's physical conditioning was a Captain Claudio Coutinho. The captain was handsome and urbane and he spoke English with idiomatic precision but his eyes never lost a look that is seldom seen outside the best

poker schools. There were disgruntled pressmen who said that
Pelé had been a big influence in tightening security to the point
of melodrama. It was true that during the interview sessions
that preceded the start of the tournament the great man tended
to stay upstairs in his room. According to Coutinho, Pelé was
'creating his mood for the matches'. The mood of the journalists,
even if they did not all realise it, was traceable to Major
Guaranys and his assistants. Turning some of us away one
afternoon when the sun was hot enough to bore holes in bone,
he said with amiable finality: 'We should like you to think of
this place as your house, to treat it as your house, but we have
rules, you see.' We saw all right. The Mexicans were saying
that when the World Cup was over they would name the motel
Casa do Brasil in honour of the celebrities it had accommodated. San Quentin might be more suitable, we suggested.
Some Brazilians who were with us felt too troubled to be
facetious. 'The military régime are taking the team over to such
an extent, trying to use them so much for political purposes,
that many of our people hope Brazil are beaten,' said a photographer from São Paulo. That statement was an exaggeration –
not of the military influence, but of the response to it. And the
very fact that this paulista could say what he did was sadly
impressive. It convinced us more than ever that regardless of
the personal extravagances of João Saldanha, the hyperbole
and the capriciousness and the violence, his removal from the
managership of the Brazilian team had more to do with politics
than with any other single factor.

Saldanha, though less outspokenly left-wing than in his youth,
had refused to co-operate with any secret service men assigned
to the *seleção*, the selection. He was continuing to pay the price
of his principles. On his way to Mexico, as a journalist and
broadcaster, he had been turned off a plane that was due to
transport senior army officers from Rio to the United States.
Friends of his said the soldiers might have feared Saldanha
would hi-jack the aircraft. At any rate, he was sent on a tortuous
four-day journey that took him through half-a-dozen countries

before he reached Mexico with a passport due to expire less
than ten days after the World Cup Final. In the midst of his
difficulties Saldanha had the satisfaction of knowing that Brazil
would go for the World Cup with his team, the men he had
chosen, doing the jobs he had chosen them to do. It could be
said that Pelé would not have been the deeply determined
footballer he was at that time if still under a manager from
whom he had become angrily remote, but there is no doubt
that until acrimony blurred their views of each other Saldanha
had seen Pelé as a vital element in his plans. He believed
implicitly in the combination of Pelé and Tostão. That was
more than could be said of Mário Zagalo, the new manager,
who argued for a long time that they duplicated in too many
phases of the game. Significantly, Zagalo tried to make substantial alterations to the team selection left by his predecessor
but in the end the only change in personnel for which he could
take credit was a highly questionable one: the recall of Félix,
the veteran goalkeeper discarded by Saldanha. The managerial
justification of Félix in the face of the criticism he attracted
from all sides during the World Cup often appeared more
emotional than logical. From the first Saldanha shrugged and
smiled his *c'est la vie* smile. 'When he was young Félix was so
quick. He was a tiger. But now he is thirty-two years old. Maybe
it does not seem too old. But he has had thirty-two years of days
and nights. Perhaps the nights have been more important.'

For all his wildness, Saldanha has a catholic, civilised mind
and at any other time Guadalajara itself, with its fine colonial
squares, would have taken up much of his attention. His sister
Ione is an internationally known artist and, though he is an
atheist, he could hardly have left without seeing Murillo's
Assumption of the Blessed Virgin in the sixteenth–seventeenth-
century cathedral or the Orozco murals in the Governor's
palace. But in those days of May and June he, like the rest of
us, was there for the football. We were unashamedly philistine.
Our concern was about whether Pelé was as fit as he claimed
to be after the luxury of training for four unbroken months

(normally he plays so many matches that he has no time to train); about whether Gérson, between smoking forty cigarettes a day and haranguing his friends with the stamina of Fidel Castro, could refute the persistent allegations that his genius shrivelled to a timid imitation of itself outside Brazil; about whether Rivelino, with a left foot that looked as if it could shuffle a pack of cards and deal its owner four aces, would emerge as a new world star; about whether Tostão had recovered adequately from his eye injury, and so on and on. For, whatever happened, Group Three was bound to be special, if only because the reigning champions, England, had been set against Brazil who, in common with Italy and Uruguay, were seeking to win the Jules Rimet Trophy for a third time and earn the right to keep it permanently.

If Brazil were for ever in England's thoughts, however, they did not make for nightmares. 'We'll beat these,' Alan Ball said and meant it. Captain Coutinho answered for 'these'. Having pointed out that Brazil's preparation had been timed to bring them to a peak at exactly the right moment, he added a simple, eloquent threat. 'We are,' he said, 'ready to explode.' Those of us who were mere observers could only stand back and wait for the shrapnel to fly.

ENGLAND v. RUMANIA

Guadalajara, June 2

There were small deserts of unoccupied seats around the steep sides of the Jalisco Stadium when, with the clattering release of a thousand pigeons, the fight to win through from Group Three was formally begun. To English eyes, the crowd was big enough. At least empty seats cannot jeer, as most of the spectators did when England took the field. The happily dishevelled little army which had crossed the Atlantic behind the team did their best to be heard but, faced with the hostile coalition of Mexicans and Brazilians, they had to settle for the role of good-humoured minority. Rumania, whose supporters hardly had to raise a murmur, were the first side to confirm that the easiest way to be popular in Mexico was to play against England.

The weather was less cruel than it could be, and indeed would be in subsequent matches. As we baked in the last hours of May, Miguel Rodríguez, head of the Jalisco State Meteorological Department, had offered hope with the assurance that the weather pattern in the area during June was so reliable that he could virtually guarantee six days of cooling rain by the fifteenth of the month. The climate was as good as his word. We did have half-a-dozen days with rainfall, two when the heavens got to work with tropical earnestness, but the effect on the temperature was always temporary and timed to be of only the most limited help to the footballers. What they needed was a steady, refreshing drizzle while they were on the field and none had the luck to encounter that ideal. However, conditions for England's first afternoon of competition were fairly encouraging, with a generous splash of rain towards the end.

Many of Ramsey's players had refused all along to share the widespread apprehension about the heat. Geoff Hurst reminded us that English sides had played in high temperatures all over the world and generally succeeded in doing themselves justice. He for one was more inclined to discuss the hazards of altitude, technical as well as physical. Guadalajara, at 5,212 feet, is located just above the level at which altitude becomes an important influence on performance. A careful programme of acclimatisation strengthened the England party's belief that they could cope with the strain on their bodies but some, like Hurst, remained keenly aware of the difference thin air could make to the behaviour of the ball. 'I found a noticeable difference at first,' said Hurst, 'especially balls being played to the chest. I found it bouncing away. The ball seems to be so damned lively, as well, quite apart from the velocity, just like cricketers playing on soft and hard wickets.' The problem was even more troublesome for Gordon Banks. His defenders have such confidence in Banks's hands ('I've never seen him drop the ball, me', Jack Charlton had said in South America) that when they see a ball fly towards him they tend to turn away, convinced there is no danger. The goalkeeper warned them that this would be a mistake at altitude. 'The ball comes much faster, more unexpectedly than it does at sea level and it's not sure to stay true. Sometimes it's going all over the place. Things I'd eat up at home I may find myself really scrambling to hold. It may be safer at times to push them away and the lads will have to be ready for that situation.'

Not everyone was sure that Rumania would be ambitious enough to create such situations around Banks. Their manager, Angelo Nicolescu, promised that they would go for a win because they had to start by taking two points to have a good chance of qualifying. The captain, Lucescu, spoke less boldly. They would have to be wary with England, he said, mentioning the young, extrovert Dinu as the sort of player who would have to be restrained. Dinu, who wears his hair long and dresses in a way that will not be seen as a good example to the youth of Eastern Europe, likes to move forward aggressively from his place beside Lupescu in the back line. 'But against England he will stay,' said Lucescu, with the firmness of a man who had laid down the law. 'England is always dangerous because it is England. The Champion.'

Equally, for the champions or anyone else, the first match is always dangerous because it is the first match. It was not surprising that nervous caution should inhibit the early sparring. Even so, chances fell to both sides. Hurst, under tight pressure, mishit a hooked shot with his left foot as he spun on to a low cross from Peters but the opening was negligible compared with that created by Dumitrache in the fifth minute. Dumitrache had twisted an ankle in training three days before the match but no one could question the completeness of his recovery as he broke with marvellous acceleration on the left wing. His high chip was worthy of the run and it appeared certain to do England some harm when Cooper, looking as if he were

H

auditioning to play one of the waking dead in a Hammer film, stood back and let Dembrowski leap in to meet the ball just outside the far post. Dembrowski should probably have lunged at the ball with his head but chose to play it loosely with a foot and Cooper, emerging from his catatonic state, had the immense relief of seeing the shot go past. That was the last memorable error Cooper was to make in the World Cup. Before the match was over he had persuaded every neutral observer that he bore comparison with the best left-backs in football and from then until he left for home he did nothing to jeopardise that status. 'I'm always liable to have a moment like that when I'm playing for Leeds,' he said of his blunder afterwards. 'I just lose concentration, go into a daze. Don Revie feels like murdering me. I just hope I don't give Alf any more cause to feel that way.' He need not have worried.

For the time being, however, Rumania had England mildly anxious. Tataru, tall and forcefully direct on the right wing, had been set to share the forward responsibilities with Dumitrache and was proving so active that the more famous centre-forward often found himself the supporting player. Having given Satmareanu the space to make a cross which Newton headed off Lucescu, Dumitrache combined fluently with Tataru to put Mullery and even the great Moore in brief difficulties. Any idea that Moore could be unduly discomfited, however, seemed more and more to be an illusion as the game wore on. Detecting hidden threats with the sensitivity of a geiger counter, defusing them with clean, uncluttered expertise, he made it easy for his admirers to insist that he is the finest central defender in the world. On his right Newton was rapidly gathering assurance after an unsteady beginning and the Rumanians, adhering in the main to a 4–4–2 formation, were finding Banks an increasingly remote target. England now felt free to show some genuine attacking vigour. Moore moved the ball through to Lee and the blond forward steered it carefully ahead of Charlton, who was making an inspired and courageous run in the inside-left position. Charlton made solid contact with the shot but a

Rumanian foot deflected the ball for a corner. Newton and Cooper were breaking regularly from behind and the Leeds man in particular was looping some alarming centres across the face of Adamache's goal. One of these reduced Lupescu to such confusion that when he dived to meet the ball he could only trap it awkwardly on the ground with his head. As it broke clear, Lee dragged it skilfully to his left and, in the moment of overbalancing, shot viciously with his left foot. Adamache scarcely saw the ball before it struck the top of his cross bar and went over. Peters and Ball had been strangely vague in midfield through most of the first half, leaving the impressively vigorous Charlton to carry the burden of constructive work there, but Peters asserted himself at the front by meeting Newton's cross with a header that rose a little too high. Tataru's characteristic break and centre at the other end drew a glancing clearance from Labone but it was by no means the most ominous gesture provided by Rumania before the interval. That came from Dumitru with a heavy foul on Mullery. Dumitru, who had been given a search-and-destroy mission in front of the back line – formed by Satmareanu, Lupescu, Dinu and Mocanu – would have received less grudging praise for his alertness and efficiency if he had not specialised in ramming interceptions that suggested he practised tackling against concrete gateposts. Unfortunately, the second half was to show that Dumitru was a gentle soul when considered alongside the left-back, Mocanu.

During the interval the great shadow cast by the main grandstand of the Jalisco Stadium broadened on the pitch, promising some additional shade to the sweating players but increasing the risk of misjudging the ball as it travelled into or out of the shimmering sunlight. Sir Alf Ramsey, already annoyed to discover the field smaller and less smooth than it had been the year before, suspected that the shadow would be an extra complication. He was proved right in the end but the evidence of this match was not disturbing. Indeed, Ramsey did not have to be seriously depressed on any count as his men drank lemon tea or sucked on oranges. The only substitution affected Banks's jersey. (In place of his yellow sweater, Banks wore a short-sleeved one in red. Apart from being cooler, it removed any likelihood of confusion with the yellow shirts of the Rumanians.)

Of course, Ramsey would not be happy about the absence of goals or of any hint that Lee might reproduce in these hot, fast conditions the brilliance that comes naturally in the wintry settings of English League grounds. The unproductive form of Peters was another lurking doubt but it was too early for deep gloom and the excellence of Moore, Newton and Cooper and the tireless, sensible industry of Mullery were reasons for optimism. So, too, was the brave persistence of Hurst, though many of us were perturbed even at that stage by the almost callous willingness with which the team (obviously acting under instructions) allowed him to be isolated in the midst of the enemy. Players such as Hurst are at their best when thundering into attack like the U.S. Cavalry, not when left hemmed in like a beleaguered wagon train.

The opening of the second half was notable for the ferocity of Mocanu, who began to behave as if he had been hired at the interval to supply patients for an orthopaedic hospital. Almost immediately he committed a prodigious foul on Newton, inflicting a knee injury that took the full-back off the field in the fifty-first minute and prevented him from playing against Brazil five days later. Wright came on for Newton just in time to see Mocanu slash the legs from Lee. Some of the Rumanian's alleged tackles were almost high enough to scalp a short man. Commendably undeterred by his maltreatment, Lee soon sprinted through to drive the ball square, but the attack brought less menace than a sudden dipping shot from Nunweiller that flew all of thirty-five yards and retained sufficient venom to make Banks push it over his bar.

Before the crowd had stopped talking about that shot, Hurst struck with one that was much less spectacular but had the incalculable advantage of finishing in the net. There were twenty-five minutes remaining when Wright moved as if to take the ball deep on the right wing and then decided to leave it for Ball. Ball swung in a high, deliberate centre angled towards the far post. As the ball fell, Hurst was on hand to drag it past Satmareanu with his right foot and slide it beyond Adamache with his left. Hurst said later that the ball had actually gone through the goalkeeper's legs. 'Nutmegs in the World Cup,' said Mullery in admiration. 'It can't be bad.'

England's position was now anything but bad, although Mocanu did his utmost to undermine it with yet another violent foul, this time on Wright. Dumitru, never shy about following such an example, chose Cooper as victim. The referee, M. Vital Loraux of Belgium, had handled the match unobjectionably while it was free of ill-temper, but once the viciousness had been injected he was revealed as hopelessly passive. His reaction suggested that the competition was not yet safe from the disasters of feeble refereeing.

Tataru had run himself out at the head of the Rumanian attack where Dumitrache, too, had faded gradually after one unnervingly splendid dispossession by Moore in the first half. Neagu substituted for Tataru in the seventy-fourth minute but, with Ball hustling into his assertive mood as Charlton's control on the midfield relaxed, Rumania were undeniably struggling. They had a right to expect much more of Lucescu. He should have been a dominating force in the middle of their team but was notably less effective than Nunweiller and Dembrowski, who were themselves erratic. Nevertheless, Dembrowski did emphasise the wisdom of Banks's cautionary words to his defence with a long, low shot that spun out of the goalkeeper's hands.

A quarter of an hour from the end Osgood came on for the tired Lee and the rain came on for everybody. The cooling downpour encouraged Wright to make a wonderful defensive header out of the English goalmouth, Ball to cross for a Hurst header at the opposite end and lastly Charlton to take the ball from Peters and drive it thrillingly close to Adamache's posts from twenty-five yards.

England went back to the Hilton Hotel feeling they had done

a competent job. Liberated to have a relaxing drink that night, they gave ample indication of their healthy morale. Mullery and Ball enjoyed telling of two rather personal exchanges on the field. After having Lucescu's elbow thrust into his face Mullery had sought instant reprisals. 'I gave him one in close, where nobody could see. He went down like a sack of potatoes. Then I tackled him hard soon after that and his boot came off. He stuck his face into mine and said "F—— i-d-i-o-t." I laughed and said, 'When you going home then? June the fifteenth?' Dumitrache, who had been predicting that he would score twice against England, had Ball to remind him of the forecast near the end. 'I went over to him and held up two fingers,' Ball told us. ' "Where's your two then, pally?" I said. "Where are they?" He just shrugged. I'm an irritating little twat, me. They must hate me, those fellas.'

For all his comedian's ways, his high voice and his Mickey Rooney exuberance, Ball is as intense about football as it is possible for a man to be, and that night his thoughts, like those of most of us, were on the Brazilians. 'England did not tear up the stadium but they're on their way,' someone said. 'Brazil say they're more worried about the Czechs than they are about us, but that's just because it's their first game. I'll bet the Czechs are worried, too.' The only people entitled to be easy in their minds were the neutrals. They had the right to assume they would see something worth paying for.

England 1   Rumania 0

BRAZIL v. CZECHOSLOVAKIA

Guadalajara, June 3

There was an undercurrent of tension in the ritual gaiety of the Brazilian supporters as they marched on the Jalisco Stadium for the first time. They knew that their team's task was not merely to win a match but to lay a ghost. The memory of Liverpool in 1966 still haunted most Brazilians, threatening their pseudo-religious conviction of their innate superiority among the footballers of the world. Of course, there had been obvious reasons for their failure to survive beyond the Group matches in England's year. Frightened selectors had opted to ride on the reputations of soiled stars from another era and had flown to Europe with a party that looked more like a Golden Age club than a World Cup squad. They chose Garrincha, whose miraculous talent had been crumbling since his club, Botafogo, took him on tour in 1963 when he should have been having rest and treatment for a serious knee ailment. They took Zito, Djalma Santos, and Bellini, all in their middle thirties, and Orlando, a veteran of 1958 who had been overlooked in 1962. Even the outstanding young players that they did have had been ill-prepared and when Pelé was methodically kicked out of the competition by Morais of Portugal an inglorious demise before the quarter-finals became inevitable.

Apart from one or two exciting goals, Brazil were left with nothing to console them but glimpses of exceptional promise in a young forward named Tostão. Now Tostão was back as a leading force in the brave new team but there were doubts about him, doubts that could be seen as embodying the general uncertainty concerning Brazil. That they had the genius to win the Jules Rimet Trophy again could never be in question and, with a unique preparation of four months in training camp, free of all club commitments, they had given themselves every chance of building up the collective condition to match the more physically orientated Europeans. After 1966, however, there was a fear that something might go disastrously wrong, that they might be in for a time of frustration following their victories in 1958 and 1962. In a country where university graduates may be found worshipping at Umbanda (black magic) altars, where great footballers have been known to lose all will to play well because their Umbandista told them they were doomed to play a bad game, there are many people willing to worry about the intervention of a malicious fate.

Even the less mystical Brazilians could see reasons for

being unsure about their prospects, although most of them agreed that the removal of João Saldanha in favour of Mário Zagalo might have given them the best of both worlds. This conclusion was as common among friends and admirers of Saldanha as among his enemies. No one was in a position to deny the healthy impact of his appointment in January 1969, but the implication was that he was replaced at a time when his aggressive independence and temperamental instability were in danger of negating the advantages he had achieved. He started by kicking aside some of the more outmoded ideas of the national football authority, CBD, using his vast experience of the game all over the world to pick a comprehensively equipped, carefully balanced group of players and insisting that they should have a thorough preparation. By putting an end to the feverish shuffling and permutating that had marked Aimore Moreira's managership, declaring his faith in a substantial nucleus of players, he laid the foundation of the challenge in Mexico. He also mounted a sustained campaign of propaganda in Europe with the intention of talking countries there into moving nearer to the South American interpretation of the Laws on such issues as tackling from behind. Saldanha's dire warnings that the World Cup would finish in uproar if the Europeans did not modify their approach undoubtedly stayed in the minds of some managers and players. (England appeared to play with an almost excessive decorum at times.)

Brazilians who acknowledged these valuable contributions from Saldanha still felt that his dismissal could be justified. One Rio journalist crystallised a widely held view when he said: 'We would have had no chance in the World Cup without João's groundwork, but he is not the man for the last lap in Mexico'. The need there, he suggested, was for a more straightforward, more technical and less romantically imaginative manager. With the grand strategy established, and a budget of $1,250,000, CBD went for a level-headed, undramatic commander in the field. Undeniably, their decision had

political overtones and the manner of its implementation
reflected no credit on those involved, but even on the basis of
football considerations a case could be made for it.

Yet there remained some misgivings about possible disruption of a winning system, and these were not diminished
when Zagalo began to say publicly that he might not choose
to accommodate Pelé and Tostão in the same team. Tostão
had been joint top scorer in the qualifying groups (with Muller,
of West Germany, who had the luxury of playing against
Cyprus) and an almost indispensable element of the side that
gave Saldanha maximum points and the amazing ratio of
23 goals against 2. Before blows from a knee and a football
brought Tostão a serious eye injury late in 1969, many good
judges, including Saldanha, regarded him as the most effective
forward in Brazil. Zagalo's hints that he might be surplus to
requirements, because he was duplicating the functions of
Pelé, had the ring of dangerous heresy. Certainly they were not
calculated to assist Tostão in his struggle to regain mental
and physical sharpness following the operation in Houston,
Texas, that corrected a slightly detached retina. The injury
cost him vital months of action on the run-in to the World
Cup, blunting the telepathic responses and extreme precision
that are the essence of his game. As late as the week before the
World Cup began, Tostão, disturbed by painless but unsightly
haemorrhaging in the eye, had a psychological crisis and was
ready to return to Brazil. A telephone call to Dr Abdala
Moura, the Brazilian ophthalmic surgeon who operated on him
in Houston, produced reassurance. The doctor, a football
addict and supporter of Tostão's club, Cruzeiro, flew to
Mexico to watch him play against a León side and told him that
even if he had more bleeding in the eye he could turn out in a
match the same day. Moura said he would take the player back
to Houston some time after the World Cup (he stressed there
was no urgency) to have the cause of the haemorrhaging
removed. He deduced that it was the result of an allergy to the
cat gut he had used in stitching.

All this renewed Tostão's confidence and, with Zagalo apparently persuaded of his importance, only the question of match fitness remained. After the pain and disappointment of the preceding months, would Brazil's centre-forward still have the quickness, the hardness and, above all, the nerve to play his old deadly game in penalty areas swarming with some of the best and toughest defenders in the world? June 3 at the Jalisco Stadium was to provide part of the answer, and no one under-estimated the bearing of that answer on the immediate future of the Jules Rimet Trophy.

There was a bad omen for Brazil in the minutes before the kick-off when one of the huge, coloured hot-air balloons so popular at Maracana caught fire on take-off and nearly incinerated the launching party, not to mention a few of the symbolic pigeons who were minding their own business in a basket at the time. Some ordinary balloons made a happier exit from the stadium, looking like a cluster of ripening grapes as they carried the green and yellow of the Brazilian flag up over the rim into the clear sky. The next memorable sight was less ethereal: Rivelino leaving Dobias paralysed with one of his complex feinting dribbles before driving the ball low across goal. Pelé reached it with his right foot but it flew over Viktor's bar. Who needs omens when little ploys like that come naturally?

But Czechoslovakia were not ready to grant Brazil an immediate monopoly of the high artifice. All at once Petras, short, auburn-haired and with an aura so electric that the air seemed to crackle when he ran, was surging and swerving in from the right along the dead-ball line towards Félix. Clodoaldo was stranded at his heels and before the others could converge to stifle the threat Petras had dragged the ball out for an angled left-foot shot from short of the near post. The shot was a betrayal of the earlier brilliance and the ball soared harmlessly behind.

Some players would have been upset for half an hour by such a miss. Petras wiped it off his conscience by scoring a magnificently impertinent goal in the eleventh minute. As

Clodoaldo loitered over collecting the ball in the right-half position, Petras spirited it away from him and galloped with killing straightness into the penalty area. Scorning both delay and elaboration, he lashed the ball with his left foot in the direction of his run and it hurtled high behind Félix's right shoulder. Petras veered away, fell on his knees and crossed himself before being buried in rowdy congratulations. Among other things, he had just ensured that Glasgow Rangers would not bid for him.

Brazil were not cowed by the early blow. Viktor was alarmed when Tostão, from Gérson's pass, slid the ball into the outside of his net, then the goalkeeper saved with difficulty from Rivelino, who had again demonstrated his ability to make menacing space out of negative situations. Pelé was the next to intervene, chesting the ball into his stride to initiate a break. But he dived hopefully in search of a penalty when he was crowded. Carlos Alberto reversed the current by receiving the ball from Félix's goal kick and giving it neatly to Adamec. The forward had room to do better than send the ball too high. The loss of a second goal then would have set a grim pattern for Brazil. Having been spared, they began to impose a design of their own by taking a swashbuckling goal in the twenty-fourth minute.

Pelé was brought down as he dribbled invitingly across the front of the penalty area and we waited for our first real glimpse of the fabled Brazilian deadliness with such free kicks. We were not let down. First Gérson and then Pelé shaped to take the kick while the Czechs hastily organised six men in a nervous row to block the line of fire, which was at a slight angle from the Brazilian right. While Gérson and Pelé were playing decoys, Jairzinho had sidled in to join the far edge of the wall. Abruptly, the shadow boxing was over and Rivelino, spurting at the ball on a run almost parallel with the goal-line, struck a murderous shot towards the yellow shirt at the end of the wall. Jairzinho leapt aside and the ball went on in a blur inside Viktor's right-hand post. The goalkeeper, who was widely criticised for taking up an eccentric position behind his own wall, bravely made contact but that only meant he had sore hands.

Brazil were now stirred to put on the style. After a penetrating exchange of passes between Gérson and Pelé, Gérson just failed to pull the ball clear of the last tackle. When Pelé passed to Tostão the centre-forward did move into the open, drifting beautifully to his left, but his crisp shot was touched over the bar by Viktor. Next Pelé, gloriously ubiquitous, came out of a challenge with the ball and raced fifty yards. Tostão and Jairzinho between them could not quite exploit the chance he made.

Undismayed, Pelé brought the first half to an amazing climax with one of the great moments of the World Cup. Moving into possession well inside his own half of the field, he gave a barely perceptible glance in the direction of Viktor, saw that the goalkeeper had moved out some yards from the posts, and struck. Pelé was still in the Brazilian segment of the centre circle when, raising his right leg in a prodigious backlift and swinging it through with a flowing, effortless precision worthy of an iron shot by Ben Hogan, he sent the ball in a fast arc towards goal. Viktor's contorted features revealed the extent of his painful astonishment as he scrambled back under the ball, then spun helplessly to see it swoop less than a yard outside a post.

Through the interval the stadium throbbed with the special excitement crowds feel when they have seen something remarkable and know there is more of the same to come. Without question, Brazil appeared capable of the explosion Captain Coutinho had promised. Pelé *had* created his mood. He was playing as many Europeans had never seen him play before. Some, forgivably misled by seeing him in his low phases when he was drained by over-use, had come to suspect that his was an inflated legend. Now they were savouring the correction. As early as this point, we could see that Pelé's statement that he was fitter than he had been for half-a-dozen years was no

mere Press release. He looked marvellous, like a hungry animal
that was quick and strong enough to kill but too wise in the
chase to start running prematurely. In addition to all his
gifts – the almost supernatural athleticism, the force and
subtlety and completeness of his play, the capacity for making
deeply considered moves as if they were spontaneous – in
addition to all this, there was an unfailing sense of relevance
in everything he did. Concentration enclosed him lie an extra
skin. He was in all important respects the most experienced
World Cup player in the competition and he knew exactly
what mattered and what did not. He knew that to try with
every fibre, which he was determined to do, he must stay
relaxed, constantly rejecting any temptation to make the
unprofitable flourish. Until the job was done, the roar of the
crowd would sound far out on the borders of his mind.

Even playing like this, Pelé did not dwarf the men around
him. Brazil's central asset, we could see already and indeed had
realised before a ball was kicked, was the plurality of exceptional talents. Gérson, his encroaching baldness and fleshless face
making him look older than twenty-nine, acted as an inspired
supply officer behind the front line. His left foot (it is an accident
if he uses his right) has the accuracy to drop the ball in a
butterfly net from fifty yards and the power to knock down a
goalpost. The other members of the team call him The Parrot
because they have never known a parrot that talked as much.
But they admit that he is worth listening to.

Alongside Gérson, although he often gave old-fashioned
justification to the number eleven on his back by thrusting
down the left wing, was Rivelino, a handsome son of Italian
parents who would be a tremendous player even if his left
foot did not shoot as hard as any in the world. Tostão, too, is
essentially left-footed, which adds to his prestige among
Brazilians. It is a matter of history that the most feared strikers
of the ball in their game, the legendary thunderers, have been
left-footed. Few of them have had the comprehensive skills
of Tostão. He is a short man with a thick torso and immense

legs that appear as big round the ankles as some players' are round the calf. There is a marked contrast with Pelé, who has massive slabs of muscle down to the knee, then tapers fine as a schoolgirl to his feet. Tostão has pleasant but rather blunt features under sparse dark hair that is curly in a wispy way. His eyes move slowly in his face, suggesting weariness with the familiarity of what they see, or hold a steady gaze as if looking through the turmoil around him to something in the far distance. There is an impression of maturity and quiet authority that makes it difficult to remember that he is only twenty-four years old. In this first match Tostão was straining to adjust. Playing far forward, often with his back to the goal, it was his responsibility to go where the concentration of defenders was thickest, so that he could employ his delicately judged one-touch manoeuvres to take opponents out of the game. At first his reactions were sluggish by his own standards but soon the barnacles accumulated by disuse were peeling away and by the end of this match there were clear signs that he would be a dominant influence on the competition.

Jairzinho had no real problems of fitness. The Negro winger admits a susceptibility to injury that surprised those who have marvelled at the great feline strength of a physique which would fit a top welterweight boxer. Part of the explanation is that following the 1966 World Cup he lost a year's action as a result of breaking the same bone in his right foot twice and only recovered after an operation had inserted a sliver of bone from elsewhere in his body. Despite this, in his determination to go through any barrier put in front of him, he exposes himself to maximum hazard. Zagalo wisely declined to pressure Jairzinho when he showed poor form in practice. 'He gave me confidence to save myself for the match and it worked,' the forward said afterwards. Even in the match itself he conserved energy, keeping his most devastating runs for the second half. It was a pattern he would confirm in later performances. He grew stronger as others wilted, and the sight of him gathering speed for one of his surges at goal came to be a major terror of defenders' lives. With the ball kept close between his feet, but bobbling deceptively loose rather than running submissively, he went at his challengers as if he found their very presence an insufferable affront. Those he could not skirt cleanly he was happy to barge aside. In these collisions he constantly appeared on the point of losing his balance but hardly ever did. That was left to the defenders.

The Czechs had encountered problems from the outset in Guadalajara. The rough field allotted to them at a local school took such a toll of their ankles that they switched to an area attached to a brewery, an act of masochism in such thirsty weather. On their return to the school Horvath, the captain and roving interceptor in the defence, and Adamec promptly hurt themselves. At the interval in the Jalisco Stadium we wondered if Horvath and Adamec might not have been better off with injuries serious enough for them to be excused duties against Brazil. The second half, we felt, was not likely to be restful for them or for Viktor.

But the score was still 1–1 and Czechoslovakia, having substituted the elongated, shambling figure of Kvasnak for the short, hustling Hrdlicka, restarted with a show of defiance. Petras made ground on the right and passed to Frantisek Vesely, who might have responded with something better than two shots against Félix's body. Brazil's answer was vivid. Pelé from the right slipped the ball short to Gérson, outside the penalty area in front of goal. The shot, struck early with the left foot, bent viciously outwards and Viktor did not move as it thudded on to his right-hand post. Gérson claimed perfect compensation in the sixtieth minute. From the depths of the midfield he aimed a long diagonal pass high towards Pelé as the great forward edged round behind Hagara. The ball, having travelled all of fifty yards, looked to be curving within reach of Hagara's jump but Gérson's judgment was so fine that it narrowly cleared the left-back's head and dropped on to Pelé's chest as he made his own leap. Pelé chested it down in front of him and took an unhurried step forward before meeting it on the bounce with his right instep to place it in the far side-netting.

Instead of crumbling immediately, the Czechs came back with their most penetrating attack of the second half. Adamec's short corner on the left took the ball back to Hagara and when he sent it sharply across goal Kvasnak had Félix at his mercy. Kvasnak closed purposefully on the ball only to slam it over the bar with his left foot. That was the last moment in which the result was open to speculation. With sixty-four minutes gone, Gérson produced another killing pass, this time from the centre circle to Jairzinho running clear well ahead of him. Jairzinho was so far clear, in fact, that the vigorous appeals for an offside decision seemed to be justified. But the referee made no gesture and Jairzinho, hooking the ball in the air to let Viktor run out under it, went on to score at leisure.

Brazil, secure in the assumption that they had beaten opponents whose sad lack of condition was being fully revealed, were about to discover the full price they had to pay. Gérson had aggravated an old thigh injury and sixteen minutes from the end he limped off to be replaced by Paulo Cézar, who had been warming up on the touchline for some time. Paulo Cézar, a player of high skill who alternates between the left wing and a more withdrawn position, much as Zagalo once did, was the accepted standby for Gérson and for Rivelino. If he and Rivelino were on the field at the same time it was natural for Rivelino to stay more regularly in midfield rather than forage freely on the left. However, Rivelino was still willing to go near enough to give Viktor a good view of his Omar Sharif moustache and oblige him to save a nasty dipping shot.

Czechoslovakia substituted Bohumil Vesely for Frantisek Vesely in the seventy-seventh minute but the change did little more than invite confusion in newspaper offices. Of similarly slight importance was the caution administered to Horvath. Gérson had received one in the first half but the match was quite without malice. Nevertheless, there was still ample legitimate venom in Brazil and Jairzinho crowned their imposing

entrance into the 1970 World Cup with a dazzling solo goal.
Given the ball by Pelé on the right, he steadied in time to
receive a bulldozing tackle by Hagara. Jairzinho's legs were
swept away from him and the award of a free kick could not
have been disputed. Wisely, the referee permitted the winger
to run on and, with courage and power to equal his control,
he bemused Horvath and Migas and thwarted Hagara's
attempt at recovery before right-footing the ball in off the
bottom of the far post. Jairzinho ran twenty yards outside the
field to accept and return the salute of the crowd.

Brazil had given fair warning to England and the rest.
True, their defence had sometimes been clumsily accommodating, with Brito and Piazza alternately hesitant and impetuous
in the middle of the back four and Félix spectacularly vin-
dicating the misgivings of João Saldanha. In this form Félix
is the kind of goalkeeper who should take a prayer mat on to
the field as others take a cap or gloves. Félix was not certain
to improve materially, but many of us were convinced that
Brito would steady to a much more reliable game and that
Carlos Alberto would show himself to be a commanding,
adventurous right-back.

Given such reasonable strengthening of the defence – and,
after all, only one goal had been lost to the Czechs, and only
two in the preliminary qualifying series – Brazil were capable
of anything. Clodoaldo, patrolling in front of the back line,
had the firmness to be a destroyer and the speed and creativity
to do great damage going forward. Gérson and Rivelino were
superb midfield players equipped to perform as superb advanced
attackers, just as Pelé had the range to be a master in any part
of the field. Tostão, too, had wonderful flexibility and it was
a tribute to his strength of character that he was operating as a
specialist front man. Jairzinho was, quite simply, the most
consistently dangerous winger in the competition. Brazil's
tactics were not so much 4–3–3 as bang-bang-bang. They were
aware of the tactical requirements of the modern game but
believed in using them to detonate rather than to smother

I

explosions. They had been assisted on this afternoon by Czechoslovakia's tendency to forget all thoughts of organised deployment and scurry into mass retreat whenever Brazil gained possession. 'They played basketball football', as Alan Ball put it.

Regardless of the deficiencies that faced them, however, Brazil had proved that the bankruptcy of 1966 was just a bad memory. Once again they had talent to burn.

Brazil 4   Czechoslovakia 1

RUMANIA *v.* CZECHOSLOVAKIA

Guadalajara, June 6

The banner of East European football was already bedraggled by the time Rumania and Czechoslovakia came together. Of the four countries from behind the Iron Curtain only Russia had taken a point at that stage and theirs had come from an inaugural match with Mexico that had all the fluid artistry of a deadlock in arm-wrestling. In Group Four Bulgaria had seen a 2–0 lead over Peru turn to a 2–3 defeat to set beside the losses of the Czechs and Rumanians. Nevertheless, there was more than scarred pride at stake in the Jalisco Stadium on this Saturday afternoon when the weather surprised no one by being more appropriate to sunbathing than football and the crowd was dressed as if for the beach. The winners would stay alive in Group Three, albeit in need of a substantial upset in the last Group matches to put them through to the quarter-finals. The losers would have a hard job to persuade themselves and other people that they had not been reduced to the status of tourists. With a fine neighbourly solidarity, Rumania and Czechoslovakia had suggested during their preparations that they had as much respect for each other as they had for England or even Brazil. Now, with that attitude looking a little unrealistic, dog would have no qualms about eating dog.

The Czechs did not hesitate to take the first bite. Within three minutes they were a goal ahead, a goal produced, almost inevitably, by the pungent opportunism of Petras. A one-two exchange of passes gave Bohumil Vesely a break into space on the right and he centred with commendable promptness. Lupescu appeared to have the cross covered but Petras dodged swiftly past him to turn a neat, decisive header low beyond Adamache's right side.

Rumania might have put themselves level at once when Neagu resourcefully ran outside the right touchline to beat Zlocha and steer the ball back for Dembrowski to volley. Vencel could manage only a lunging, slapping save and he seemed to be unlucky when the ball travelled to Dumitrache. But it reached the centre-forward waist high and he could not contort himself sufficiently to keep it under the cross-bar. Soon afterwards Dumitrache saw another shot turned away by Vencel but throughout the first half Petras was the most conspicuously effective attacker. Only twenty-three years old and playing his third senior international (he had been ordered from the field during the play-off with Hungary that won Czechoslovakia a place in Mexico), Petras already had two World Cup goals to his name and seemed likely to take more. His socks at his ankles, his fair head a beacon for any aggressive-minded man in his side, it was he who lent validity to the Czech policy of letting the Rumanians have more of the ball on the assumption that after taking a few harmless blows the Czechs would get home a punishing one of their own. The theory was put under stress by some perceptive passes from Dinu, one of which released Lucescu from midfield for a centre that nearly gave Dembrowski a scoring header. Yet the somewhat isolated assaults of Czechoslovakia did remain more menacing until the interval and Dinu's excellence was mainly to be seen in defence, alongside Satmareanu, who was playing brilliantly at right-back. Neither they nor the other Rumanian defenders could do much in the thirty-eighth minute when Jurkanin was sent clear by a wonderfully spontaneous return pass from Petras. Jurkanin delayed his shot as if intent on seeing the whites of Adamache's eyes. Instead, he felt the weight of Lupescu's tackle and a glaring chance was missed.

As the first half was ending a hero behind one of the goals waved a tiny Union Jack and brought a swelling angry whistle from thousands of spectators. England did not have to play to be abused in Mexico.

When the teams came out to begin again we were quickly made aware of the weariness that was spreading through the Czechs, bringing a raggedness to their 4–3–3 and affecting even Petras. His legs no longer pumped as eagerly as they had done in the first half hour and we were forced to conclude that he was not immune to the general lack of stamina that had been so blatant against Brazil. Now it was Neagu who emerged as the most dangerous forward. Just how dangerous was shown in the fifty-third minute when Dinu gave the ball to Nunweiller and he in turn thrust it ahead into the inside-left position. Neagu spun to flick the ball past Migas and, steadying carefully, used the side of his foot to guide it just inside the far upright.

Adamec had come on for Jurkanin at the interval and he provided a threat with a corner that appeared to hypnotise Adamache into immobility. Kuna, moving up from the middle of the team, failed by an inch or two to connect with a telling header. In the succeeding minutes chances fell to both sides, the best of them to Rumania, who must have taken the lead if Lucescu had been at his sharpest. Predictably, Lucescu was replaced by Tataru after sixty-nine minutes but that change, the simultaneous substitution of Frantisek Vesely for Jokl, and the later summoning of Gergely in place of Dumitru all left the basic trend of the match unaltered.

What did have a significant effect was the increasing discomfort of Zlocha, whose promotion to take over from Hagara, a stubborn left-back against Jairzinho of Brazil, had been unexpected. From the start Zlocha had been unhealthily stretched by the task of restraining Neagu and with twelve minutes to go he gave way to desperation. As Neagu was striving to get away yet again, the full-back wrestled him down and the Mexican referee, Diego de Leo, immediately signalled a penalty. Dumitrache's high, hard shot was made doubly sure by the fact that Vencel (one of two unimpressive Czech goalkeepers) elected to move the wrong way.

Our last memory of the match was fitting. Trying to reach a centre from the right as it dropped temptingly in front of him, Kvasnak, a survivor from the side that lost honourably in the Final of 1962, fell backwards in an awkward heap. He – and Czechoslovakia – were making an untidy exit from the World Cup. They could still be saved, of course, if England and Rumania failed to win any further points and the Czechs themselves finished with a two-goal winning margin against England, but Guadalajara was not swarming with people willing to bet on such a turn of events. The Czechs looked like a team who had trained for forty-minutes matches. They should have been two goals up on Rumania at half-time but the potency of their strikers steadily diminished after the first flourish. Rumania gradually shed the vagueness that had afflicted their early play and found the authority to penalise the tiredness of the opposition. Satmareanu, Dinu and Neagu had served them splendidly, Nunweiller and Dembrowski had worked the midfield selflessly in a temperature well above 90 degrees and Dumitrache had been exciting in bursts. But in their last Group match Rumania would meet Brazil, an exercise likely to yield lessons rather than points.

Rumania 2   Czechoslovakia 1

BRAZIL *v.* ENGLAND

Guadalajara, June 7

The days leading up to the meeting of England and Brazil had that intensity of nervous excitement that settles on a crowd in the minutes before two heavyweight boxers enter the ring to fight for the championship of the world. It is an almost painful sense of anticipation, as much to do with dread as exhilaration. The time of preparation, filled with comforting repetition and the luxury of analysis and prognostication, is over. Someone's ambitions and dreams, perhaps even someone's dignity, may soon be broken. A man you have talked with and admired and grown to know in the quiet of the training camp may be battered helpless in front of you. Even those who can keep their stomach muscles loose and their throats from drying up, do not feel like talking much. Such moments are not morbid but they have a solemnity that no amount of cynicism can undermine.

Football is very different from boxing. Its beauty is not burdened with the same physical and indivisibly personal penalties. Defeats for the most part bring only psychological suffering (the financial loss is rarely important to the players) and even that can be shared among eleven men. Yet at its highest levels the game can acquire something akin to the concentrated drama of the prize ring. Players go into some matches with the certain knowledge that the result will stay with them, however submerged, for the rest of their lives. Defeat will deposit a small, ineradicable sediment, just as victory will leave a few tiny bubbles of pleasure that can never quite disappear.

Brazil *v.* England was that kind of match. There was never any possibility that it could be mundane. Apart from the status of the two countries as champions and former champions, and their fierce pride in their separate philosophies of the game, there was the realisation that the football world was watching for a sign. This scrutiny imposed the greater strain on England. Four years of Latin American scepticism would spill over into

outright derision if England failed to answer the challenge of
Brazil's rediscovered exuberance. Mathematical interpretations
might appear to diminish the importance of the match (either
side could lose and still qualify for the quarter-finals) but there
was no sense in denying that it had a retrospective as well as a
current relevance. England's validity as world champions had
been persistently and sneeringly questioned since 1966 and
those who argued that the dice had been blatantly loaded at
Wembley would not forget to gloat if they fell. While the battle
was still comparatively remote the hotel lobbies of Guadalajara
were loud with English – and, disconcertingly, Scottish –
voices insisting that this could not happen. Tommy Docherty
and Charlie Cooke wagered on England with an enthusiasm
calculated to cause mass resignations among Scottish Nationalist
election agents. The city buzzed with hyperbole and esoteric
tactical theory, like a saloon bar on a Saturday night. But as
Sunday drew near, banter gave way to tension and in places to
bitterness.

On the Friday and Saturday nights crowds of Brazilian and
Mexican youths congregated outside the Hilton Hotel for a
raucous assault on the peace of the England team. The footballers were kept awake into the early morning and some were
forced to change rooms. When the malicious cacophony was
at its worst on the Friday night the England team bus – whose
importation from Britain had been seen by the Mexicans as
yet another provocation ('Do you think we have not yet
discovered the wheel or the internal combustion engine?')
– was driven off as a decoy, but without much success. The
policemen assigned to protect the England squad stood passively
inside the glass doors of the hotel, apparently satisfied that
they were doing enough if they prevented the mob from barging
their way in. 'If I'd been there I would have directed the bus
to the Brazilian camp and given them a taste of that mob,'
said one British journalist. 'But I suppose the bastards would
have whispered three cheers and gone home.'

As it happened, the Brazilians had a problem sufficiently

serious to keep them off their sleep. The pulled muscle in his right thigh which had caused Gérson to leave the field before the end of the match with Czechoslovakia was still restricting him painfully and he was arguing against pessimistic medical opinion. 'This is the match that stands between us and our third World Cup,' Gérson declared publicly. 'The pulled muscle is not severe at the moment. If I am to damage the leg badly it is better that I should do it against England. There is a chance that I could help to defeat them before I come off.

In his desperation to play Gérson underwent the most intensive treatment he had ever received. He agreed, for the first time, to have cortisone injections and he submitted readily to the constant attentions of Mário Americo, the vast, waddling Negro who has been repairing the violated muscles of Brazil's great footballers since 1950. Americo, whose bulk and hairless head give him the appearance of a darker and more benevolent Odd Job, ministered to Gérson, a tough, independent man, with the gentleness of a mother. Even while Gérson slept Americo slipped into his bedroom, turned him over delicately and applied a short-wave machine to the injured thigh.

It was easy to understand the depth of Brazilian concern over Gérson. Apart from his brilliance as an individual – the alertness with which he read situations, the subtlety of his running, the deadly variety of his left-footed passes and shots – he contributed a sophisticated tactical intelligence and a fierce, infectious will. He, even more than Pelé, was the team's formative thinker on the field, compulsively driving, instructing and cajoling throughout the ninety minutes. Many Brazilians felt that, in the context of a match so tense that even those who would only watch were inclined to catch their breaths at the mention of it, Gérson could be more influential than Pelé.

That tribute was the measure of the disappointment when the doctors made their pronouncement, for they decided that Gérson could not be risked and Paulo Cézar was named in his place. Rather, Paulo Cézar, a gifted player with a refined and powerful right foot, took over from Rivelino as a midfield man with a licence to run free on the left whenever possible. Rivelino inherited for the time being Gérson's more general responsibilities in the middle of the team, leaving Brazil confident in their strength. They were becoming impatient about being told that if Kvasnak had not missed an easy chance for Czechoslovakia shortly before Jairzinho scored an apparently offside goal to give Brazil a 3–1 lead, the previous Wednesday's match would not have turned into a joyful rout. 'We were always going to have too many goals for Czechoslovakia,' Mário Zagalo said tersely. 'Maybe we will have too many for England also.'

The English players did not think so. According to Alan Ball they had been 'frightened to death' of having a bad result against Rumania and their win had rid them of their nerves. 'We got the hardest over and now we think we can beat these,' Ball said. 'I only hope England can go ahead as early as the Czechs did because England would beat Brazil by three or four. I think the Latin Americans have to be a success to play in a game.' Jackie Charlton though the Brazilians did enough ball-watching in defence to give England a good chance of taking a lead, especially if the combination of Hurst and Peters operated at full efficiency. And he was sure Zagalo had been deprived of his best player by the injury to Gérson.

At Suites Caribe, squinting into the sharp sunlight by the swimming pool and moving his head occasionally to prevent a microphone from going down his throat, Gérson acknowledged that England would be more difficult than Czechoslovakia. 'Their defence will not be so naïve. They will not play a straight line across the field like old-fashioned soldiers. But if England gain an advantage by having so many men in front of their goal, such depth in defence, are they not handicapped by having only two men in attack? How long did they take to have a real shot against Rumania – half an hour?' Gérson agreed that it was not too much of an over-simplification to say that when England lined up against Brazil the finest defensive team in the world would be confronting the finest attacking team. He considered that Brazil's infinitely superior ability to make the killing break would settle the match. Even without him there would be Pelé, Tostão, Jairzinho, Rivelino, Paulo Cézar – all regular scorers of goals – and Clodoaldo, Carlos Alberto and even Everaldo capable of coming threateningly from behind. There would, Gérson and many others suspected, be one menace too many for England to watch.

The new menace that had emerged since England lost narrowly to Brazil in Rio a year previously was Rivelino. He had the handsome, moustachioed and sideburned face of a playboy but his body was thickly athletic and the legs bulged with power. On the field his left looked dainty enough to put a match football in an egg cup but the shots when they came were intimidatingly violent.

'Is Rivelino going to be a world star?' Pelé was asked at the Suites Caribe. 'Rivelino *is* a world star,' Pelé said quietly. The greatest star of all had made a late descent from his room into the babel of a Press session. There was first a hush and then an engulfing clamour. He took it all as natural, even when reporters unashamedly asked him to autograph their identification cards. He repeated that he was in the best condition he had known for six or seven years. Yes, it was true that the improvement in Brazilian organisation compared with 1966 had restored his appetite for the World Cup. Yes, he believed Brazil could win it and he could do much to help.

When we recalled seeing him score superbly unexpected goals over the heads of goalkeepers who had drifted off their line, and asked if his unforgettable looped shot from his own half against the Czechs had been an attempt to realise a lifelong ambition, he looked even happier than before. It was an eloquent affirmative, but for those with English sympathies there was something disturbing in that expression. This was a different Pelé from the dejected figure of 1966. The smile was back on the face of the tiger.

That smile could only be widened by the conditions at the Jalisco Stadium on Sunday June 7. Some time before noon the ground was filled with close on 75,000 people and a hard, inescapable heat from the high sun. The Guadalajara climate, like the population, was giving its vote to Brazil. It is a mistake to think that Brazilians, white or Negro, actually enjoy playing football in high temperatures. Most matches in Rio are timed for the cool of the evening and some in the far south of the country can be played on snow. All players prefer the mild, still weather that allows them maximum exertion. But extreme heat is a fact of life for most Brazilians to an extent that it can never be for people from northern Europe. Psychologically as well as physically, they are familiar with it and they do not find it alarming, whether they are walking in the street or playing football. That was Brazil's advantage. Since the sun was an enemy to England, it was an ally for them. The alliance was strengthened as the thermometer climbed to an enervating 98 degrees Fahrenheit.

England had other problems but nothing to produce despondency. Mocanu, the Rumanian left-back who, as Pelé remarked, appeared to confuse tackling with street fighting, had succeeded in making Newton an invalid. But Wright, despite his rather stodgy physique, was seen as a competent deputy, especially against the Brazilians who might have punished the openness of Newton's game.

The hostility of the crowd would have dented the spirit of most teams. Partisan aggression was to be expected of the Brazilians, with their flags and chants and the tireless rhythm of their drums, but through all this there ran the harsher, more gratuitous enmity of the Mexicans. They dearly wanted to see a Latin American side humiliate England, but in the absence of Latin Americans Martians would have done. There were, of course, two or three thousand friendly voices, led by that of Ken Bailey, the quasi-official mascot. Dressed in a tail coat of hunting pink, with a black top hat, and showing an expanse of Union Jack across his chest, Bailey carried a cloth bulldog and flaunted the ensemble as publicly as possible wherever he went. But he and his flag were all too easily submerged in the mass opposition of the locals. At the Jalisco Stadium the cheers of the British sounded small and plaintive as the voice of a genie locked in a bottle.

In this setting the demeanour of the England team, their unforced indifference to the strident resentment evoked by their presence on the field, was an extraordinary achievement. As they kicked around before the start, several of them gave the crowd a slow, appraising look, then turned back to the ball as if they had seen nothing worth their attention. And when the game began they went to work with a relaxed matter-of-factness that controlled and concealed the extreme tensions they must have felt. For ten minutes the ball was rarely out of their possession. Passing it unhurriedly from one to the other, they sought skilfully to eliminate the risk of those early errors that so often settle such a match. They probed cautiously but without nervousness, like a good climber securing holds on a treacherous rock face. Soon they were steady enough for Ball and Bobby Charlton to emphasise the edginess of Félix. Then, in the tenth minute, the mountain almost fell on them. Carlos Alberto gave the ball along the right to Jairzinho and the winger accelerated dramatically beyond Cooper to the byeline. From there his centre was pitched towards the far post, some seven or eight yards out. Pelé, reading the situation flawlessly and moving as perhaps only he could, had come in on the far side of Mullery and now he rose in an elastic leap, arching his back and neck to get behind and above the ball. The header was smashed downward with vicious certainty, aimed just inside the upright Banks had been obliged to neglect as he went to the near post in an effort to cover Jairzinho's cross. Pelé, Mullery reported later, shouted 'Goal' as the ball flew off his head. So did nearly everyone else in the stadium. But Banks, hurling himself back across his goal at a speed that will never cease to awe those who were there or the millions who watched on television, was already twisting into range as the ball met the ground two or three feet from his line. When it rose again venomously he managed to flick his right hand at it

and divert it miraculously over his crossbar. Much later
Banks was to bring an incredulous expression to Cooper's
face by saying the ball had been about shoulder height when
he reached it, then amending his assessment to thigh height.
In fact, the ball had been a foot or at most two feet off the
ground when he saved it. He had reacted so quickly, so
instinctively, that even his own mind did not have time to
record the exact details of what he had done. There was no
confusion, however, about the uniqueness of it. 'That is
without question the greatest save I have ever seen,' said Bobby
Charlton, who has seen a few.

Charlton was one of the players most immediately encouraged by Banks's virtuosity. With the surviving strands of
blond hair glistening behind him, the face strained by effort,
he was to be found wherever there was action. He had made
a vigorous start and now, incredibly, he was stepping up his
pace, running like a man who had recently passed twenty
rather than thirty. It was a sign of his effectiveness when
Rivelino, who was regulating the pulse of the Brazilian midfield
in the manner of Gérson, came so far out of character as to
attempt a foul on Charlton. Even that did not work, for
Rivelino merely succeeded in hurting himself. When his verve
carried him through on goal Charlton forced Félix to save at
his feet, then hurdled two rough tackles before shooting too
high. The Brazilians were at their most dangerous when
Jairzinho and Paulo Cézar were dribbling or sprinting wide of
Cooper and Wright to turn the ball back into the penalty area.
But the covering in England's central defence was quick and
sure. Moore, as always in this World Cup, was magnificent,
interpreting the designs of the opposition with clairvoyant
understanding and subduing their most spirited assaults with
brusque authority. Mullery was marking Pelé with the good
sense and energetic persistence he had shown in Rio a year
before and, though the Brazilian attack was ripplingly alive
with one-twos and sharp progressive triangles, England were
doing more than holding their own.

It was already a marvellous football match, tensely balanced
and overflowing with high skills and intelligence. It was, as
Mário Zagalo would say later, a match for adults. Far from
being negatively defensive, England were retaliating with
swift breaks that promised a goal. When Wright's cross was
edged on by Lee, Peters headed over the bar from a position
he would normally consider a scoring one. After thirty-one
minutes a fine pass along the right wing by Mullery saw Wright
spin on the bye-line to screw back a wonderful centre that left
Félix's goal open to Lee. Unfortunately, the ball came to Lee's
head, which is by no means his most powerful weapon, and
the header was well taken by Félix. Lee, running in, kicked the
goalkeeper and was warned by Abraham Klein, the Israeli
referee. The forward's impetuosity, which had earlier produced an undamaging kick at Everaldo, brought retribution
from Carlos Alberto, who went violently across the ball to
foul him. (Carlos Alberto apologised at the interval and the
match was never again to fall below its impressive level of
integrity.)

Ball, who was pumping ceaselessly alongside Charlton in the
middle, exposed a great gap in the left side of Brazil's defence
with a superb pass forward to Hurst and we waited for the
famous athletic rush on goal. But the big man loitered almost
diffidently before pushing the ball on to Lee and a definite
chance was lost. There were Brazilian demands for a penalty
when Mullery, finding his job more taxing by the minute,
crashed into Pelé and both sprawled face down in the box. The
referee might have been more sympathetic if Pelé's fall had
looked less like a crude impersonation of the cliff divers of
Acapulco. No one, however, could question the award of a
free kick when Cooper fouled Jairzinho just outside the area.
Employing the ruse that had been so successful against
Czechoslovakia, the Brazilians put Jairzinho in the English
wall but Moore, who could play tag with a fox and never
get caught, simply stood behind him. As Rivelino's shot raged
through, Moore killed it as coolly as he would have taken a

lobbed tennis ball and strode upfield. The word 'majestic' might have been invented for him.

At the interval the ferocity of the conditions was graphically indicated when the shadow of the public address loudspeakers, which were suspended on wires high above the middle of the pitch, was seen to be resting dead in the centre circle. Brazil delayed their appearance for the second half, leaving England to swelter in the vertical glare but Ramsey's players sat around in unconcerned groups, casual as sunbathers. They are too mature in the ways of international football to be affected by a little gamesmanship.

There was nothing gradual, however, about the entry into the second half. Almost at once Hurst went close to making decisive contact with a Peters cross and then Paulo Cézar struck a long right-footed shot that dipped and swerved before Banks lunged to push it round the post. A through pass by Pelé, quick as a mongoose to punish any hint of vulnerability, sent Jairzinho raking through to the edge of the penalty area but Banks careered out to kick the ball away. Soon Pelé, jinking and jostling through a pack of white shirts, was only stopped by Mullery's final tackle. Then Banks had to punch out a worrying shot from Rivelino.

Yet, for all this momentum, Brazil's goal when it came after an hour had a quality of surprise. Its immediate origins were deceptively innocent. In fact, it began with a lucky break of the ball. Tostão, spurting at Moore out on the Brazilian left, played the ball through the English captain's legs and had the satisfaction of seeing it ricochet between them and bounce out conveniently on the other side. Even then, Tostão seemed to have nowhere to go but, twisting and pivoting away from the closing defenders, he turned back brilliantly on his right foot and centred. He admitted later that he had aimed the ball for the danger area rather than for any specific player. Disastrously for England, it went straight to Pelé. With Labone looming in front of him and Cooper straining to come across from his right, Pelé decided against a shot. Instead, letting

himself fall away to the left, he stroked the ball delicately at a
slight angle in front of Jairzinho on his outside. Cooper's last
hope of an interception went when he lost his footing and
Jairzinho was clear for a shot. As Banks came plunging off his
line and Peters struggled vainly to reach the ball Jairzinho
hammered his cross shot in high with the right foot.

Sir Alf Ramsey had detected signs of tiredness in his team
as the pressure on the defence mounted and he had one
substitute warming up on the touchline before the goal was
scored. Now, with twenty minutes left (and soon after Jairzinho
had brought further alarm by shooting over, following passes
by Paulo Cézar and Pelé) he put Astle on for Lee and Bell for
the overworked Charlton. Astle's principal virtue (some would
say his only virtue) as an international forward, is his ability
in the air. Hoisting himself above defences as smoothly as a
performing seal rises from the water, he heads the ball with
tremendous power and flexibility. That skill showed with
heartening promptness for England when he knocked the ball
back towards Ball. Unluckily, it was on Ball's left foot and the
attempt at a volley was abortive. The other side of Astle was
then sadly revealed. Everaldo, in a moment of terrible aberration, rolled the ball to the Englishman near the penalty spot,
leaving him with generous time and an unobscured target.
An equaliser seemed assured but Astle hit the ball slackly with
his left foot and it slid past Félix's left-hand post. That, for
England, was the most disappointing miss of the World Cup.

But they were not beaten yet. With twelve minutes left and
Roberto on the field in place of Tostão, Moore went driving
down the left, steadied and crossed for Astle to head on to Ball.
A little way inside the eighteen-yard line and at an angle on the
left, Ball made a calculating pause and carefully passed rather
than shot the ball high beyond Félix's left shoulder. It was a
beautifully deliberate effort and Ball was entitled to his
agonised gesture of frustration when the ball, having beaten
Félix completely, bounced on the top of the bar. Soon afterwards, as the goalkeeper punched the ball away, the small

red-haired forward volleyed it back but again it did not stay low enough. He was playing splendidly, demonstrating every asset a great, foraging player needs, except luck.

To help wash the taste of injustice out of English mouths, Brazil finished with a flourish. Roberto, fed by Clodoaldo, made Banks dive to save at a post, then Pelé sent one of those sinister chips close to Banks's crossbar. But it would have been blatantly wrong if Brazil had taken a two-goal victory from a match which, ideally, should have ended in a draw. England, who lost because they did not take the chances they made, had the substantial consolation of knowing they had conducted themselves like world champions, sharing equally in the honour of a genuinely great match. After watching the film of it, Bobby Charlton said: 'Even *we* were impressed. You could take that film and use it for coaching. That is what the game at the top is all about. There was everything in that, all the skills and techniques, all the tactical control, the lot. There was some special stuff played out there.'

There was indeed, and despite this setback England were still very much alive and ready to provide more special stuff.

Brazil 1   England 0

BRAZIL *v.* RUMANIA

Guadalajara, June 10

A grasp of advanced mathematics was as relevant as a knowledge of football in any discussion of what was likely to happen when Brazil completed their Group programme against Rumania. In the English camp particularly, the hours before the match were filled with convoluted speculation on how the Brazilians might manipulate the points advantage they had established by beating Czechoslovakia and England. Their maximum points total was reinforced by robust statistics in the goals column. They had scored five and lost one while England and Rumania had each lost precisely the same number as they had

K

scored. If the Brazilians chose to be devious, it was argued, they were in a position to put great pressure on Sir Alf Ramsey's team. For instance, if Brazil could contrive to lose by one goal to Rumania, then England would be obliged to defeat the Czechs by at least two goals next day to be sure of qualifying for the quarter-finals. The fate of countries tying on points was to be settled by goal difference: the figure produced by subtracting the number conceded from the number scored. Even if the Rumanians took a draw, nothing short of a victory in the last group game would see England through without the necessity of drawing lots. Every bar in Guadalajara was an arena for the conflicting theories about Zagalo's intentions. Some of the attempts to relate psychology to figures, pride to practical calculations, were enough to tax the combined understanding of Freud and Einstein.

Perhaps the only people who did not bother to consider the highly imaginative range of possibilites were the Brazilians themselves. As many of us had suspected, their one concern was to put their own name among the list of quarter-finalists as outright winners of the group and let the others squabble for what was left. Any nonsense about allowing Rumania a victory would have jeopardised their own life in the competition. In any case, if they won their last match and so earned the right to play their quarter-final in Guadalajara they would know that England, at best, faced a hazardous journey to León to meet Peru or West Germany. Brazil needed no more complicated incentive. There were many remarkable ambiguities about the afternoon's electrifying events in the Jalisco Stadium but none of them involved Zagalo's motives. He sent his men out to go for the throat of the Rumanian side and for nearly half an hour they did so with a zest that was to provide some of the most brilliant (several good judges would say *the* most brilliant) football they played in the World Cup. That early surge exhausted itself with dramatic suddenness, opening the match to fierce tensions, but while it lasted it had the thunderous excitement of a tropical storm. The essence of the coruscating attacks that all but overwhelmed Rumania within twenty-two minutes was the comparatively new Brazilian emphasis on one-touch plays, an emphasis that the shiningly intelligent Tostão had done much to foster. The ball would be moved effortlessly all over the field, from one Brazilian to another, in short or long passes of casually achieved accuracy, from Carlos Alberto at right-back to Paulo Cézar at outside-left, and all the way back, with the Rumanians incapable of offering more than token interference. When they did make a more forceful retort by conceding a free kick two or three yards outside their penalty area, and almost in a line with Adamache's left-hand post, they were summarily punished. Such kicks were always liable to be deadly weapons for the Brazilians. This time, with Rivelino unfit and on the sidelines, it was Pelé who struck, smashing the ball brutally with his right foot to send it high and wide of Adamache's right shoulder. Three minutes later Paulo Cézar, whose right-footed bias frequently tempts opponents to misread his manoeuvres on the left wing, left Satmareanu looking ponderous as a stage policeman as he swept past on the full-back's outside. Pursuit was no more than a gesture. Paulo Cézar too kthe ball briskly to the bye-line and turned it in low and hard for Jairzinho to run it into the net at the near post. The reaction to this goal was significant. Jairzinho was smothered in congratulations while Paulo Cézar, who had loaded the gun and placed it against the victim's head, was ignored as he ran back for the kick-off. Then Pelé realised what was happening and raced to give Paulo Cézar his due. Inevitably, all the others followed. Once again Pelé, the omniscient, omnipresent father-figure of the team, had identified the priorities of the moment. Paulo Cézar, a highly gifted player who required an injury to the great Gérson to put him in the side, was in far more need of public gratitude than Jairzinho.

Having made such a beginning, Brazil appeared poised for one of those sustained exhibitions in which the subtle, mounting rhythm and bright crescendoes of their game are made doubly intoxicating by their own almost trancelike pleasure in the performance. In fact, what they exhibited was the seed of self-destruction that was always present in the eccentricities of their defence. It is an acceptable oversimplification to say that the problem with the Brazilian defence in this World Cup was that the backs did not trust the goalkeeper and the goalkeeper did not trust the backs. Each side had a case but most of us had to agree that the greater weakness was with Félix. In younger days he was a goalkeeper of fierce alertness, quick enough to catch swallows, but now at thirty-two his reflexes were so ragged that at times he behaved like someone under heavy sedation. Admittedly, the behaviour of the men assigned to protect him was occasionally sufficiently weird to send the strongest man to tranquillisers. The strangest lapses tended to occur in the left centre-back position and these were never stranger than against Rumania. Piazza, a midfield player with experience as a troubleshooter in front of the back line, was asked to be the regular in this deeper position after Zagalo rejected both Fontana and Joel, a large truculent Negro who does not believe in living a monkish life. Zagalo's difficulties were compounded when Gérson and Rivelino were declared unfit to face the Rumanians; Piazza had to join Clodoaldo in midfield and Fontana had to be brought in at the rear. According to a slightly bitter joke circulating in Brazil at the time, Fontana, tall, blue-eyed and handsome, had been picked in the hope that he would be able to pose with the Jules Rimet Trophy after it was won, in the line of those other unmistakably white heroes, Bellini in 1958 and Mauro in 1962. That Fontana is a finer model than he is a footballer was adequately demonstrated against Rumania. He is known as 'the sheriff' in his own country. 'We call him that,' explained a Brazilian journalist, 'because he plays very little but behaves as a tamer of cities. He tries to impress as a good commander, shouting and gesticulating all the time at his own team-mates while kicking the opponents' legs – hardly ever the ball.'

His introduction to an already dubious defence was the equivalent of stitching a wound with rusty wire, and in the decline that began soon after Jairzinho's goal the patient was in real danger of dying. The fringes of Brazil's penalty box became an area of confusion and the uneasiness spread to the middle of the team. Pelé and Tostão, sensing the shakiness at the base of the side, must have felt like men trying to launch rockets from a plywood platform. They had already persuaded the Rumanians to withdraw Adamache after the second goal and send on the huge Raducanu as substitute goalkeeper, but they were having little opportunity to worry him and soon had to fall back and assist the panicking garrison behind them. The change that had come over the match was stunning. In that opening passage the ball had moved among the Brazilians as delicately as a point of light. Now it was as cumbersome as a cannonball at their feet and the strenuous, rather military football of the Rumanians was in control, looping countless orthodox centres into Félix's area. One such predictable assault gave Rumania a goal eleven minutes from the interval. A high cross from the right dropped short of Carlos Alberto and seemed to be at his mercy but he delayed complacently. Dumitrache did not, dashing in front of the defender to meet the ball with a first-time shot that drove it past Félix's right thigh from a dozen yards. There were few other occasions in the World Cup when Dumitrache lived up quite so vividly to his reputation.

Brazil should have been thoroughly steadied after sixty-five minutes when Pelé recovered their two-goal lead by taking Tostão's curved pass to volley powerfully beyond Raducanu's bulk from about fifteen yards. Instead, they degenerated again into helpless turmoil. Seven minutes from the end they lost a goal as conspicuously avoidable as Rumania's first. Satmareanu spurted along the right into a vast space created by the inexplicable absence of Marco Antonio. The full-back's centre was again humbly orthodox, soaring towards the six-yard area where Fontana and Brito were apparently waiting to intercept. But Fontana remained mysteriously immobile and Brito's vertical jump was made pointless by the abrupt intervention of Dembrowski. Coming between the two startled defenders, Dembrowski connected with a header that was merely respectable. Félix, however, had completed the muddle in the Brazilian defence by mistiming his advance off his goal-line and he and the ball passed each other as cleanly as trains on separate tracks. We were to find that, without exception, the goals scored against Brazil in the World Cup were the direct product of foolish mistakes by their defenders. Only England failed to take advantage of their reluctant philanthropy. A more imaginative and fluid team than Rumania would have taken further profit from the feverish uncertainties of those last minutes but they adhered rigidly to a pattern of play that was mainly dull, though sporadically violent. The least skilled of the countries in Group Three (their defeat of Czechoslovakia was a matter of condition rather than talent), they were certainly the roughest. Brazil were there on that day to be played into trouble, not kicked into it, and they suffered the physical excesses of such as Mocanu and Dinu more happily than they would have received subtlety and sharpness in front of their goal. As it was, they were able to survive the depredations of their own defence and finish their Group programme with a perfect record. The result had the effect of easing the burden on England the following day. Now a draw would be sufficient to take Ramsey's team through. But a draw, as it happened, was to be no easy target.

Brazil 3   Rumania 2

ENGLAND *v.* CZECHOSLOVAKIA

Guadalajara, June 11

In the concluding match of Group Three Czechoslovakia were in the position of a dying man who is still capable of firing one last killing shot. Their own goal figures were so miserable that they had to beat England by four to qualify outright for the quarter-finals, three to enter a lottery with Rumania for the remaining place behind Brazil. Such overwhelming wins could not be considered serious possibilities on the basis of their previous form, especially as that form was inseparable from a blatant lack of physical condition. There was, however, a danger that a late upsurge of pride among the Czechs and a reaction among the England players to their memorable but unrewarded struggle with Brazil would combine to bring a narrow defeat for Ramsey's team – and any defeat might be fatal. If England lost by one goal, their goal difference (the discrepancy between the number of goals scored and the number lost) would equal Rumania's and lots would have to be drawn to decide who qualified. If Czechoslovakia beat England by two goals, then Rumania – on the strength of a four for, five against scoring record – would go through with Brazil. In short, Ramsey's vital concern was to avoid losing, a situation in which his teams have rarely set spectators' hearts jumping in their rib cages. As the sun burned into the Jalisco Stadium with the crowding heat of a blow-lamp, the British in the stands voiced expectations of unspectacular effectiveness from England while the Brazilians relaxed and in a gossiping mood, contributed tales of Czech revelry that had lasted into the early hours of that morning. Neither the forecast nor the gossip remained convincing once the match was under way.

Ramsey, apparently balancing the wish to blood recruits and rest regulars with the practical demands of the moment, made five changes in the side that had gone down honourably to Brazil. Recovery from injury restored Newton automatically, and Jack Charlton came in for Labone, Bell for Ball, and Clarke and Astle for Lee and Hurst. Surprisingly, Peters, who had yet to show a glimpse of his best form, was retained, presumably in the belief that more, not less, action was his need. The Czechs reshaped their team even more drastically. Only four of the players who lost to Rumania took the field against England and three of the other seven were making

their first appearance in the World Cup. Hrivnak emerged
from the reserves to take Horvath's place in the middle of the
back line and concentrate on marking Astle. Capkovic was
given his first chance to apply his swift directness on the left
wing. But it was the third newcomer, Pollak, who had an
immediate and lasting impact. It was not merely the slim,
deceptive frailty of his build or the fact that he was down to
the last remnants of his fair hair that suggested comparisons
with Bobby Charlton. Pollak brought much of the same fluid
control, graceful running and untiring eagerness to the Czech
midfield as England's usually gained from the Manchester
United man.

Almost from the start of the match admiration for Pollak
was increased by the dismal evidence that on this afternoon
not even Bobby Charlton could impose constructive order in
the middle of the English team. Sadly, it was equally obvious
that the second Charlton, that attenuated pillar of the 1966
team, had lost some of his certainty and was liable to bring
perilous disorder to the defence. Jack began by whacking
Petras hard on the left leg but his aim was less assured when he
went for a tackle shortly afterwards. When he missed it,
Adamec picked up a rebound and nearly broke through.
Moore, intervening, reduced the cost to a corner. England
retaliated with Mullery's pass to Bell at inside-right and a
quick shot that Viktor pushed over his crossbar, then with a
Cooper centre and a header by Bell that lifted too much. But
the Czechs were carefully steadying the game to their own
rhythm. Hagara, reproducing the excellence he had displayed
against Brazil before being strangely omitted for the match
with Rumania, was giving intelligent support to the speed of
Capkovic down the left. When the winger met one low centre
from the full-back at the near post Banks had as much cause
for anxiety as when Pollak's cross let Petras in for a volley.
Each time the ball flew over.

England had little but copious sweat to offer in answer to
Czechoslovakia's composed possession game. Already it was a

matter of wonder that a footballer of Pollak's quality had been left unused so long, saved to provide one last meaningless flourish, like a bright flag in the hand of someone about to drown. Petras, too, one of the major unrealised talents of the World Cup, was free with the farewell gestures. Whenever he went near the ball he put Jack Charlton in difficulties, once spinning smoothly round the centre-half only to be pressured into pushing the ball too far ahead. England's discomfort might have been reflected on the scoreboard if Adamec had matched the enthusiasm of those alongside him. But the petulance that had afflicted him since the beginning of the competition was rampant now, and more than ever its source seemed related to a profound uneasiness when faced with physical contact. When urgent voices from the bench called him on to one quite reachable ball, Adamec stopped to engage in a shouting argument. Moore, the insatiable retriever of the English defence, must have been glad of such helpful lapses. His shirt, originally coloured pale blue in the hope that he and his men would absorb as little as possible of the sapping heat, was blackened with sweat. His work load was being multiplied by the unwonted inaccuracy of the passing in front of him. Later we would be told that the vast shadow which virtually bisected the pitch longitudinally had produced a kind of sun-blindness in the players, who found it hard to identify figures flitting between the fierce glare and the twilight beyond. At the time, however, many of the misdirected passes indicated errors of touch more than vision.

Adamec did succeed in rousing himself sufficiently to steer the ball skilfully to Frantisek Vesely, who had still to reveal in Mexico the destructive aggression that had shattered Hungary and taken Czechoslovakia to the Finals. Now Vesely cleverly heeled the ball down to Capkovic but the winger did not keep his shot low enough. This recurrent failure and a tendency to shoot from optimistic distances prevented the Czechs from alarming Banks deeply but they did occasion him more disquiet than Viktor was likely to experience when confronted

by an English attack led with ponderous incompetence by
Astle. Ostensibly Astle had been drafted in to supply the vigour
and particularly the heading power that regularly come from
Hurst. Unfortunately, this was one day when Astle's head
found the rest of his body, and especially his feet, an un-
manageable encumbrance. He stumbled from one blunder to
the next and, with the midfield incurably ragged, Peters
inconsequential and Clarke promising rather than punishing,
England's first-half performance was calculated to bring a
hopeful flutter to Rumanian breasts. Yet, just on the interval,
they contrived the most satisfying concerted attack of the
forty-five minutes. Taking the ball out of defence with his
habitual coolness, Moore sent a fine diagonal pass to Bell,
who responded with a reverse diagonal into the path of Clarke's
thrillingly intelligent run. The shot, efficiently struck, was
beaten down. Predictably, there was minimal reaction from
the Mexican majority in the crowd. Their one explosive roar
had celebrated the announcement on the scoreboard of a goal
for Mexico against Belgium.

When they came noisily alive again at the start of the
second half it was to communicate one of their favourite
emotions: contemptuous anger towards England. The flood
of derision from the steep terraces of seats was released by a
goal that would have caused controversy anywhere. It came
after forty-eight minutes from a penalty awarded when Kuna,
having attempted a rough tackle on Bell as the forward moved
inside the area on England's right wing, slipped and put his
left hand on the ball as he fell. To many it seemed that the
initial handling was unintentional and even the subsequent
televised evidence, that there had been a dragging movement
of the arm while still in contact with the ball, was not conclusive. Confused by an awkward fall and unnerved to find
his hand landing accidentally on the ball, a man could easily
fail to withdraw it cleanly, trailing it off as someone might
unwittingly drag a finger along a surface that was burning
it. The laws of the game decree that handling must be deliberate

before it is an offence. Only a bold man would argue dogmatically that Kuna's action was a thoroughly conscious one. Watching Roger Machin, the French referee, point to the penalty spot, we assumed that he was such a man. But French journalists reported Machin as saying afterwards that he had penalised a foul by Kuna on Bell. There had been more than a hint of the illegal in the way Kuna went for Bell but hardly enough to justify a penalty. One had the feeling that M. Machin was betting each way.

At least there was no trace of compromise in Clarke's execution of the kick. Before the match he had volunteered confidently to accept the responsibility if it arose, speaking out above the reluctance of more experienced players. It was characteristic of Clarke, whose belief in himself as a scorer of goals is unshakable, that he should step brashly towards a severe challenge in his first international, then make good the implied boast by smashing a faultless, rising shot to Viktor's left.

With fifty-nine minutes played, Astle was mercifully pulled off and replaced by Osgood. Five minutes later Bobby Charlton, having laboured through a thankless hour to earn the one hundred and fifth cap that equalled Billy Wright's record number of appearances for England, made way for Ball. Between these changes Banks went behind his goal in an effort to reason with the crowd, who were throwing fruit and coins in his direction. Moore, his sweat-soaked shorts clinging to his thighs like swimming trunks, brusquely informed the goalkeeper that he was wasting his time. Banks rebuked his abusers more eloquently by turning a free kick from Petras over his crossbar but he had to be grateful for rescue when Petras once again beat Charlton with disturbing ease and passed square to Adamec. Cooper came racing across to take the ball off Adamec's toes. A more determined forward would have made the job more difficult.

Czechoslovakia had a right to be satisfied with the amount of trouble they were giving England and it took an injury to

bring about their first substitution. Capkovic was carried off
bleeding from the mouth after a collision with Mullery twenty
minutes before the end and as the left-winger lay back on the
trainer's bench to have treatment Jokl was sent on in his
place. Jokl asserted himself quickly, moving on to a pass from
Petras for a shot that Banks dived to save. There was much
greater concern at Viktor's end, however, when Hagara,
inexplicably losing concentration, swept the ball across the
field to Clarke. From Clarke it went briskly to Ball and he ran
on to shoot powerfully with his right foot. Viktor knew little
of the shot until the ball had bounced out off the bar above
his head.

Dobias, who had been an impressive right-back in all three
of Czechoslovakia's matches, now achieved two contrasting
distinctions within a few minutes. First he was cautioned for a
foul on Bell and risked giving the referee ironical applause.
Then he did something infinitely more remarkable: he made
Banks look slightly foolish. As Banks reached above his head
to take the full-back's sudden twenty-five yard shot the ball
ricocheted out of his hands and thudded back off the underside
of the bar. The goalkeeper said later that the ball had gone
'all over the place' as it came towards him. There had to be a
touch of the extraordinary about a shot that produced his one
notable mistake of the World Cup.

The crowd, seeking new ways of expressing the resentment
that had simmered since England's goal, had taken to keeping
the ball when it went behind at either end. Twice they simply
refused to give it up. In the midst of this hostility, like a man
intent on arranging his own lynching, Ken Bailey, the self-
appointed leader of the English supporters, was waving a small
Union Jack. While the ball was on the field the Czechs continued
to make more able use of it. A good long shot by Clarke was
less dangerous than Jokl's free kick from the right to the far
post or Kuna's complementary header that went narrowly
wide. Nearer the finish there was another threatening free
kick, this by Adamec, but it carried into the side-netting

The last blow of the ninety minutes came, predictably, from the Czechs. It did them no credit, for Jokl's boot was aimed unmistakably at Osgood's leg.

Such a late misdemeanour was unlikely to stifle praise of a performance that deserved better than defeat. Josef Marko, the Czech coach, was at last entitled to be light-hearted at his Press conference. Capkovic, he said, had been hurt under his teeth but was not worried. 'He is already married,' said the Americanised translator. 'He has no broad in town.' There was only a tinge of bitterness in Marko's joke about the referee. 'He was fair about everything – except the penalty.'

England were not in a mood for jokes. With a handful of exceptions (Banks, Moore, Newton, Cooper, Mullery) they had, in the words of one of them, 'played rubbish'. And within three days they would have to cope with the greater height and heat of León, not to mention a West German team who had scored ten goals while England were struggling for two. Of course, there were strong men waiting on the sidelines. They would be needed. One hundred and fifty miles of dusty mountain road lay between Guadalajara and León, and at the end of it there was sure to be another rough ride.

England 1   Czechoslovakia 0

GROUP THREE

	P	W	D	L	F	A	Pts
Brazil	3	3	0	0	8	3	6
England	3	2	0	1	2	1	4
Rumania	3	1	0	2	4	5	2
Czechoslovakia	3	0	0	3	2	7	0

5 Group Four

Bulgaria, Morocco, Peru, West Germany

The sun set over León. The young people came out to parade round the square in the *paseo*, the dating hour; the Mariachis added their strolling music and there was such peace that one wondered how this little town had become caught up in the World Cup. In fact it never really did so. It still retained its air of old Mexico and with it mellowed the visiting supporters. There was never such wild enthusiasm in León as there was in other centres.

The supporters of Peru might have stirred it up but a heavy depression set in when the news came of the disastrous earthquake in their country. The day after Peru met Bulgaria forty-five Peruvian supporters were called home to members of their families who had been killed or seriously injured. They were from a party of 150 people from the fishing town of Chimbote where around 1,000 persons had been killed.

León lies, minding its own business, 5,934 feet above sea level and 240 miles north-west of Mexico City. There are 300,000 inhabitants, with shoe-making the chief occupation. It was the hottest of the World Cup sites, and the temperatures were a much greater inconvenience than the altitude. The town is proud of its modern stadium. It holds only 25,303 seated spectators but this was enough for the town and more than enough for the needs of Group Four. It was never filled for a Group game.

Helmut Schoen, the West German manager, went to look at León before he brought his squad to Mexico and decided it was a nice town to stay out of. He heard of a hotel at Comanjilla sixteen miles away across sandy scrub land which had a pool

159

heated by a thermal spring. He booked the whole hotel for the duration of the Group Four matches. It was a fine training situation, fresh and exciting, and with ample facilities to combat boredom.

There was one little inconvenience. The place was under constant armed guard during the Germans' stay. There had been a threat by extremists to kidnap some of the players and the ultra-cautious Mexicans left nothing to chance. They had nine armed policemen on guard twenty-four hours a day. They patrolled the grounds, hid among the trees and overlooked the frolics in the pool. Visitors were carefully vetted before they were allowed to pass the guard at the entrance.

There was an intensification of the guard when the West German ambassador was kidnapped in Rio de Janeiro, and the Bonn Federal Interior Ministry sent out two men to live with the players. Everybody seemed impressed by the threats except the players themselves. They were carefree but dedicated in their preparation and the harmony was remarkable as old alleged enmities were dissolved.

Seeler and Muller, who had been built up by the Press as incompatibles, shared a room. Beckenbauer and Schulz, who in the past had each wanted to play in the same position in the middle of the defence, worked out a compromise for the good of the team. The cooking was to their liking for the party had brought their own chef with them, the same one who came to London in 1966.

Helmut Schoen was satisfied with the hotel and with the spirit of his men. He had reservations about the condition of the players. They had come jaded to Comanjilla after crushing many postponed matches into the last month of the season. West Germany had had the worst winter in memory and football was badly hit. He hoped that the players would play themselves in during the tournament.

Peru during their stay were heartened by promises of healthy bonuses. Before they arrived in León they were promised 200 dollars for each player for each victory. For their match with

19 Allal Kassou punches a dangerous ball clear from the head of Bulgarian forward Mitkov

20 Cubillas of Peru is tackled by Beckenbauer of West Germany

21 Gerhard Muller lies on the pitch as his header curves into the top corner of the net to register his hat-trick against Peru in the Group Four match. In the centre is Peruvian back Orlando de la Torre, and falling behind the post is goalkeeper Luis Rubiños

22   Mexicans, here thronging Mexico City's 'Reforma' boulevard, celebrated throughout the night of June 11 following their country's 1–0 victory
over Belgium which put them into the quarter-finals

Bulgaria that was raised to 300 dollars and against Morocco a rash burst of national pride sent the figure to 400 dollars. The reward for reaching the quarter-finals was to be 1,250 dollars for each player.

The officials had originally booked Peru into a hotel in the town of León but quickly they discovered that the atmosphere there was more conducive to socialising than to strenuous training. The girls were particularly lovely and friendly – there were rumours of involvements but these were terminated when the squad was taken thirty miles out of town.

There was a strange incident later when Señor Roberto Ramirez Otorolo, the president of the Peru delegation, stormed into León to squash stories of disharmony in the Peru team. He denied that two Peru players had fought over a girl, but many were unconvinced. Nor were many inclined to believe that Didi, the coach, had not suggested that he would manoeuvre to play England in the quarter-finals rather than Brazil, with whom he had won two World Cup medals as a player. There was never a dull moment around the Peruvians, but there was a regrettable one when some of the players were robbed in their hotel.

There was also a lighter moment when a Mexican star-gazer predicted that, as Peru's stars corresponded to Gemini, there was an indication they would reach the semi-finals. He added a much more relevant point. He had watched them practise for fourteen days and they looked good.

Bulgaria came to León after a most thorough and expensive preparation for the competition. There had been altitude training and a South American tournament but then they learned that heat in León was the major problem and they were not prepared for that. Maybe that accounted for the surly mood throughout of the manager, Dr Stefan Bozkhov, a physician. He refused to meet the Press after matches, while Helmut Schoen took advantage of the reaction with splendid co-operation with the Press. He also became a near-national hero when he was tossed into the hotel pool fully clothed by his

L

players. This human touch was highly publicised and endeared him to the Mexicans who were always wanting someone to like.

Morocco, on the other hand, very much the country cousins, were starry-eyed in their hotel, which was a busy one overlooking the main square. Blagoviev Vidinic, the former Yugoslav international goalkeeper who was their manager, tried to raise them in mind above their amateur status but he never really succeeded in making them believe that they had a right to be in the World Cup, even in such a humble little town as León.

BULGARIA v. PERU

León, June 2

Apprehension hung heavy over the Guanajuato Stadium when Peru played Bulgaria in the first match of Group Four. Reports had come back from Mexico City branding the goalless opening match as dull. There were fears that over-strict refereeing would destroy the action. Many wondered if this would be a tame, inhibited World Cup. Bulgaria set minds at ease.

Before that sunny Tuesday Bulgaria had not been noted for stimulating excitement but within twelve minutes they had scored the first goal of the tournament, and when the news was flashed on the scoreboards of the other three venues that the well-fancied Peru were a goal down the beat of the competition was raised and it was never to subside.

The game had been tense and untidy until that twelfth minute. The reports beforehand suggested that the Peru defence did not match the dashing forwards in competence and so it seemed as Yakimov dragged the ball around and defenders with it. Peru struggled to find a rhythm.

They conceded a free kick. Dermendjiev was on to the ball quickly as it was flighted into the penalty area and he scored coolly. Peru did not react in like manner. They went furiously for the equaliser, scorning heat and altitude as they tried to shake off that barb that had pierced their pride.

Mifflin tried to bring sense to the activity and Challe moved strongly to back the strikers. Bulgaria were forced into defence. León and Cubillas joined with Gallardo in long-striding passing movements that took them to the Bulgarian penalty area. But their over-anxiety was their undoing.

These were stirring forward dashes that the powerful León led but they were frustrating ones, for the raids that did not break down usually finished with the galloping Gallardo. His shooting was powerful but wild. Shots hurtled straight at the competent Simeonov, seasoned in twenty-five internationals. Others finished high in the crowd or wide of the posts. The giant Dimitrov struggled to plug the middle of that Bulgarian defence but the roused Peruvians could not be kept out and only their own shooting failings thwarted them.

Towards half-time the play of the Peru forwards was more settled and they went into the second half with controlled speed. But still the final pass lacked precision and the final shot was wild.

And then, with but five minutes of the half gone, the harassed Bulgarians scored again. It was a flukey goal but one that was to raise cries of wonder in the other grounds, for who had thought that Peru with their method based on that of Brazil could go two down to this poorly rated Bulgaria?

Bonev had struck his free kick with plenty of power and over the wall of players but it seemed no more than a spectacular effort, for Rubiños saw it clearly and had it covered. But the ball was to deceive him as it sped fast through the thin air and it leapt out of his hands and into the goal: better goalkeepers, and few were not, would later be deceived similarly.

Didi, the Peruvian manager, could be seen showing his worry on the track and panic was near, but the cold Mifflin took charge to shoot away long passes and get his wingers running. He worked with no fear of what was happening behind, for the captain Chumpitaz had taken control of the penalty area.

And within a minute the Peru forwards were to get their rhythm right and so brilliant were they in the next fifteen minutes in their speed and articulation and effectiveness that the German manager, Helmut Schoen, said their football was the best he had seen since Brazil charmed everyone in the 1958 World Cup.

Gallardo, who had squandered so many chances in the first half, at last got his shooting on target and a tremendous right-foot shot sped to the roof of the net. Simeonov made no move. Gallardo had had better chances in the first half.

Bulgaria were under heavy pressure then and their tackling became rougher and more desperate, and in the fifty-sixth minute they conceded a free kick which produced much jostling and gamesmanship as the defensive wall was formed.

Two Peru players forced a space and through it Chumpitaz shot with an accuracy unsuspected in such a stout defender. The ball found the net and Peru were level and living again.

And up went the pace. The wingers pulled the Bulgarian defenders around and Cubillas was unstoppable as he took on one, two and three men. Bulgaria hung on dourly, settling for the draw and apparently incapable of regaining their lead against those furies who were punishing them with their speed and dash.

Then Cubillas was away on another weaving run, hitting a low right-foot shot to the left of Simeonov. The goalkeeper could not reach it and Peru at last had come back from the dead and led. It was a great moment for them.

Peru players piled high on the delighted goal-scorer and the Italian referee, Sbardella, pulled at them as he tried to bring order out of hysteria and get the game started again. And all the time Bulgarian players stood despondent that the cup had been dashed from their lips.

There was no holding the ecstatic Peru then. León pranced through the middle, a magnificent athletic figure, Gallardo sprinted powerfully and Cubillas added his artistry, and with the substitute, Sotil, who came on for Baylon, joining in the cavorting Bulgaria were outclassed. Asparoukhov came on for Bonev and Marachliev for Popov, but to no avail.

Twice more Peru had the ball in the net but offside was given. They finished sound winners of a game they seemed to have lost. It was a fine match to get Group Four going and to rouse the little town to World Cup enthusiasm.

Bulgaria 2   Peru 3

WEST GERMANY *v.* MOROCCO

León, June 3

Morocco, the amateurs who had survived two play-offs and the toss of a coin to reach Mexico, raised wild hopes that they were another giant-killing North Korea when they scored in the twenty-second minute and then had West Germany, the finalists of 1966, wallowing in confusion and indecision.

West Germany's approach to the match had been apprehensive. After their worst winter in memory the players had left for Mexico jaded and short of the international match practice they had had before the 1966 tournament. Schoen explained that he wanted them to find their feet during the Group matches. They would start against Morocco playing simply, then if their game came right they would try for a spectacular score to create a good impression among their opponents.

It seemed a reasonable request but simplicity is not in the make-up of such as Beckenbauer and Haller and others of the team, and, good though their intentions were, they were elaborating before they were settled. The nippy Moroccans scuttled among them to whip the ball away and found this ever easier as German nervousness increased.

Overath and Vogts, cold men and solid men, tried to bring order and sense to the German build-up, but Haller seemed to have lost his nerve, Beckenbauer still sought a rhythm and the strikers Seeler and Muller were locked in a tight hard defence.

Then in the twenty-second minute the 2,000 German supporters in the thin 8,000 crowd were shocked. The German defence fell into confusion and Houmane pounced on a disastrously misguided header by Hottges to turn the ball in. The Moroccans danced wildly, belaboured the scorer, and one collapsed with excitement.

The Moroccans had no time to savour their goal before the Germans were at them. Indignity had settled their nerves. The play was aimed straight at goal but Morocco knew how to face such stern attacking.

A fine midfield player, Bamous, dropped back to organise the defence. Lamrani, Benkhrief, Khanoussi and Slimani dug in behind him and space was hard to find in that Moroccan penalty area.

Overath tried to direct the attacks to the wings and turn the defence, but inaccuracies in the passing destroyed progression. The Moroccan forwards were ever alert to break with neatness and speed and Germany had to be careful in defence. They could not commit themselves completely to attack.

Half-time came and still Morocco led and they had gone into the fifty-sixth minute before that astonishing veteran, Uwe Seeler, came back and eased the tension with a goal that was acrobatic and unexpected. There was a tight bunch of Moroccans covering the ball when he pushed in among them, turned quickly with it and scored as he was falling over backwards.

The unhappy Haller had been left in the pavilion at half time and Grabowski, who came on for him, brought a fresh directness to the German play. He led the fierce assault after Seeler's goal that was to show the quality of the goalkeeper, Kassou Allal. Even the worried German supporters cheered his inspired saving.

And so the siege of the Moroccan goal went on. With fifteen minutes to go Schoen took off the full-back Hottges and put on another forward, Lohr, and three minutes later the goal he craved was scored.

Yet another shot was hurled at the goal which struck the cross-bar, and that master of the half-chance, Muller, sprang to head the rebound to the net. It had taken West Germany until the seventy-eighth minute to lead these speedy African amateurs.

It was West Germany's game then; but not because they were better in method or skill but mainly because they were physically superior to the slim Africans. The Moroccan coach, Vidinic, the former Yugoslav international, later made this concession.

Helmut Schoen admitted his discomfiture and blamed the disorganisation of the team on their trying to make difficult passes. He seemed to be seeking consolation when he said, 'The game wasn't very good but the work of our players was'.

Morocco had shown in a strange match that they were competent in the technical side of the game but in attitude and physique they were indeed amateurs. Yet their technique and speed were to trouble others in León's stadium.

West Germany 2   Morocco 1

PERU *v.* MOROCCO

León, June 6

A humble crowd of 27,000 could pack the pleasant little León Stadium but on a sunny Saturday afternoon less than half as many were there. It was difficult to relate the scene to the World Cup. Those who were there were colourful and gay and they might have been gathering in the town square to sway to the Mariachi band. Morocco had stirred little enthusiasm.

The coach, Vidinic, had made some brave talk to rouse his team and maybe win some support. He explained, 'My players are better than they looked against West Germany. They were overawed then. They know German football and Beckenbauer, Overath and Seeler are gods to them. They did not believe in themselves even when they led.

'Peru is different. They know nothing of Peruvian football and they will not be repressed.' He made it sound good but there was little substance in the pronouncement. Vidinic made his own reckless assessment of Peru. 'Their second-half recovery against Bulgaria did not impress me. I remembered how bad they were in the first half.'

The theorising finished when they kicked off in the heavy heat and if the Moroccans did not show awe at least they showed apprehension in the way they scurried back immediately to crowd their penalty area. Whatever was their formation, at least the striking line was 1.

Peru had the midfield conceded to them, and in a faint imitation of the Brazil football samba they weaved unmolested through it, at first cautiously for it was so easy it smelled of a trap. Then they reached the penalty area and their troubles started. Space was difficult to find. They probed and the sudden change from freeway to jungle entanglement stirred frustration and that brought the slack pass, the recklessly hit shot and, to disturb the mood further, Morocco showed a neat swift flurry of raiding when the attacks broke down.

Crisp speedy passes built up the counter-attack but when it broke there was again the undignified race for the penalty area with one attacker staying behind. A monotonous pattern developed. Peru, like a wave, surged and ebbed and came again, eroding a little in the process but not noticeably until late in the second half.

In such a packed penalty area Peru's attempts at crisp short passing on the run broke down and what they could not do with sophistication they tried to do with power. They brought up the heavy shots. Tremendous drives were hurled at goal, but recklessly, and at extreme range.

Three times the powerfully built León shot wide. Gallardo sent the ball high into the terracing behind goal and it seemed for a second or two that it was going right out of the stadium. That was wild shooting. The shots that were on target were taken in the safe hands of Kassou Allal. A fast, sure-tackling back, Lamrani, was ever ready to turn the flow.

And so, with nothing to trouble them in the midfield, Peru attacked almost incessantly but without inspiration and inventiveness and the shooting of León and the dashes up the right by Gallardo were no more than spectacular. They worked sullenly to half-time with nothing but frustration and sweat to show for their dominance.

The second half started ominously for Peru. Ghazouani rose high at a corner kick and headed wide when it seemed easier to score. There was an uneasy moment when León, in the clear, shot against the goalkeeper's feet as he lay on the ground and Gallardo shot across the exposed goal. The omens were against Peru, and their supporters became impatient and whistled, but whether in derision or anxiety was not clear.

On the field a strange change was taking place. Morocco began to see themselves with a chance and became more adventurous. There were confident thrusts into attack. In the rear, however, Khanoussi and Maaroufi were showing signs of wear in the middle of the defence and they began to wilt. And so when it seemed that Peru were in most danger at last they scored. They had worn the wall thin.

Predictably Peru's goal was untidy and scrambled. In the sixty-fifth minute León's poorly hit shot came back off the goalkeeper's legs to Cubillas, who scored easily. The referee awarded the goal to Sotil, but after film clips had been examined the organising committee named Cubillas as the official scorer. And once they had one Peru soon had another. Challe scored four minutes later with a straightforward run and shot. It was easy when the tension was eased.

Peru had Cruzado on for Mifflin and then in the seventy-fifth minute Ramírez for Gallardo, and in that minute they scored a third goal. Cubillas, ever dangerous on the run, hit a swerving shot that flew off the goalkeeper's hands to the net. Having three, Peru eased off, and Morocco with nothing to lose dropped their inhibitions and made such a show of neat attacking that Peru lived dangerously until the end.

Startling gaps were torn in the Peru defence and one wondered what would have happened had Morocco gone at them
from the start. When considering the future it seemed reasonable to remember the defensive weaknesses exposed in those
closing minutes and the struggles of Peru to open a tight
defence when it was strong.

And so Peru advanced uneasily towards the quarter-finals
and they showed their concern over their form by the excuses
they made. 'Morocco were fast and made us work.' 'Only our
nerves and bad luck kept the score down.' There was no
mention that Morocco were amateurs.

Peru 3   Morocco 0

WEST GERMANY *v.* BULGARIA

León, June 7

The cautious attitude of West Germany before the match was
a hang-over from the disturbing game against Morocco. They
dared not be optimistic, they dared not be associated with any
words of confidence. Helmut Schoen set the mood: 'Bulgaria
will be fighting for survival. They will be difficult but it is in
our favour that we know their style of play and the strengths
and weaknesses of their players. They will be easier to contain
than the unorthodox Moroccans but we have to do more than
that. We want to lead this Group, so we must win.'

Stefan Bozhkov, the coach of Bulgaria, had a more compelling line to his apprehension. Bulgaria had spent much money
on the preparation of the team. There had been high altitude
training and a South American tour. Bulgaria had failed to
survive the Group matches in the previous World Cup tries in
1962 and 1966 and should they fail to do so again then Bozhkov
himself could scarcely hope to survive in his job.

Schoen brought back to the team Reinhard Libuda, the
winger who had scored the goal against Scotland which had
sent West Germany to Mexico. Schulz was out with an injury

which some said was political. He would not want the indignity of being dropped.

On a day when the temperature went over 90 degrees Fahrenheit a sparse crowd of 8,000 was all that mustered to watch the play. It was too hot for spectating, except for the fully committed such as the German supporters, whose well-fed bodies sweated in the fierce heat. It was cruel weather for football.

The Germans had sweated for another reason when their team played Morocco, and again their worries started early. Bulgaria scored in the twelfth minute. A free kick had been conceded just outside the penalty box. Nikodimov took it and his shot swerved into the left-hand corner of the goal with Maier scrambling but beaten. Bulgaria were elated but were given little time to enjoy the sensation before white shirts assailed their goal in what seemed to be hordes.

The Germans had forgotten the heat in the indignity of once again going behind. They stirred up the action. Beckenbauer, the elegant one, and Overath, the fighter, took command of the midfield. Seeler, with the cunning of experience, worked between them and the front striker, Muller. They plugged the ball to Libuda on the right wing, setting him to run his side of the defence to confusion. He did just that and, as he beat the full-back Gaganelov consistently, the Bulgarians began to look uncomfortable. In the twentieth minute he found another chink in the Bulgarian defence.

From Seeler's pass Libuda raced away with the defence scattered and trailing, but his shot was not of such quality as his run. The ball flew straight at the goalkeeper, Simeonov; he seemed to gather it, then let it slip under his body and it rolled slowly over the line. A defender kicked it clear but the Spanish referee, Mendibil, rightly awarded a goal. That was a depressing moment for Simeonov and he was not to recover from it.

Already the players were showing the effects of the heat. They were shorn of adventure and tried to work the ball as slowly as was possible. Only Libuda was prepared to carry it

and chasing him was a task that did not appeal to Bulgaria.
He worried them into conceding the second goal in the twenty-
eighth minute. Again the unfortunate back was beaten and the
ball crossed to the lurking Muller with the defence pulled out of
position. He hit the ball on the volley and it flew to the net.
A run down a wing and a cross into the middle was simple and
old-fashioned but, even in a World Cup, effective if there was
such a winger as Libuda and such a single-minded finisher as
Muller. They were to prove this often.

At half-time Bulgaria, outplayed and fatigued, replaced
Dermendjiev with Mitkov, but they could not get rid of the
torment of Libuda and soon he was at them again worrying
deep into their defence. He outplayed the tiring Gaganelov and
was racing clear on goal when the back tripped him from
behind. It was a penalty kick and Muller scored from it.

In the fifty-ninth minute Grabowski came to the left wing in
place of Lohr and it was no surprise when Bulgaria decided
that Gaganelov had had enough and he was replaced by
Chalamanov. Having done the damage on the wings, West
Germany, when the pace slowed almost to walking midway
through the second half, developed short passing progression in
the midfield and Bulgaria, hot and tired and demoralised, were
at their mercy.

Leisurely interpassing brought the fourth goal in the sixty-
ninth minute. Overath and Beckenbauer developed the movement and Overath's pass into the goalmouth eluded Jetchev
and Seeler glided the ball into the net. It would have been
merciful to have taken the players off then. They wilted in the
heavy heat, had scarcely the energy to push a short pass, and
no inclination to do anything more strenuous. Bulgaria had
trained for altitude, but heat was the enemy.

Beckenbauer had had enough and he went off. He deserved
the relief for, after Libuda, he was the most effective of his
team and he had added to effectiveness the pleasing elegance
of his individualism. He and the hard-working Overath, by
their mastery in the midfield, had made West Germany a more

impressive team than had seemed possible on the day they
played Morocco. Weber was substituted for Beckenbauer.

They played out time in the sultry heat but clearly their
minds were more on the cold shower in the dressing-rooms than
the World Cup, at least all except Muller whose thirst for goals
was greater than the one the others found so compelling. In the
eighty-sixth minute he was eager enough and alert enough to
score his side's fifth goal and his own third. It was the first
hat-trick of the tournament.

Nobody cared much when almost from the kick-off Bulgaria
made ground and Kolev scored. The final whistle released
them at last from their torment and, like legionnaires in a film
coming in from the desert, they waved to one another with
casual, limp gestures and were gone to the cool of the
dressing-rooms.

And so West Germany and Peru had qualified for the
quarter-finals, for their four points were beyond the reach of
the others and the last game would decide who won Group Four
and stayed on to play in León. Schoen, working well on the
public relations side, met the Press afterwards and said that he
thought his team had played better against Bulgaria because
the Eastern Europeans were a stronger side than Morocco. He
added, 'You might think that the sun makes me talk like that
but it is true.' The Press had time to work that one out for the
Bulgarian coach, Bozhkov, refused to be interviewed. He wanted
to suffer alone and contemplate his future.

West Germany 5   Bulgaria 2

BULGARIA *v.* MOROCCO

León, June 11

The teams had different motivations in this match which was to decide the third and fourth places in Group Four. Bulgaria, after their expensive preparation, had to avoid the ignominy of finishing bottom in the section and without a win. Morocco, the amateurs, just wanted to beat someone and anybody would do, even Bulgaria. They kept very quiet about their team selection but it did leak out that the agile Moroccan goalkeeper, Kassou Allal, would not play. Bulgaria could boast of some kind of a record for they were the first squad to book a passage home. They had their return tickets before the match.

Predictably the game was a dull one. Fewer than 4,000 spectators bothered to watch it and they saw Bulgaria dominate the play. They saw them twice hit the goalpost but generally their finishing was so poor that the reserve goalkeeper, Hazzaz, was seldom troubled. The first half was drawing to a frustrating close when Bulgaria received the stimulation of a goal in the fortieth minute. Jetchev was the scorer. It seemed then that Bulgaria must at last win a match.

That view was altered during the second half when Morocco found unexpected reserves of spirit and stamina to take the offensive. Bulgaria's second-half sag, which had shown in all their games, was again apparent. The Moroccans seemed to thrive on attacking and they were delirious when in the sixtieth minute Ghazouani scored a goal to tie the score.

Near the end Morocco had control of the play and were the fitter team and several times they came near scoring the goal that would have given them victory.

It would have been wrong, however, had either team won such a game. The Moroccans considered that they had scored a moral victory. They waved to the crowd and accepted their sympathetic cheers. The Bulgarians trudged dejectedly to their dressing room, as well they might, for one point was a disquietingly small return for such a meticulous preparation.

Their thoughts were obviously of home.

The Bulgarian coach, Bozhkov, was in surly mood when he said that the referee had done a poor job in a poor match. He would not elaborate but the referee was far from being the worst performer. In an epic of understatement Bozhkov said that the team could hardly expect an enthusiastic welcome home. He seemed ultra-confident when he said that he did not think that his job was in danger.

Morocco could expect a happier return for they had performed creditably and King Hassan, an enthusiastic supporter of football in his country, would be pleased that they had not been humiliated. The coach, Vidinic, declared 'A great day for African football' and hinted that professionalism might be introduced.

The disappointed Bozhkov said as a summing-up, 'It seems that some of our players are too old but if you lived in Mexico for twenty years you would not get acclimatised to the altitude and the heat.' Some did, and in much less than twenty years.

Bulgaria 1   Morocco 1

WEST GERMANY *v*. PERU

León, June 10

Some of the people who had gone to León to watch the early performances of West Germany and Peru brought back with them, over the 150 miles of narrow mountain roads to Guadalajara, classic travellers' tales of the wonders they had seen. If they had just come upon the Yeti brewing himself a can of tea in a Himalayan ravine they could not have conveyed a deeper sense of awe than they did when speaking of Peru. These players, the deprived listeners in Guadalajara were told, were clearly on the point of inheriting the leadership of South American football from Brazil. Drawn by accounts of the grace and athletic elasticity, the explosiveness and deadly guile of the Peruvian attack, many of the reporters who had been covering the England Group decided to forgo the Brazil–Rumania match and drive to León for the meeting of West Germany and Peru.

They journeyed hopefully. Had not Walter Winterbottom said the Peruvians on the aggressive were the best team he had seen since the Brazilians of 1958? Had not Eric Batty confessed that he found it difficult to be moved by the heroic dimensions of England versus Brazil because he had been spoiled by experiencing the magic of Peru? Who is Eric Batty? Well, to be fair, it must be said that Mr Batty is an outspoken, not to say pontifical critic who declared in the March 1970 issue of *World Soccer* that Brazil had yet to prove themselves to him. (One could imagine much wringing of hands in Rio de Janeiro.) Unlike 'more gullible' observers, wrote Mr Batty, he had been unimpressed by Brazil's development of their national side since the fiasco of 1966 in England. Having acknowledged that they had 'a more than useful centre-forward in Tostão', he listed as grave weaknesses Carlos Alberto at right-back and 'a grossly overrated midfield pair in Gérson and Rivelino; talented yes, but so eager to show off their ball skill they seldom bothered to look about and play off the first-time ball which has become a cornerstone of the modern game'. In justice, however, Mr Batty had felt at that time, barely three months before the World Cup, that he should mention 'a young and talented right-winger in Natal (from Belo Horizonte), whose intelligent distribution and running off the ball proved conclusively that there is at least one real coach working in Brazil. But strangely enough this young man has been conspicuously absent from Brazil's team since Aimore Moreira lost control.'

Considering what Gérson and Rivelino and that other young and talented right-winger, Jairzinho, had already shown in the opening matches of the competition – and the fact that their thrilling accomplishments merely confirmed what some of us had known about them for years – testimony from Mr Batty was liable to be attended by doubt. However, his enthusiasm for Peru was shared by many witnesses and those on their first visit

23 The Uruguayan goalkeeper Mazurkiewicz just gets his fingertips to this cross and ends a Russian attack during the quarter-final game. The players are (*from left*): Puzach of Russia, Ancheta, Matosas, Mazurkiewicz and Ubiñas of Uruguay, and Bishovets of Russia

24 Mexico's goalkeeper Calderón strains to recover the ball as Italy's Luigi Riva (*left*) shoots his country's fourth and last goal in the quarter-final match at Toluca

25 Martin Peters scores the second goal for England in the quarter-final against West Germany

26 With characteristic economy, Tostão scores Brazil's second goal in the quarter-final against Peru

to the Guanajuato Stadium were ready and willing to be
dazzled. The first minutes of the match (which would settle the
placings at the top of Group Four and so decide whether West
Germany or Peru would travel as runners-up to meet the winners
of the England–Brazil Group) left plenty of room for optimism.
Peru were obviously capable of swift, exciting attack. Cubillas
had the control, the perception and urgency to bring the ball
through tellingly from the midfield and Perico León at centre-
forward and Gallardo at outside-left responded with skilful
vigour. León is built along the lines of a heavyweight boxer
and Gallardo is exceptionally tall for a winger, but they and
Cubillas brought a sureness of touch and subtlety of intent to
the close triangular passing manoeuvres and ferociously quick
one-twos that were their team's favourite and most effective
ploys. Unfortunately, those alongside Cubillas in the middle
three, Challe and the widely praised Mifflin, did not approach
his standards on the day and the predictability of Sotil on the
right wing made the attack noticeably lopsided. This weakness
was emphasised when it became evident that the full-back with
the pace, ball control and ambition to break from behind was
Fuentes on the left.

Initially it seemed that the fluent overlapping of Fuentes
might be a decisive menace in itself. He found and used space
without hindrance twice soon after the kick-off, and first León
and then Gallardo just failed to do West Germany vital harm
as they converged on the centres at the near post. However,
having been so vividly warned without having to pay with the
loss of a goal, the Germans set about coping with these precisely
identifiable threats. And soon they were taking the game away
from the South Americans, refusing to let them kindle the slow
fuse in midfield that would run towards those explosions of
activity on the edge of the penalty area. Overath, so confident
of that great left foot that even on the ball he can carry his
head up, searching for openings like a hunting animal seeking
prey, began to be as prominent as his gifts always entitle him
to be. He did not have to wait long for strong support from

M

Beckenbauer and from Seeler, who was withdrawn behind the
forwards to give Muller more room to exploit the power,
courage, positional awareness and speed of reflex that make him
one of the most prolific scorers in Europe.

Once the Germans were moving forward smoothly their basic
strategy was unmistakable. They meant to use their wingers,
Libuda and Lohr, to stretch the Peruvian defence and then
assault the weakened middle by aiming high crosses at Muller.
These methods were calculated to test the accuracy of the
diagnosis made by a minority of observers who had seen
crippling flaws in Peru. 'Any side that can throw plenty of high
crosses at them will murder them,' one Scottish journalist had
announced baldly. There was no prolonged agony of suspense
about whether he or the eulogists would be vindicated. After
a straightforward chip over an unresponsive wall of defenders
had seen Muller run in on a good chance, only to find Rubiños
saving at his feet, West Germany went one better by scoring a
goal of embarrassing simplicity in the twentieth minute. Libuda
– now breaking freely on the right with a low, sweeping action
that stirred memories of that much greater winger, Finney –
swung in a high centre that left the Peruvian defenders craning
pointlessly, like tourists in New York, as it sailed over the
penalty spot. When the ball had cleared De La Torre, Muller
had adequate time to chest it down and slide it beyond Rubiños,
who was already giving weight to the widely held belief that
he was the worst goalkeeper in the World Cup. Six minutes
later Muller was turning the ball in for an equally easy goal
after Lohr out on the left touchline had come away from
González as if the full-back had run the previous leg in a
relay race. The same winger made another opening for
Overath, who shot excitingly but wide, and Libuda passed for
Seeler to execute a bicycle kick that sent the ball close to
Rubiños's crossbar. With so much danger coming from the
flanks, Peru's central defenders were stumbling around like
men waiting to take delivery of guide dogs. Even Chumpitaz,
a stocky, spirited player capable of thrusts into the midfield

and beyond, was frequently at a loss. The aerial attack could hardly have been more damaging if mounted by the Luftwaffe.

Chumpitaz did bring respite by forcing the ball through to Gallardo in a promising position but Gallardo, under heavy pressure, put it past. Then, with seven minutes of the first half remaining, West Germany scored a third goal and again the Peruvian defence showed themselves lamentably vulnerable to a spurt on the wing and well-directed centre. There seemed little to worry about when a throw-in on the right reached Seeler. But, as he hesitated to consider alternatives, he saw a gap and darted through cunningly at inside-right. The cross was cut back in a high, measured loop and Muller had an air of irresistibility as he rose in a muscular leap, straining to get behind the ball and hammer his reverse header in a killing arc over the goalkeeper. This goal said much about the qualities that cause Muller to be feared by the best of defenders, a company to which the Peruvians scarcely belong.

By now the small Guanajuato Stadium, which has something of the pleasant, almost pastoral ambience of Fulham's Craven Cottage (though there is no cooling river at hand to dilute the drugging heat of the Mexican summer), was loud with German klaxons and bright with the broad slashes of red and yellow on their national flags. A goal for Peru in the last minute of the first half only put a momentary stutter in their cheering. It was rather clumsily surrendered. De La Torre was tripped as he came through on the offensive and the free kick by Cubillas, struck from about twenty-five yards out and in front of goal, was confusingly deflected – both Schnellinger and Fichtel, who are ambiguously blond, were accused – and the ball spun past Maier.

Attendants in white coats had waited on the sidelines with canisters of oxygen, their solicitous alertness recalling the distressing scenes that marked the climax of so many Olympic events in 1968. They were not needed here but the players were being visibly drained by the heat and it was inevitable that both teams should call on substitutes. At the interval some of us thought the Germans would be tempted to replace Vogts, the brilliant little full-back who had punished himself relentlessly in containing Gallardo and helping to carry the fight to Peru. But Helmut Schoen had justified faith in the ability of Vogts to maintain his self-sacrificing mobility and the substitution made at the beginning of the second half was that of Patzke for Hottges, the left-back. By the fifty-sixth minute León, whose legs are less than sound, had made way for Ramírez and the two further substitutions that were permissible followed soon afterwards: Cruzado for Challe after seventy minutes and Grabowski for Libuda when seventy-four minutes had been played. In the meantime, Cubillas, apparently realising that he must assert himself more pointedly in the goal area if the match was to be salvaged, wasted a good opening by allowing Maier to save at his feet after receiving the ball from Ramírez. Cubillas made and missed a much more glaring chance when he left three defenders groping, then shot carelessly wide. Fatigue was blatant among the Germans in the final quarter of an hour and without the energy of their fresh recruits, particularly the superb Grabowski, who was already established as the star substitute of the World Cup, their predicament would have been serious. As it was, they were often profoundly uncomfortable and Schnellinger, who had the job of sweeping up trouble behind the main line of the defence, needed all his composure and experience. Sotil had now thrust himself into the game and when he was put through at inside-right Maier had to make a good diving save. The goalkeeper could do little but pray when the winger worked a one-two with Cruzado that left Cruzado in a scoring position. Cruzado obligingly toe-ended the ball past Maier's right hand post and we knew that Peru's surge had come too late to do more than alleviate the embarrassment of those who had been smothering them in tributes.

Helmut Schoen said later that he had not been surprised to find people raving about the Peruvians. 'For twenty minutes against the Bulgarians their football was like an ecstasy. They played like men in a trance, in a beautiful dream in which they could do nothing wrong. But the Bulgarians permitted them to play their game, let them build towards those quick passing moves on the edge of the penalty area. We did not. We took the ball away from them in the middle of the field and we hit them with those high balls they do not like. We played the game our way.'

The Brazilians, we suspected, would play the game their way when they met Peru in the quarter-final. Zagalo would not be misled, as so many early observers of Peru had been, into overlooking their shortcomings in defence. However, given the peculiarities of Félix's goalkeeping and the occasional lapses of the men immediately in front of him, a high-scoring match was in prospect. Schoen, relaxing in the shade of tall trees beside the thermal swimming pool in the Germans' tranquilly isolated camp, was understandably cautious about forecasting what would happen when his men met England. All he felt sure about was that the match would be hard and close. Had he known how hard and how close it was to be he might have been inclined to take two or three sleeping pills that night.

West Germany 3   *Peru 1*

GROUP FOUR

	P	W	D	L	F	A	Pts
West Germany	3	3	0	0	10	4	6
Peru	3	2	0	1	7	5	4
Bulgaria	3	0	1	2	5	9	1
Morocco	3	0	1	2	2	6	1

6 *The Quarter-Finals*

As Mexico City came blinking out of its hangover on the morning of June 12, marvelling at the memories of the overnight tumult that had followed Mexico's defeat of Belgium, one question dominated the streets: would Mexico now play their quarter-final at the Aztec stadium?

It had been widely known for several days that the lobbyists had been at work, anticipating the possibility of a situation like the one which now confronted the tournament. The gist of the argument was that it was entirely reasonable for Mexico to play all their matches at Aztec, regardless of the rules. After all, more than three times as many people could watch the team in Mexico City as could be crammed into the stadium at Toluca, the other quarter-final venue for Groups One and Two. The cynics were in no doubt that Mexico would rig it somehow. There was abundant confidence that Mexico would not be denied the formidable backing of that blazing Aztec crowd.

In Group Two the position was plain: Italy, having finished first, would receive the second-place team from Group One at Toluca; Uruguay would meet the Group One first-place team at Aztec. But Group One was deadlocked. Both Russia and Mexico had five points, and each had the same goal *difference*, 6–1 in Russia's case and 5–0 in Mexico's. (Difference, of course, not goal average, was used to decide between tying teams in this World Cup.) So on Friday morning the draw was made in a small suite in the Maria Isabel Hotel to decide first and second places. Outside the windows a mass of cheerful students danced in the decorative, shallow pool, waving flags and chanting in happy conviction that soon they would hear the announcement they wanted. They got a deflating one instead. The televised ceremony was short and brisk. Russia's name came out first. So Mexico would play Italy in Toluca, and the Aztec stadium would stage a match that few people in Mexico City wanted to see.

The news was absorbed calmly. The hysterical abuse of FIFA predicted so solemnly by some foreigners did not occur. There was a sense of resignation, or perhaps of surfeit; a feeling that Mexico had already had its day. More materially there was also the fact that Mexico had tried, and failed, to reverse a similarly disagreeable decision two years before. When they reached the football quarter-finals of the Olympics they were determined to have their venue changed from Puebla to Mexico City. A wrangle with the FIFA Amateur Committee began one night at 8pm. and ended at 3am. At that point Guillermo Cañedo, the president of the Mexican F.A., conceded to Helmut Kaser, FIFA's General Secretary: 'This is the first time in my life I haven't got what I wanted.'

So now, as then, the lobbyists discreetly withdrew and the wishful thinkers were disappointed. But there was one sly, amusing exercise of pressure from an oblique angle. The resourceful Governor of the State of Mexico, the same Carlos Hank González who had made sure that Toluca, his capital, would not be by-passed by the World Cup, was now suddenly seized with concern about the safety of the town's stadium. He thought it vital, before it could be trusted to bear the weight of the full house the Mexican national team would bring, that the place should be examined by his engineers. It was a brave try. The boy would surely go far.

U.S.S.R. *v.* URUGUAY

Aztec Stadium, June 14

On a bright, cloudless Sunday morning the half-empty stadium was buzzing with transistor radios and portable TVs tuned in to Toluca. The blue and white flags of Uruguay and the solitary

Russian flag among its tiny huddle of Soviet supporters failed to draw even the customary whistles of derision, but when the teams emerged there was a vast cheer for the Uruguayans who, with a neat sense of public relations, were carrying a large Mexican flag. First round to them.

The teams squared off like Sumo wrestlers, afraid to make the first positive move in case they were overthrown. Among them stalked the spare figure of the Dutch referee, Laurens van Ravens, quiveringly alert for the first sign of trouble. He did not have long to wait. Uruguay's back four of Ubiñas, Ancheta, Matosas and Mújica had the powerful, slick look of a long-serving bunch of night-club bouncers and they swiftly went about their intimidating work. Evriuzhikhin, small and quick, was not quick enough to escape a Rugby tackle after pushing the ball past the balding Matosas. Mr van Ravens was on the spot instantly to lecture the Uruguayan, who was all shrugs, smiles and apologies. Montero Castillo was next to be warned for a violent body-check on Khmelnitski; and when Afonin was hurt the referee threw away the Russians' water bag which other players were using as they gathered round the injured man.

Russia, at their strongest with the return of Kaplichni in the back line, had early opportunities, mainly from wing bursts. Once Khmelnitski overran a cross by Evriuzhikhin right in front of the posts, and he was again at fault in failing to control a centre when Bishovets swerved out to the right, taking a posse of Uruguayans with him. But in their canter through Group One the Russians had run into nothing resembling the ruthless professionalism they now faced. Uruguay were content to blunt Russian threats, which they did with increasing assurance, inflict a few bruises (invariably followed by a pat on the head or an attempted handshake with the stricken victim if they had been spotted by the referee) and rest their attacking case on the unexpectedly subtle skills and speed of the portly little right-winger, Cubilla.

Uruguay, paying passing service to the 4–3–3 system, did not hesitate to pull back the midfield three – Montero Castillo, Maneiro and Fontes – into the defensive umbrella at the slightest hint of danger, and when Ubiñas impeded Khmelnitski near the penalty area they withdrew the entire team to deal with the kick, which Muntian lobbed wastefully into a mass of blue shirts.

Muntian, the smallest player on the field, beat Matosas and forced Mazurkiewicz to a leaping save, but when he tried to repeat the gesture by dribbling round Montero Castillo he was savagely fouled. The violence wasn't one-sided, however. Asatiani, a long way from the assured all-rounder he had looked in the Group games, was cautioned by Mr van Ravens for 'feet up', and at half-time – greeted by boos and a slow hand-clap – the thirty-two fouls so far committed had been shared equally, though most of the Russian offences had been trivial.

Having buffeted Bishovets and intimidated the other small strikers, Evriuzhikhin and Khmelnitski, Uruguay now set about the second part of their campaign, springing instantly into smooth attack. Cortés put Maneiro's inviting square pass high over; Fontes's awkwardly bouncing shot was well stopped by Kavazashvili; a menacing cross from the left was hurriedly pushed for a corner by Kaplichni. Behind most of these raids was Cubilla, roaming hungrily and revealing some unsuspected gaps in Russia's covering. He would manoeuvre himself into impossible-looking positions, crowded right on the touchline at a full stop and shielding the ball with his thick body. Then brilliantly, swiftly, he would dart away into a space or flick off a telling pass. Russia's left flank was beginning to creak under this assault and once Kaplichni leapt on to Cubilla's back in desperation.

As the electric scoreboard started to flicker the tale of goals in the other quarter-finals, Russia almost conceded one. In a bizarre reversal of roles, Khmelnitski fouled Ubiñas inside the Russian area and an indirect free kick was awarded. It was backheeled to Mújica, who drove left-footed just past the near post.

The battle was rarely eventful, always interesting, as Uruguay patiently chipped away at the Russians' confidence and determination. Morales wasted a fine chance from Cubilla's cross, heading backwards to a non-existent team-mate when he might have scored himself, then Kavazashvili sprang to turn away left-handed a fierce Maneiro shot. With twenty minutes remaining Gavril Katchalin took off the disappointing Asatiani and brought on Kiselev. Soon afterwards Russia replaced Khurtsilava with Logofet.

Bishovets battled on bravely against the forest of Uruguayan defenders, but his temper broke when he was again fouled by Ancheta. A pushing match followed, with Mr van Ravens throwing more punches than the players in keeping them apart, and the incident ended in the inevitable handshakes. Unrepentant, Ancheta and Matosas combined to crush Bishovets, injuring Russia's leading scorer as he chased a high centre.

As the whistle blew for the end of regulation time both sides sank to the grass, but it was the Russians who looked in worse condition. Some were having towels flapped in their faces to revive them, like amateur boxers who have ventured into their first ten-round fight. Russia had used both substitutes and played their hand in all senses. When the extra period began that famous Soviet discipline had drained into the Aztec turf. They looked ragged and were shirking the heaviest tackles.

Uruguay, who had brought on Gómez for Morales in attack at the start of extra time, now varied their theme, mounting a mortar assault on Shesternev and Kaplichni at the heart o Russia's defence. Centres and hefty clearances rained into the Russian area, and one long punt from Matosas found Cubilla, whose sharp header was well caught by Kavazashvili. Now Uruguay made their second, vital substitution. Fontes was pulled out of midfield and Espárrago added to the attack. At once he raced forty yards, only for Kavazashvili to beat away his angled kick.

After almost two hours of inconclusive combat, and with the match apparently to be settled by drawing lots, the ball was in the net twice in as many minutes. First, Bishovets drove in Muntian's lob but the East German linesman, Rudi Glockner, had his flag up and Bishovets was offside.

Then Muntian fouled Montero Castillo on the halfway line. The kick was thrust forward to Cubilla, who had sprinted into what used to be called the inside-left position. He shuffled down to the dead-ball line to the left of Russia's goal, turned his back on the posts and went into his screening, tip-tap routine, trying to work an opening as Afonin hovered behind, unwilling to risk conceding a corner by intervening forcefully. But for once Cubilla misjudged his juggle and the ball ran briefly but clearly out of play. Afonin turned away and the rest of the Russian defence paused; Cubilla, granted the space he had been seeking, chipped over his centre and Espárrago, on the near post, headed in by the far one.

Russia's attitude when they saw Mr van Ravens point towards the centre was unexpected only in its savagery. Bishovets, who had absorbed such a battering, complained so violently that he became the only player to be booked in the game – for 'disputing the referee's decision'. The linesman concerned was the Scot, Bob Davidson. The action was three-quarters of the pitch's width away from him and Cubilla's shielding bulk could not have helped his view, but Mr Davidson said afterwards that though the ball was partly out of play it had not gone completely over the line. From the Press seats the line was clearly visible between the ball and Cubilla's boot.

As the whistle blew, after Bishovets had persuaded one final save from Mazurkiewicz (who had kept goal with a competence and lack of flamboyance which evoked comparison with Gordon Banks), the Uruguay reserves and officials came capering from their dug-out. Kisses smacked on to haggard cheeks, tears were wiped away, ecstatic supporters mauled their heroes. The Russians turned their backs on this match of seventy fouls to begin their preparations for 1974.

Though Uruguayan relief was profound, they had deserved to win. They had measured their opponents, and then outplayed them, outgunned them, outlasted them – and outkicked them.

U.S.S.R. o   Uruguay 1

ITALY *v.* MEXICO

Toluca, June 14

For this match Toluca was barely recognisable as the half-aware town we had grown used to. As the crowd milled in the streets around the stadium trucks came rolling up to deliver squads of soldiers equipped for a shooting war to join the five or six hundred policemen in and about the ground. There was a crackly tension under the sun. An hour before the game started the stands were packed and the intermittent chanting battered the close, confining walls like sea waves. And the volume increased until, in the last fifteen minutes before the kick-off, the unbroken roaring of 'Me-hee-co' made the ears ring. The Italian supporters, for once, were compressed into timidity in their block of seats beside the Press stand.

The Mexican players had already outstripped their country's pre-tournament hopes for them. Even allowing the dubious nature of their win against Belgium they could fairly be commended for having lifted their football to an unexpected degree of shrewd organisation. There was some individual flair, too, from Munguía, adroitly initiating attacks out of midfield, and from Pulido, Valdivia, González, less intelligent but vivacious when going forward. Gratified supporters among the rich Mexicans had already disbursed about £200,000 around the squad; Raul Cárdenas, the manager, had also been given a house, and players had received expensive presents ranging from plots of building land to cars and dining-room suites.

Forty-eight hours before this quarter-final Cárdenas had talked with relaxed good sense about Mexican football, and about the alarming conduct of the spectators at Aztec. The sport was still inadequately taught in Mexican schools, he said, and poorly understood by much of the population, so that their fanatical concern for local players was little tempered by appreciation of others' skills – particularly the undramatic ones. He knew that the team had greatly benefited from being together under his coaching since January. There was a sense of restrained self-satisfaction about him then, as if defeat by Italy now would not offend him any more than it would surprise anyone else.

But Mexico's supporters in Toluca, far from being satisfied, were panting for more. And when González gave them an excellent goal after twelve minutes their deafening optimism seemed well justified. Italy had started with some crisp moving of the ball, which the Mexicans had disrupted only by the most combative interventions, notably from Peña and Vantolra. But Italy's own tackling suggested they had underestimated the opposition badly when Mexico launched their first, and telling, attack.

Fragoso was permitted a substantial run forward with the ball, Munguía was given time to aim his flicked pass for Valdivia's sprint on the left, and the Italian defence was suddenly outwitted. Valdivia crossed quickly to the unmarked González, who hit the ball with the outside of his right foot to beat Albertosi's dive. The goalkeeper thumped his fists into the turf, while the crowd bayed and danced.

It was the first goal Italy had conceded in the tournament, and in three matches they had scored only once. Riva had been saying after his several near-misses against Israel that he felt if he could score one he would get twenty. But it was clearly going to need a change of gear from Italy if they were really to come boldly from behind now. They were self-conditioned to constraint.

Twenty minutes passed before Riva hit Italy's first threatening shot. It flew wide of the far post, and the crowd whistled and hooted in happy derision. A few seconds later their view of things appeared all the more supportable. Pulido improved greatly on Riva's attempt with a ferocious drive from thirty

yards, which Albertosi pushed round his left-hand post with a
dive the width of the goal.

Impressively Mexico were able to group seven men quickly
into defensive positions, to smother Riva and Boninsegna by
sheer numbers as the long balls came floating up from De Sisti,
Bertini and Mazzola. Every breakdown of an Italian move was
accepted with piercing contempt from the stands. Perhaps the
crowd had not noticed that those deceivingly lazy attacking
moves were now so frequent they were nearly the whole of
the play.

In the twenty-sixth minute this slow, deft use of the ball put
Italy level, although Mexico were not helped by Calderón's
inattentive goalkeeping. Boninsegna took De Sisti's forward
pass, then hit a long, diagonal one which Riva followed to the
right of Mexico's penalty box. Riva, usually the determined
soloist, this time pushed the ball into Domenghini's stride from
the touchline. Domenghini's low shot seemed to take seconds
to reach the goal, yet it crept between Calderón and his near
post. The crowd muttered and brooded.

Immediately Mexico's work looked more ragged, the running
far less prompt for Munguía's cogent passes and the resolution
ebbing out of the marking by Peña, Pérez and Vantolra. But
Mexico could still manage to discomfort the Italians with
individual enterprise. Valdivia turned up suddenly with the
ball inside the Italian penalty area, and stabbed hard across
the face of the goal. De Sisti had to kick desperately away for
a corner, while Burgnich and Albertosi argued with angry
gesticulation about personal responsibilities.

But we were now seeing the familiar Italian exercise in
professional patience. The number and variety of skills at their
command lifted the side outside Mexico's class. They were
playing the game as if waiting for time to reward them. And
Mexico escaped twice in the closing minutes of the first half.
First Domenghini mis-hit his cross wide, as Riva and Boninsegna
waited in perfect timing and positioning in front of goal; then
Calderón pushed Facchetti's shot straight at the jostling figures

of Riva and Peña, and the referee, Rudolf Scheurer of Switzerland, gave a free kick to Mexico when a penalty for Italy would have been no more questionable.

For the second time Rivera appeared for half a match, now replacing Mazzola. This time his arrival was spectacular. Within twenty seconds he stole away on the left to hit a big cross that cleared the unprepared defence. Riva rose to it and headed hard downwards against Calderón's knees. The goalkeeper seemed to have made a save he knew nothing at all about.

This mixture of stealth and cold strength in the partnership of Rivera and Riva had been urged persistently on Italy's coach, Feruccio Valcareggi. If that kind of thing could be often repeated he would surely not require any more persuasion. The problem for Valcareggi was that while the persistence of Rivera's propagandists could be relied on the player's own was less dependable.

Not for the first time it was Domenghini, wispy and darting, who claimed most attention now. Of all the Italians he had always seemed least inhibited by Toluca's altitude, exceeding even Mazzola's willingness to trade pace. It was Domenghini's run and swift cross that gave Boninsegna the chance for a flying header, putting the ball narrowly past a post. One felt that if Domenghini had the strength of personality to dominate his side and persuade them into his optimism Italy might have entertained much more than they did, and overwhelmed their opposition the more easily.

But there was no doubt that the Italians had control of this match. With Munguía in the dressing room, replaced by Díaz after an hour, Mexico were increasingly disordered. The Mexicans still managed to interrupt Italy's composure, as when Pulido's sharp header beat Albertosi and had to be headed out from under the bar by Cera; but there was lead in Mexico's legs, and as much tiredness in their thinking.

Riva's goal in the sixty-fourth minute was typical of his physical power. Taking a short pass just inside the Mexico penalty area he was half stopped by Peña's heavy obstruction, the ball trickled away from him and he had to break free to regain it. He turned to shoot low, close to the far post on Calderón's left.

Five minutes afterwards Riva's gathering speed in an unusual, long run, after he snapped up the ball near his own penalty box, made Italy's third goal. Riva once more forced his way out of a tackle, still in possession, and prodded the ball forward for Boninsegna. Calderón was fifteen yards out of his goal, but three shots were blocked in the confusion of bodies around him before the fourth, from Rivera, found the net. Rivera disappeared under a wriggling pile of Italian players.

The fourth Italian goal also had Rivera's care and Riva's belligerence. Rivera ended a run clear of Mexico's defence with a low pass exactly at Riva's feet on the right. Vantolra was evaded and then Riva dragged himself away from the Mexican's despairing hand on his shirt. Riva's first shot came back off Calderón's body, but the second went in from three yards.

There were no more goals. But Riva reinforced the image he had given us of muscularity in fluent and threatening movement: a run through three tackles from Peña, Vantolra and Guzmán, as he carried the ball into the goal area to force a corner. Yet as memorable was Domenghini, tottering in exhaustion from the pitch four minutes before the end and slumping against the trainer's bench to be revived by the water bucket as if he were parched vegetation.

The Mexican crowd also had a shrivelled look. But its sound was depressed, not bitter. There was a defiant chanting of 'Me-hee-co' at the final whistle, just to drown the smug delight of the Italian following. For an Englishman with news of the sickening events then occurring in León, any kind of delight was offensive, of course.

Italy 4   Mexico 1

BRAZIL *v.* PERU

Guadalajara, June 14

Waldimir Pereira, the coach of Peru, took his team reluctantly
to Jalisco Stadium for the quarter-final against Brazil. He had
not wanted to meet Brazil until later, and how could it be
otherwise for he was of them? As Didi, he had been a lauded
notable in the great Brazil team of 1958, a giant in 1962. He
was twice a World Cup winner with Brazil, convinced then of
their invincibility, and such notions die hard.

He had reckoned that Brazil would win the Guadalajara
Section and said he wanted his team to win the León Section
to dodge them. He preferred to take his chance against England
but the three goals by Muller had kept West Germany at León
and sent Peru to Guadalajara.

And so Peru moved from the small-town peace of León to
the exciting rhythms of the capital of Jalisco, and the many
fountains of that beautiful city seemed to dance to the samba
beats of the South American supporters as the red and white of
Peru was added to the already entrenched Brazilians. Saturday
night was one of noisy revelry, yet the Mexicans were perplexed – both teams were South Americans and they could not
take sides.

There was one hidden factor that could be decisive. Gérson,
the Brazilian master of the midfield, was recovering from the
injury that had kept him out of the match against England.
Brazil needed him. Didi wished him no harm but would as soon
have had him limping as fit.

The young Rivelino, too, had been injured and there was a
frantic search for news of those formidable backers of the
Brazilian attackers. Zagalo seemed to clear the air when,
unusually, he announced a team; then he quickly clouded
matters again when he added, 'At least that will be the team
unless the doctor vetoes any of my four injured players, Gérson,
Rivelino, Clodoaldo and Everaldo'. So there were four with
their fitness in question.

The doubts were maintained until the Brazilian team was released at the stadium and then Didi learned he had to face the full might of Brazil. It was a heavy thought.

At least the weather was right. A day of sun and pleasant heat was perfect for these teams who scorned defensive theorising and wanted the ball to run fast. It suited, too, the colourful spectators and their stirring beats were only silenced when the anthems were played and the pigeons released for their flapping flight round the field.

Brazil kicked off and were immediately menacing as some jungle cat prowling with power leashed ready to explode into attacking fury. They built a terrible tension as Peru manoeuvred to keep their goal adequately covered.

Then Gérson, stalking in the midfield, had the ball and Pelé was moving out of his languorous meandering and Gérson noticed and hit a long pass to where he was heading. The defence was startled and Pelé had the ball on his chest and in that astonishing way of his was taking it past the man who covered him. Chumpitaz, the captain, was left perplexed and trailing and the sleepy cat was awake and gliding in on goal. Rubiños, the goalkeeper, came out but majestically Pelé clipped the ball past him. A goal was acclaimed on the terracings but Pelé, who sees more than most, knew differently. He saw the ball was going to strike a post and he raced for the rebound while others were flat-footed. He was first to the ball and back-heeled it with difficulty to Tostão. The defence had recovered and the shot was charged down.

The game had gone but four minutes, but even so soon there had been a gem of the genius of Pelé. To make the chance would have been enough to stamp greatness on any player but, in such an instant of wild excitement, to read so precisely and swiftly that the ball would strike a post was beyond the ordinary call of greatness.

And having put Peru under pressure Brazil squeezed. Tostão lay deep in the Peruvian goalmouth, laying off so calmly the balls that were driven at him, and then he moved into the clear as Pelé came through and the ball was flicked to him. Before he could move he was swept down and Brazil had a free kick in that danger area just outside the penalty box. The defensive wall was set and inspected. Pelé was to the right of the ball, Rivelino of the swerving, blasting shot was on the left. They raced on diagonal intersecting courses. Pelé ran past the ball but Rivelino hit it and had it raging past the line of defenders. Rubiños dived, but instinctively, for he could have no clear view of the ball in such speedy flight. Luck favoured him and the ball hit his knees as he stretched out parallel with the ground. The ball went for a corner and from it Pelé was diving to head when he was pushed. Already Brazil might have scored three times and they had been playing but six minutes.

The play then came down to a more temperate level and there was time to note that when Didi had said, 'We don't know how to play defensively,' he had spoken truthfully. Peru were striking with León, Cubillas and Gallardo and there was steady support for them in Baylon and Fernández.

And as Peru, looking big and powerful in their white with the red sash exaggerating their chests, struggled to bring order and equality to the play a great shout of exultation rose from the terracings, a startling shout for the cause was unknown. Soon it was. Radios in the crowd had blared the news that Mexico had scored in their quarter-final against Italy.

And in just another minute, the eleventh of the match, that roar of acclaim was made to seem as a mere whisper. Brazil scored. Predictably it was a magnificent goal created apparently from nothing. Jairzinho was lumbering with the ball on the right. He stopped and started, hesitated, then sent a harmless looking pass inside to Tostão. At least it seemed harmless, but we should have known that no situation is harmless when Tostão is in the middle of it. Rivelino was moving on his left but Tostão seemed coldly unimpressed as he stroked the ball; then it was rolling right into Rivelino's stride and the goal was exposed twenty yards away. Such as he could scarcely miss and his superbly struck shot went in off a post.

Rivelino was hugged and smothered by the arms and bodies of team-mates who showed in their grotesquely exaggerated congratulations the tension they were under. Then, with the strain eased, they swept into rollicking happy attack.

Pelé and Tostão bewildered the Peru defence with fleet, intricate interpassing. Pelé was pulled down when slipping clear. There seemed no other way to stop him. Then an astonishingly cool pass from Tostão to Rivelino brought a corner kick. Tostão took it and played it short to Rivelino and got the ball back. He dallied and the defence got set and waited for the pass as he moved along the bye-line. Then he stroked a shot through the gap between the goalkeeper and the near post and it was as simple as that. Simplicity is the mark of Tostão.

Brazil led by two goals and some thought by three when Rivelino, with another spectacular shot, sent the ball to the net from a free kick. It was a non-scoring free kick and he had been looking for a deflection. They had played sixteen minutes and the contest seemed over.

Peru would not concede that. They worked at getting their forward passing right. León and Cubillas could break smartly, and Gallardo joined them. Their passing through the middle was slick but lacking the individuality and panache of Pelé and Tostão. And then in the twenty-third minute Peru did get the move right and the last pass was precise and Cubillas was clear and shooting. The ball struck the goalkeeper's knees, the rebound struck Brito and flew to the hands of the startled Félix. Didi must have found that moment hard to take.

The scare that ran through Brazil was quickly eased by wonder at the insolent genius of Pelé. He tried to chip into a gap little bigger than the ball itself showing high in the goal, and only he would aim at such a ridiculously small target.

But not by genius alone are games won, as Gallardo showed in the twenty-eighth minute when he scored and brought the contest alive again. He galloped past Carlos Alberto and beat Félix with a simple shot. It was a clean straightforward goal.

Brazil were roused and the pressure on Peru was furious till half-time. Tostão wriggled through on a fifteen-yard run. Pelé's great shot leaped from the hands of Rubiños and struck a post. He dropped to smother it. Only on the right were Brazil not striking effectively. Fuentes was controlling Jairzinho.

Brito, who had been playing safely, lapsed and was slow to cover Fernández and there was much furore for nothing when an indirect free kick was conceded. Almost on half-time Rivelino's shot beat the goalkeeper but Fuentes, coming across, saved desperately although he seemed to be knocking the ball into his own goal. Rubiños got back in time to save. It was a fittingly exciting end to a first half of stirring attacking.

Peru had been as committed to attack as the happy Brazilians. They had been persistent and fast in probing the middle of the defence. They would send four or five men into the interpassing in front of goal but they had no Pelé, no Tostão – but who had?

There was no fun in Brazil's play at the start of the second half. They wanted a goal. They stirred up the action and added speed to the sophistication of their play. Rivelino had another free kick but his shot was blocked. Pelé speeded towards goal but was tripped. Carlos Alberto charged through, but his shot was deflected. Peru were living dangerously.

Yet in the midst of such hectic action again Brazil brought disaster to Peru with another lethal moment of calm. Jairzinho lumbered along. Pelé sprinted clear and Jairzinho reacted as the move demanded and gave him the ball running alongside him. The shot was on and the defence seemed to cower from it. But that unpredictable one instead squared the ball nonchalantly to Tostão who, from a position made easy, scored almost with diffidence. The second half had gone seven minutes.

Again there was pressure on Peru and as they tottered Brazil sought to floor them. Jairzinho for once raced clear but wasted the chance. Félix sent apprehension through them to dampen the fire when he dropped the ball from a thirty-five yards free kick. Tostão tried to get at Rivelino's hard cross but Rubiños smothered the ball and was hurt.

The sorely harassed Peru brought on Sotil for Baylon and

then Reyes for León but not until the sixty-seventh minute did Zagalo make his change. Gérson, who had dominated the midfield with lordly presence, was substituted by Paulo Cézar. Cézar came on to see a great shot by Pelé deflected and then his free kick played over the bar by Rubiños.

But as the heat and the intensity of the play sapped strength the fresh men began to be noticed. Sotil was lively and ran and held the ball to the discomfiture of the Brazil defence. He was in the centre of the work that made another goal for Peru in the seventieth minute.

At the first speedy thrust the ball was blocked, then it was retrieved and sent out to the lurking Cubillas. He hit it on the volley, a magnificent shot, and Brazil were pulled back to a single-goal lead.

But always they had something in hand. Always one was aware of a streak of fiery individualism waiting to break through. Such a flash earned Brazil their fourth goal when Rivelino came striding through the midfield and sent Jairzinho racing clear into the left penalty area. That was an unusual position for him. Rubiños raced out, but the big fellow beat him to the ball and took it past him, and it seemed too far, to the bye-line. Tostão raced in, inviting the cut back, and Jairzinho posed for it but, as the defenders closed on his target, calmly and unexpectedly he turned and pushed the ball into the narrow slice of net that was showing. That was typical Brazilian cheek.

Tostão might have had another goal when he had a good chance but he tried to beat two more men to make certain and was crowded out. And so they went into the last five minutes drained of energy as were the 55,000 crowd who, on the hot terracings, had thrilled to the persistent attacking, the magnificence, the goals. There were heavy limbs on the field, thick throats up above. And in these minutes Peru made their last defiant gesture. Cubillas shot and it seemed a goal, but Félix dived to his left to save instinctively and crush some of the mounting criticism of his goalkeeping.

When it was all over we remembered how healthy and clean was the play, how the ball skills were allowed to be developed and for that we thanked an excellent Belgian referee, Vital Loraux, who impressed even those he had alarmed and disappointed in England's opening match with Rumania. In such a satisfying game as this quarter-final there had to be a good referee.

Brazil 4   Peru 2

ENGLAND *v.* WEST GERMANY

León, June 14

When the England party arrived, as inconspicuously as thirty people can, at the back door of the Motel Estancia in León shortly after one o'clock on the burning afternoon of Saturday June 13, Mrs Beckenbauer was with the wives of other German players by the swimming pool. Bobby Moore pleased the waiting photographers by walking across to talk with her for a few minutes. As Sir Alf Ramsey and Dr Neil Phillips joined the trainers, Harold Shepherdson and Les Cocker, in ushering the rest of the group to their rooms around the pool, the scene conveyed a sense of routine calm. There was nothing to betray the private anxiety that already threatened English confidence. Anyone who studied Gordon Banks closely might have noticed that his colour was less than healthy. But the goalkeeper's complexion is never the kind that shines from the pages of holiday brochures and, given a natural expression that is almost orientally impassive, it was unlikely that a casual observer would pick him out from the bunch as a man whose personal distress could spread to leave millions feeling sick.

For an hour or two at least, we could concern ourselves with the historical and psychological factors that must always affect matches between teams from England and Germany. The ultimate question to be answered in the enfeebling midday heat of the following day was whether generations of history

could be outweighed by a fortnight of current form. If the
alarming inadequacies of England's qualifying performance
against Czechoslovakia were compounded by the effects of
travelling to a city that was about 1,000 feet higher and
appreciably hotter than Guadalajara, there would be little
chance of interrupting West Germany's confident advance
towards the semi-finals of the World Cup. But when the
English and the Germans meet on any competitive field echoes
of previous battles, more distant and more bitter than the
Wembley final of 1966, sound in the blood. This may be
regrettable but it is inescapably real, and there is no doubt
that the unique tensions that pulse beneath the surface of
these occasions have done more damage to Germany than to
England. The Germans carried into the quarter-final the
knowledge that their only victory in previous full internationals
with England was in Hanover in 1968. And then they needed
an untidy, slightly fortuitous goal to beat an English side
deliberately weakened in recognition of imminent exertions
in the European Nations Cup. Of the other ten meetings,
England had won nine and drawn one. The Germans, however
defiantly they insisted that they were broken in the final of
four years before by an illusory goal, would be obliged to
ignore more omens than Julius Caesar on assassination day.

Yet when one encountered an economics adviser from
Brazil who wanted to bet two hundred dollars on West Germany
the only surprise was his name: Pedro MacGregor. Mac-
Gregors have been known to go in at worse than evens against
the English, but they are rarely recruited from Brazil. The
justification for the boldness of Pedro, and for the smiling,
relaxed optimism that greeted anyone who drove through a
wilderness of scrubland to visit the Germans at their spa hotel
sixteen miles outside León, was in the contrasting courses Sir
Alf Ramsey and Helmut Schoen had found themselves taking
to a place in the last eight. Ramsey's men had come to León
with the disconcerting awareness that their best display in
three Group matches brought a defeat. The achievement of

losing only one goal was put in unimpressive perspective by their failure to score more than two, including one from a dubious penalty. In the meantime, West Germany, after making a melodrama of beating Morocco, had settled to a virile rhythm and thrashed Bulgaria and Peru. The Germans' scoring record was ten against four and, despite the irresolution of their opponents compared with those faced by England, the figures reflected a willingness to go after goals and a capacity for getting them.

The exuberant spirits of the German camp at Comanjilla were exemplified by Schoen's excuse for being late for a Press conference before the quarter-final. He had to change after being tossed into the thermal swimming pool by two of his more boisterous players. 'How would Sir Alf Ramsey take that?' we were asked archly by Wilfried Gerhardt, whose intelligence and unofficious competence as a Press officer raised him to the level of respected helper at the manager's right hand. Sitting under the palm trees bordering the pool, Schoen, a tall, bald man with a quiet, articulate manner, admitted that he had come to Mexico with no more than 'an idea of a team', having had his preparation eroded by the bad winter and the extended league season that kept his squad in Europe until May 19. But he was satisfied that they were now a cohesive and vigorous force. By persuading Beckenbauer to operate with Overath in midfield, leaving Schnellinger or Schulz as sweeper, and convincing Muller that it was no disadvantage to play with the legendary Seeler, Schoen had given his side a solid base from which he could exploit the exciting form of his wingers, Libuda and Lohr, and the dramatic interventions (through carefully planned substitution) of Grabowski. The wingers' main function was to feed the aggressive appetite of Muller. Playing an unequivocal centre-forward game – with Seeler switching tirelessly between the middle three and the front line – Muller took seven goals to emerge as clearly the leading scorer in the Group matches. He had shared the same honour with Tostão of Brazil in the qualifying stages of the World Cup.

Anyone tempted to think Muller merely adept at punishing weak defences had to consider his 138 goals in five years of German league football and especially his record-breaking thirty-eight in the 1969–70 season. In Germany they say there should be a law against him inside the penalty area, where his thick, heavy-thighed physique does not stop him from demonstrating a swift, economical agility on the ground and in the air. His positioning is inspired and, if his control is moderate, he is one of that rare breed of apparently ordinary forwards who become giants when presented with the remotest chance of scoring a goal. The English strikers, who had found scoring about as easy as ski-ing on marmalade, were sure to envy Muller. It went without saying that the English defence would worry about his presence. Now, on the eve of the match, however, everyone was suddenly absorbed by the likelihood of another man's absence.

Gordon Banks did not take part in a light training session at the Guanajuato Stadium on the Saturday afternoon and Ramsey admitted that the goalkeeper had stomach trouble. He was, in fact, suffering from the complaint described, with grim facetiousness, as Montezuma's Revenge, a condition that usually brings bouts of nausea and the need to sprint for the lavatory with exhausting frequency. The illness must have hurt Neil Phillips almost as much as Banks. Having protected the players with unremitting care through nearly two months in Latin America, guarding them against every foreseeable hazard, down to the ice that arrived automatically in their soft drinks, the doctor found the enemy's first serious victory flattening one of the most vital men in the party. Phillips was not likely to endorse the views of those at home in England who suspected a plot to put Banks out of the match, least of all the theory of one well-known figure who muttered that the C.I.A. had an interest in keeping the Brazilians happy. But he could be forgiven for cursing his luck. There seemed a chance that it had changed when Banks passed a good night and rose on Sunday morning to do a little light practice with a ball. He was

officially in the team when the players assembled for the pre-
match meeting in Ramsey's room. While the meeting was in
progress, however, the goalkeeper suddenly took a turn for the
worse again and it became clear that he could not play. With
less than an hour to go before the party left the motel to travel
the few hundred yards to the stadium, Peter Bonetti learned
he was about to play in a World Cup for the first time. It was a
bitter irony that an ambition so long cherished should be
realised in such unfavourable circumstances. Perhaps some
players would prefer to be thrust unexpectedly into that kind
of challenge, without time to brood on its implications. But it
is reasonable to suppose that most would benefit from a more
gradual psychological preparation, from having time to cleanse
the shock and personal excitement of the promotion from their
minds, leaving their concentration keen and uncluttered. No
one could fail to sympathise with Bonetti as he lined up under
the high, hard sun with a number 12 on his back, knowing he
was the only one of the twenty-two who had never before
experienced the unique pressures of the World Cup. Five of
the England men beside him had worn the same red colours at
Wembley in the final of 1966 when German resistance was
ground down over two exhausting hours. None of them had
any doubts about Bonetti's talent – he was by all acceptable
standards of comparison among the best half-dozen goalkeepers in the tournament – but they could not escape a slight
twinge of uneasiness over the absence of Bank's relaxed, rather
shambling figure. Through the early matches of the competition,
indeed as early as the short tour of Colombia and Ecuador, he
had confirmed that his gifts were unimpaired, still without
equal in the game. It was simply impossible to believe that
anyone in the history of football had ever done the goalkeeper's
job better. And beyond his great worth as a member of the
team, Banks was a potent talisman. True, his finest save, the
miraculous interception of Pelé's header at the Jalisco Stadium,
had not averted defeat but there was a persistent feeling that
this big man, apparently capable of catching mortar shells,

could make his side nearly invulnerable. Banks shares with
Moore the remarkable distinction of drawing from fellow
internationalists the effusive tributes that normally come from
star-struck fans. And Moore himself gets about as close as he
ever can to rhapsodising when he talks of the goalkeeper. On
their way to keep a date with Pelé after the Brazil match,
Moore and Bobby Charlton agreed that they had never known
anyone in football quite like Banks. 'He is the only keeper I
know who never wants to play in another position, even when
we are having a little practice game,' said Charlton. 'Most of
them are desperate to play out of goal, to show you what they
can do on the wing or knock in a few goals. They often fancy
themselves on the ball. But Banksie just wants to stay in there
and let you try to beat him. He would have you shooting at him
all day. We all lined up on the edge of the area this morning
and hammered shots at him and we couldn't put one past him.
He was unbeatable. He loves that. If one does get by him, even
in a little kick around like that, he gets needled with himself.
Starts muttering and trying to work out what went wrong. He
thinks you have no right to score against him.' The Germans
had managed it twice at Wembley four years earlier but they
were unlikely to be depressed by the thought that now, as the
screeching of their supporters' klaxons became louder and the
red, black and yellow flags isolated the Union Jacks on the
terraces, Banks lay in a darkened room along the road. He
would follow the match by means of a delayed transmission on
television, trailing far behind its breathless fluctuations.

There was a stuttering start when the referee had to replace
the unsatisfactory ball with which the Germans kicked off.
Less than a minute had been played before the change but it
was time enough for Hottges to give Lee some harsh treatment.
The discomfort inflicted on Newton immediately afterwards
was more legitimate. Lohr's speed, used first individually and
then as the cutting edge of a one-two manoeuvre, twice left
the full-back straining in pursuit. Moore's alertness doused
the threat in the second situation. The England captain was

giving instant evidence of his commanding form and when
Muller pushed the ball through his legs, obliging Labone to
clear, one felt that the German should receive some sort of
prize for his nerve. There seemed no likelihood of any other
reward for Muller. When he took to drifting away from the
spearhead position, withdrawing or going wide in an effort
to pull the central defenders out of their places, he found a
wary response. Labone stayed back to block the way through
the middle, alternating with Moore in picking up Muller as
he came within menacing range. With Newton repeating the
pattern of previous matches, swiftly overcoming a nervous
beginning to play with assured brilliance, the defence soon
assumed a look of solidity. England, as usual, had a minimum
of four men in the midfield and if this inevitably left the front
line under-manned there was obvious compensation in the
subduing effect on the German builders, Overath, Beckenbauer
and Seeler. Harassed by the vigorous mobility of Mullery and
Ball and the swooping interventions of Charlton, they had
little opportunity to develop the measured passing moves that
should have fed the wingers and Muller. They might have
been swamped entirely if Peters had equalled the efficiency
of those alongside him. But he was again a lifeless imitation
of himself, questioning with every tentative gesture the wisdom
of Ramsey's insistence on using him in all of England's games.
Even the sight of Hurst at his most effective could do nothing
for Peters. Indeed the first of many breaks marvellously
engineered by Hurst was ruined the moment Peters joined
him. There was a faint stirring of hope when the familiar slim
shape slipped, almost unnoticed, behind Maier in anticipation of Newton's inswinging centre. The goalkeeper, possibly
distracted, dropped the ball but recovered it. With that chance
gone, Peters sank back into vagueness.

The fact that Lee was the least impressive of the other
England players ensured that the burden on Hurst was huge.
Still unable to reproduce the electric aggression of his home
form in these crudely alien conditions, Lee was permitting

his frustration to express itself in petulance, complaining about collisions he would hardly acknowledge if things were going well. He may have been entitled to grumble, however, when he had his name taken following an incident with Maier. Lee closed with Maier after Hurst headed Charlton's centre across goal and the goalkeeper went down as if he had been hit with an axe. Later the forward claimed he had merely patted Maier teasingly on the cheek. If so, the referee, Angel Coerezza from Argentina, made certain that the joke misfired. Before the match many of us had felt, remembering 1966, that there was an unnecessary risk in asking an Argentine to be referee. Apart from the open wounds left by the circumstances of England's victory over Germany in that World Cup final, it had to be recalled that most Argentines remained convinced that they would have beaten the English at an earlier stage and gone on to win the Cup if their captain, Rattin, had not been wrongfully ordered from the field. That the referee who dismissed Rattin was a German added to a welter of ironies calculated to make the head reel. And all this was made more disturbing by Coerezza's performance in the Aztec Stadium the previous Thursday, when he allowed the host nation to ease into the quarter-finals by awarding them a penalty which neutrals present agreed was one of the most ludicrous they had ever seen. Fortunately, he was showing no such malleability here. Some briefly suspected that he was being influenced by the Mexican support for Germany when he reacted favourably to Overath's histrionic allegations against Ball and gave a free kick. But that misconception was rapidly corrected when Muller, who had retreated far into his own half to foul the same English player, had his name noted under Lee's in Coerezza's book. Ball was irritating the opposition in more ways than one at this point, once almost getting a destructive pass through to Hurst. Schnellinger and Overath combined to give Seeler scope for retaliation, and for a change the old warhorse found himself free of Mullery's smothering presence. But the shot was shut out by Moore. A long ball from Schnel-

linger soared over Labone's leap and set Muller chasing but
the ball ran too far left and, though a chip by Beckenbauer did
give the forward a shot, he had still to do his first real
damage. A fairly simple punching save above the heads of
Seeler and Muller was the only notable effort required of
Bonetti so far. Maier, admittedly, had not been called upon to
be much more energetic but there was far greater substance
in the attacks that did reach his area. Hurst, collecting and
shielding the ball with flawless economy and aplomb in the
tightest positions, constantly alarmed the German defenders.
The memory of his three goals against them in 1966 seemed to
have doubled his flow of adrenalin. It was difficult to think of
any other forward in the tournament, apart from Tostão and,
of course, Pelé, who could have achieved half as much in
advanced isolation – and even Tostão rarely functioned as far
ahead of the main body of his attack. With half an hour
played, England were in control and gaining the confidence
to back Hurst by sending other players through from behind,
as Ramsey had promised they would do in the sudden-death
state of the competition. Ball climaxed one progressive dribble
by edging the ball right to Charlton, who promptly swung at
it. When Hottges put his foot firmly in the way both crumpled.
The referee awarded Charlton a foul but it was a doubtful one.

German satisfaction at surviving that free kick without cost
did not last long. In the thirty-first minute England took a
deserved lead with a magnificent goal. The build-up began
when Cooper, deep and wide in his own left-back position,
pushed the ball inside to Mullery. Having sent it forward to
Lee, Mullery moved on to a short return in time to hear
Newton's intelligent call from far out on the right, near the
halfway line. Mullery's left foot carried the ball crisply in the
air across the width of the field for Newton to bring it down
and stride ahead. As the full-back did so, Mullery was already
committed to a surging diagonal run and he met the angled
centre as it fell on the edge of the six-yard area opposite
Maier's left-hand post. Mullery said later that all the time he

was running he was waiting to be blocked or diverted. 'I couldn't believe they would let me run as far into their box without interference. I kept thinking, "Any second now I'll be clattered." ' But he was not and as the ball dropped his right instep made perfect contact ('I knew I'd got it just right – it was a great feeling') to sweep it high past Maier's left shoulder. It was Mullery's first goal in over thirty internationals for England. He could not have wished for a better or more important one.

Muller, finding Moore's regular attentions too much for him, was inclined occasionally to push like a Japanese wrestler but when the Englishman uncharacteristically complained the referee advised him to get on with the game. Overath received a similar admonition after voicing his opinion of a free kick given for a foul by Libuda on Cooper. It almost took the misdemeanour to remind us that Libuda was on the pitch. Cooper, maintaining the excellence of his performances in Guadalajara, made it hard to realise that this was the winger who had wrought so much havoc in the Group Four matches. Seeing Beckenbauer reduced to a succession of long, meaningless shots and Lohr become steadily more innocuous on the left wing, we were forced to conclude that the weight of history was going to prove stronger than recent form. Seeler, with the sweat glistening on his bald head, was still pumping his short, thick legs all over the field and the great Overath continued to probe hopefully for weaknesses, like a doctor struggling with a difficult diagnosis. Vogts was fast and enormously aggressive from full-back. Having seen his inaccurate drive needlessly headed behind by Labone, he stayed upfield to meet the corner with a dangerous header. But there was no concealing the apprehension that had spread through the German team. Their main tactic now was to lift long speculative passes forward from midfield in the manner of a quarterback in American football. They did not trust themselves to keep possession for a controlled, concerted assault. The shouts of 'Uwe, Uwe' that had urged on Seeler

o

and his men in the first half hour were significantly muted before the two sides headed gratefully for the comparative cool of the dressing-rooms at the interval.

When they came out again both teams applauded the announcement that Bobby Charlton was establishing a record by playing his 106th match for England, one more than Billy Wright's total. The other information conveyed by the public address system was that Schulz was replacing Hottges. Predictably, however, Schulz lined up in the middle of the defence, concentrating on Hurst. Fichtel, who had been given the unpleasant job of marking Hurst in the first half, switched to left-back to fill the gap made by the departure of Hottges. Schnellinger's responsibilities were still mainly those of sweeper. With Moore usually managing to repel Muller before he could move close to Bonetti's goal, Labone was similarly free for general policing duties in the England defence. Mullery, having another of the faultlessly reliable matches that made the World Cup a personal triumph for him, gave first priority to watching Seeler but used his overspill of vitality to drive on the English forwards. Their healthy urgency appeared to have carried England into the semi-final of the World Cup when they scored another goal after only five minutes of the second half. Moore dispossessed Seeler and passed to Ball, who steered the ball on to Hurst. As Hurst pressed through powerfully in the inside-right position, Newton made a furious run on the outside, checking momentarily and then accelerating fiercely again to outflank the defence. Just when it seemed that Hurst might hold the ball a fraction of a second too long he passed with perfect timing and Newton, from near the bye-line, clipped a sharp centre just beyond the far post. Peters, rediscovering his gift for materialising as an executioner, forced the ball past Maier. Some British Pressmen stood up in the stands, faced the German supporters and shouted 'Auf Wiedersehen'. At the time it struck us as a logical if slightly offensive comment. But strange things were about to happen.

The Germans were in urgent need of stimulation and

Helmut Schoen was lucky in having a man at hand who could provide it. Jurgen Grabowski had already earned the reputation of being the most influential substitute in the World Cup. Schoen had made a habit of introducing him at crucial points and he had never failed to galvanise the side. This match was no exception. As soon as Grabowski took over from Libuda, in the fifty-eighth minute, the course of the game was profoundly altered. The hard, low shot he struck immediately from the right was only a hint of what was to come. Cooper stopped that effort but Grabowski's runs became increasingly troublesome as the back tired in the heat. Whereas Libuda had a standard technique for evading tackles, his replacement exhibited endless variety, going past defenders on either side with killing fluency. Enlivened by Grabowski's example, the whole German team began to generate a mounting rhythm. Beckenbauer, always at his magical best when riding a tide created by others, emerged excitingly from his detached mood of the first hour. His best shot so far cannoned off Moore's head before going wide. But there were hardly more than twenty minutes left. Surely it was too much to expect the Germans to penetrate the strongest defence in the world, not once but twice, in such a short time. It would have been, if that defence had not suddenly revealed a mortifying weakness. Bonetti, so long insulated from the pressures of his unique situation by England's overall superiority, was now asked a relatively simple question. His response was fatally hesitant. He was like a boy who goes into an examination knowing every answer, then sits staring at the hypnotic blankness of the paper, forcing his mind to focus and his hand to move only when it is too late. Beckenbauer's goal in the sixty-eighth minute, the goal that transformed this match and perhaps this World Cup, was the result of a shot that would not have given the goalkeeper a moment of anxiety on a normal day. Beckenbauer was a little fortunate to find room for it in the first place. He had tried one from short of the eighteen-yard line on the right wing and seen Lee fall in pain as he took the ball between the legs. The rebound went to

the German but when he swerved to his right, outside Mullery
and into the extreme corner of the England penalty area, he
seemed to be a negligible threat. Both Lee and Mullery recalled
afterwards that they stopped worrying when he turned away
from the target, especially when they were aware of him
shooting early from that inauspicious angle. To us on the
sidelines it appeared that the right-foot shot was a reflex at the
end of the run, something to round it off rather than a determined, optimistic attempt at scoring. 'He shot because there
was nothing better to do,' said a Brazilian in the Press stand.
Given the angle and the unfrightening speed of the ball,
those accustomed to the excellence of Bonetti's goalkeeping
waited for him to take two brisk steps to the side and pick it
up or at least fall firmly on it. Instead, he dived in a slow arc
over the ball and left it to travel on into the side of his net.
The impact of that goal was immense. Apart from encouraging
the Germans to hope that their rally could give them more
than an honourable exit, it hit the English with the full chilling
realisation of what it could mean to be without Banks. 'With
a two-goal lead, you would have felt you could let them come
and shoot in at Banksie, that he could have held them out on
his own,' one of the players said later. That blissful illusion of
impregnability merely created yet another burden for Bonetti
to bear on the most unpleasant afternoon of his career.

The alarm that was being kindled in England was not
stifled by Ramsey's decision to substitute Bell for Charlton
within a minute of the goal. Bell had been warming up on
the touchline before the blow but seeing one of their most
feared enemies withdrawn at that point could only raise thd
Germans' morale, persuading some of them that they coule
detect panic in the opposition. Charlton himself was not a
happy man when he reached the bench. 'They're pissing about
too early,' he said as he sat down.

However, Bell did make a spirited entrance. Taking a pass
from Moore, he struck a low shot that Maier saved and then,
served by Ball, broke on the right to precipitate one of the

crucial moments of the match. Hurst dived brilliantly to meet
Bell's low centre at the near post, leaving Schulz and Maier
flailing around his ankles, and flicked his header for the other
side of the goal. It looked guaranteed to go in or at worst
bounce back from the upright (Lee confessed that he waited,
hypnotised, for it to come off the post, instead of following up)
but at the last second it bobbled over the bye-line. English
hearts dropped further when Muller, finding himself one-to-
one with Newton, beat him and steadied for the shot. But when
it came, Bonetti dropped skilfully on the ball.

There was no time to savour the relief. With eighty minutes
played, Peters was belatedly taken off and Hunter shunted into the competition for the first time. That Ramsey ignored the
possible implications of an injury already suffered by Newton,
who was on the ground when the change was made, indicated
that he was extremely anxious to introduce Hunter in place
of an attacking player. His idea, presumably, was that the
most vigorous challenger in British football should win the
ball from the Germans in midfield, above all from the ubiquitous
Grabowski, and hustle them out of their growing confidence.
The idea soon looked sick. Hunter had been on the field only a
few seconds when England lost another goal. The substitution
apparently extended a period of disruption in the defence and
there was a hectic flurry of abortive clearances on the right-
hand side of the penalty box. At last the ball fell conveniently
free in front of Labone and he seemed sure to lift it out of
harm's way. In fact, he swung at it hastily and slid it straight
to Schnellinger. The reaction was a quick, left-footed cross
aimed high towards the far edge of the six-yard area. There
Seeler had slipped behind Mullery – into a position that may
have been offside – and he leapt for a typical back-header.
He did well to make solid contact and could not be choosey
about where he placed the ball, obviously being content to
guide it into the mouth of the goal. That generalised menace
was made murderously specific by Bonetti, who stranded
himself in the no-man's land half-way between his line and

Seeler. The ball looped over the goalkeeper and under the bar. England felt they were the victims of something close to a black miracle. The Germans, who had pushed them into extra-time with a late goal in the Wembley final, were doing so again. Indeed they almost did worse. In the nine minutes that remained (there were barely two after the equaliser in 1966) Beckenbauer's left-foot shot swept just wide of a post and Lohr's high header from an Overath free-kick was sufficiently near to make a few Englishmen close their eyes.

The German surge carried over into extra-time, led first by Lohr and then by Beckenbauer, whose drive from twenty-five yards was touched over by Bonetti. There followed three corners in quick succession, five in two or three minutes, and the English weariness was blatant. Grabowski was veering and and spurting like a power-boat among paddle steamers and even a fresh Hunter, though pounding around strongly, could not subdue him. No one was more distressed now than Labone, but he did manage to move upfield for a shot from Bell's low cross. A marvellously persistent run in on the bye-line by Lee brightened England's prospects a little more but once the change of ends had put Bonetti back in his unlucky goal pessimism swiftly took over again. A centre from Ball that went through Maier's hands should have brought England more than a corner. Another centre, this time high and diagonal from Grabowski deep on the German right wing, should have brought England less than defeat. But this unsubtle stroke killed them. As the ball fell beyond the far post, Lohr rose and forced the tired Newton to head across goal. Muller, so ineffective for so long, had started to move towards the far post but now, with spontaneous perception, he spun round and overtook the ball on its return journey. He was unhindered as he hoisted himself off the ground for a muscular volley. The cameras caught Bonetti in a helpless pose that might have been mistaken for supplication. There were eleven minutes left and England filled most of them with furious aggression. Lee jockeyed the ball round Schnellinger on the bye-line and pushed it across for Hurst to score but the goal was inexplicably disallowed. Lee was not offside and we had seen no foul on Schnellinger. Argument being pointless, England resumed their assault. Mullery, hammering the ball on the run, saw it rise inches too high and Ball, coming in on Hurst's downward header, could not keep his shot from going wide. Appropriately, Newton, who had contributed much to his side's two goals, provided the last flourish by galloping on to Ball's pass and blasting the ball towards Maier. The goalkeeper was beaten but the ball stayed fractionally outside his posts.

So history had repeated itself, with an agonising twist for England. Here it was Beckenbauer who rolled over ecstatically on the turf, much as Ball and Stiles had done at Wembley. Here the German supporters brought their flags and their jubilant klaxons crowding into the centre circle. It was for England to find consolation in the memory of that first hour and of some splendid performances by their players. And to reflect on what might have been, what must have been if Gordon Banks, or for that matter if the real Peter Bonetti, had been in goal.

Almost as soon as they were back at the motel the England players re-emerged from their rooms in swimming trunks and lay on the lawns by the pool, drinking bottles of beer, well within range of the loud and happy conversation of German journalists and supporters eating in the alfresco restaurant. The footballers were making a late gesture towards tanning bodies that had stayed glaringly white under the restrictions imposed to curtail the damaging effects of the sun (Thompson and Sadler had long since emphasised by their colour that their membership of the squad after Quito was honorary). They were also, understandably, making sure that their disappointment remained communal. Not all the victims were there to share the pain. Bonetti was conspicuously absent. He, Moore, Peters and Hurst had been given permission to leave immediately after the match so that they could join their wives and travel on to Acapulco for a holiday. It was not until a day or two later that Bonetti learned, in the course of conversation, that he was being held particularly culpable for what had happened. The men who were left at the Motel Estancia were concerned with their mutual loss rather than recrimination. They were glad of company, their own and that of anyone else who was available. To be alone was to invite a private showing of a horror film in the head. It was better to be out blinking in the sunlight, with other people's voices butting into their thoughts. Their faces had that look of controlled relaxation that comes when men try to keep a distance between what they feel and what they show. Most of the conversation was unnaturally casual, the way it is at funerals. They talked rationally, sometimes lightly, when they must have wanted to scream. All returned to the same unoriginal but acceptable analogy to describe how they felt. It was like being in a nightmare, waiting for the reassurance of waking up. Alan Ball, red stubble glinting on his chin, plunged into the small pool as if that would do it. 'Look at the pace of 'im, look at that *pace*,' he snorted as he splashed across. Later Ball would tell us that he had thrown the medal awarded for competing in the World Cup out of his bedroom window. His father, sitting up to an ungodly hour to telephone from England, had told him before the match, with that wet-eyed sense of drama that goes with the toughness of the family, that he should 'go out and die for England' if he had to. Ball never lacks such willingness but this time it had not been enough and he came back out of the water to join in reconstructing the nightmare. As in all nightmares, the central figures and events were at once familiar and unfamiliar. Bonetti was somehow not Bonetti.

'The Cat didn't look like the Cat out there,' somebody said. 'That first goal were a Weetabix goal,' one of the players added. 'And the second wasn't all that much. But you've got to feel sorry for Peter. He was only told he was in about half-an-hour before we left for the ground. No wonder he was a bunch of nerves. If he'd had a lot of the ball early on he might have sorted it out but there was hardly anything to do before

Beckenbauer stuck that one in. In that sort of situation goal-keepers have no chance to find their feet.'

The afternoon had brought its own special misery to Banks, too. On his television set, England were still a goal ahead when his room-mate, Alex Stepney, came in with the shattering truth. Banks would not believe that there was no joke involved. Neil Phillips, as if his own memories of the day were not bleak enough, had the task of convincing him.

As the players sought to dissect the calamity, they wondered if they had attempted a containing game too early and if the timing and the nature of Ramsey's substitutions had been right. Several were apparently in agreement that, despite the skilful efforts of Bell, Bobby Charlton should not have been called off when he was. There was doubt about whether Lee should have played out the full two hours. Perhaps neither Peters nor Lee should have been fielded in the first place. Out of five-and-a-half hours' football in the World Cup Peters had not shown his true quality in more than a few minutes and Lee freely admitted that *his* performances had been an insult to his abilities, that he had never been able to get started in Mexico. But these points had to be set beside the paramount fact that the holders were out because the best goalkeeper in the world turned sick and one who is only slightly less gifted was over-whelmed by the suddenness of his promotion. In sport disaster often feeds upon itself; but this was a sickeningly gluttonous example.

Those who chatted smugly in distant television studios about the tactical blunders of Ramsey were toying with the edge of the issue. His theories are open to severe criticism but the quarter-final with West Germany can never be seen as a condemnation of them. Errors there were. Ramsey, preoccupied with saving Bobby Charlton for the semi-final, almost certainly withdrew him prematurely, removing the one midfield man whose vast experience told him that England were permitting their rhythm to become too languid. On the other hand, if the manager had decided it was time to rest Charlton on the bench, as was indicated by the sight of Bell warming up on the touchline, he should have done so without delay. Instead, he hesitated, Beckenbauer scored and the substitution that followed immediately had the appearance of a panic measure. When all this has been said, however, Ramsey still has a right to his claim that his side were felled by something close to an act of God. It is true that at his Press conference after the match he seemed to many neutrals too anxious to exonerate himself. 'He lost his last chance of a moment of grandeur,' wrote one Latin-American journalist. 'He was ill-mannered to Mexican officials and the Press alike. He dismissed the German victory as a lucky one, saying their first two goals came from defensive mistakes. He said he had never seen England give away goals like that. He hinted that no tactical instructions from him could have averted defeat. All of this most of us believed to be true but it was not for him to say it. It was as if he was disowning his team in defeat.'

This was another classic instance of Ramsey misrepresenting himself. He is capable of much that is regrettable but never of disowning the men who play for him. His provocative insistence that he does not have to be diplomatic to anyone, the near-paranoid suspicion that civility is likely to be confused with weakness, that every question is a booby trap, every questioner (especially a non-English one) is a potential assassin of his character – this attitude combined with the objective knowledge that the match should never have been lost produced an impression of ungracious bitterness. But there is another side to Ramsey. Many will be reluctant to take the trouble of finding it, just as his retort would probably be that he never asked them to bother. Yet it seems a pity if the warmth he is able to evoke in his players and his close assistants is confined to that inner circle, mystifying the majority beyond it. In those hours after the suicide in León, outsiders had a glimpse of an attractive Ramsey. After waiting for a time in his room, receiving a discreet flow of sympathisers, in a silence so deep that one could almost hear the bubbles in the champagne that was being drunk, he came out to sit among his players and drink a little more of the wine Bobby Charlton had bought to mark his record number of caps. Ramsey did nothing remarkable. Mainly he talked quietly of his pride in managing men who have proved they were no false world champions. Whatever he had suggested at his Press conference, he now emanated a sense of complete identification with them, a loyalty emotionally reciprocated when several players threatened physical harm to any reporters who dared to criticise him. Unmistakably, he was suffering as much as anyone. He was not angry or remorseful. He was sad, and the simple human vulnerability the emotion conveyed made up for many moments when he had seemed arrogant and antisocial. Like many of us, Alf Ramsey is a poor judge of the parts of his nature that should be shown to the world.

That night most of the British who were in León got rather drunk; not tearful drunk, or roaring resentful drunk, just defiantly high. The players sang and danced (with or without partners) and spontaneously turned the wake into a party. They were out, but they had no doubt they were at least the second-best team in the competition and they were not inclined to slink away from Mexico. It was strange that the final impression left by those noisy, lubricated hours should be one of dignity. Quite a few people, including some who would deny being sentimental as vehemently as they would deny being English, felt it was a privilege to get drunk with them.

England 2   *West Germany 3*

7 *The Semi-Finals*

ITALY *v.* WEST GERMANY

Aztec Stadium, June 17

Italy had been eloquent against Mexico, once stung into heightened action. Yet in considering the likely nature of this semi-final one was still gripped by the sense of enigma about the Italians. There seemed little doubt that West Germany had now exposed the full range of their strengths and weaknesses; that they had indeed been stretched to the point of peril. It was not the case with Italy. Israel, unexpectedly, had made them hurry; Mexico had provoked a chastening retaliation. But stubbornly they remained the half-known force of the tournament, the extent of their full power still concealed. The components of imagination, speed and physical aggression had all been seen impressively at work. But one was left wondering whether they could all be brought to function simultaneously; and, if so, how formidable would be the unit?

What was not in question by this stage was that Italy had been determined to impose their pre-decided pace on their matches. They had intended to last, and had not been deflected. Feruccio Valcareggi, the coach, made a comment after the quarter-final win that expressed the party's approach to the whole tournament. 'The tactic here must be to be strong at the end,' he said.

Italy had exorcised that grisly spectre of their recriminative collapse in 1966. But Italian football has for too long nourished its role as the raw nerve of the game. It was beyond hope that the national side could contest this World Cup without the distractions of public bickering in which the Italian Press traffics with the sinister skill of the *agent provocateur* and the hysteria of a deceived lover. Gianni Rivera, the definition of romanticised Italian youth, with the faun's eyes and the delicate symmetry of build, provided the material for a quarrel in the Italian camp which threatened to cripple the squad by fractiousness as the competition began. Rivera, a truculent, handsome, engaging and proud hero, reacted to Valcareggi's dismissal of him from the first-choice team with bitter resentment. Valcareggi was on the point of sending him home, which might have ended the dispute or provoked mutiny. The president of the Italian F.A., Artemio Franchi, made a soothing intervention. Rivera stayed. The quarrel was overtaken by football, but its divisive influence never left the Hotel Parque des Princes, where the party stayed in tense luxury, all through the tournament.

In the hotel garden, around the swimming pool, the Italians had the look of cliquishness, of too many brittle temperaments in too confined a space. Rivera, seeming younger than twenty-six, was a princeling with a knot of favourites; Riva, built like a quick heavyweight, with a promise of great violence in the shut face, was a brooding, unapproachable king; Bertini was some kind of aspiring contender, flexing his big muscles in the pool's reflection.

But Giacinto Facchetti, the team captain, was a centre of easy, frank common sense, the long figure extending bonily in every direction out of a high-backed chair. The plain manner, the firm opinion, the disregard for quibbling diplomats: added to his build and the long-boned face, they increased his similarity to Jack Charlton, who also likes to deal exclusively with the tangible. Facchetti shrugged through his confirmation that Italy's unforgettably dull, defensive performance against Uruguay – surely the most cynical event of the competition – had been exactly according to instructions. Yes, it was true that the team had been seriously frightened by the exhausting effects Toluca's altitude had on them in their first match, against Sweden. The two doctors with the party had recommended the use of oxygen at Toluca, but the players had rejected it, mostly because they felt they might come to rely on it too much. But they got over that fright, and even against Mexico they had been the less affected, he thought.

Facchetti reflected a team which had started the tournament by masking its fears and had eventually expunged them. The dissension still hovered in the background, Rivera insisting forty-eight hours before the semi-finals that he would never accept being 'half a player'. But clearly there was extreme professional discipline in a squad which could suffer these psychological pressures and still pursue their plans so relentlessly. One had more respect for Italy as one became more familiar with their weaknesses.

This semi-final was the more fascinating in prospect for the strong contrast between the teams. There was an open-faced simplicity about the West Germans, in such direct opposite to the Italians' wariness and stealth. Germany were the most popular of the European sides in the tournament because of their vivacity, their high optimism. They were the most free-scoring team in the competition so far, with ten goals; Gerhard Muller, their exciting striker, was the leading individual scorer, with seven. Clearly there was no lack of enterprise here. But the team had been seriously damaged by that two-hour match against England three days before. Horst Hottges, injured then, was not now available to the defence; Klaus Fichtel had to be replaced in midfield because his extreme tiredness after the England game still lingered. These two losses were troubling.

Now as the game started, in a stadium nearly full in a cloudy warmth, it was quickly one particular Italian asset that held the eye: the attackers' capacity to conjure instant danger. Hottges had been replaced by Schulz, who was given the job of marking Roberto Boninsegna. The Italian, so light and nimble, exploited the German's slowness without mercy. But it was Boninsegna's immediate response to opportunity that brought him the game's first goal in the eighth minute: a deflection off a German body, the ball invitingly loose, and Boninsegna swung his left foot hard, the shot swerving in low to beat Maier's dive.

That considerable shift in the flight of the shot suggested that Boninsegna might have benefited twice from fortuitous German contact with the ball. The goal was no less significant in this player's career. He had been called into the Italian party only a few hours before it left for Mexico, when Pietro Anastasi had to be hurried to hospital with an intestinal cyst. Boninsegna had already justified his inclusion by his selfless persistence alongside Riva in all Italy's games; but this goal was his first, and it was overdue.

Riva himself soon repeated the Italian message about their avidity for the German net. A long cross from the right seemed to be dropping too far away from him to be of use, but with an extraordinary, elastic lunge he achieved a left-foot volley which Maier reached only by a dive.

Such a beginning by Italy, with De Sisti, Domenghini, Mazzola and Bertini all pressing forward with a concerted urgency, plainly disconcerted the Germans. Their end of the field for the first quarter-hour had a flustered, over-manned and under-organised look, with Beckenbauer scurrying inelegantly around the edges of the penalty area and Lohr and Muller poised impatiently for the passes which took so long to arrive from that tangled defence. It needed a personal contribution from Beckenbauer to end this confusion.

Suddenly he was running clear with the ball, his team breaking free behind him. He swerved away from Facchetti and was almost in the Italian penalty area when a tackle from behind brought him down. The ball trickled away and over the byeline. The Germans appealed for a penalty. The referee, Arturo Yamasaki, of Mexico, gave a goal kick. The run had given Germany the relief they needed, breaking into Italy's confidence just as it was threatening to be overwhelming. And within two minutes Beckenbauer was going forward with the ball again. This time Mazzola stopped him.

27   West Germany's Gerhard Muller volleys the goal that put England out
of the World Cup

28 Schnellinger scores the first goal for Germany in the semi-finals, equalising in the last minute of normal time. The Italian goalkeeper Albertosi looks rigid on his line

29 The goal that got away . . . Germany's Muller collides with Albertosi in the semi-final, but the ball rolls along the line and past the post. Muller finishes in the net

The crowd sensed a grudging struggle in the making, and there was a hum of tense expectancy in the air. For most of the 90,000 people in the Aztec Stadium no one on the field had any claim on their emotions except by boldness, by the thrill of the invention or the belligerence. Yet the crowd would be close to derangement in their exhilaration before this tempestuous match was over.

As the half hour was passed the pace was notably lifting on the impetus of Overath, Muller and Grabowski, all three involved in plunging runs at the Italian penalty area. Italy's gaping goalmouth was cleared by Bertini, hurtling between Muller and Seeler as the three of them competed for the loose ball. Quickly after the corner kick that followed Muller ran to Patzke's thoughtful short pass and his shot swung away from Albertosi's right post.

Muller's ceaseless mobility was making as much labour for Rosato as Boninsegna's abrupt turns and fleetness were for Schulz. But the German defender was showing the greater frustration. His crushing foul on Boninsegna in the thirty-eighth minute was sour with personal defeat.

Albertosi's goalmouth was taking on the appearance of siege. A six-man wall of Italians cringed at Lohr's free kick; then Riva burst free from the line to collide with the German as he was about to strike at the rebound. Again the wall was formed; this time Lohr put the ball just over the bar.

Yet the first half left us with a memory of the same kind of Italian enterprise with which it had begun. Riva, baulked by the short, thick figure of Vogts, paused for an instant and then stabbed the ball abruptly between Vogts's legs. Maier, astonished, was late at the far post as the ball barely cleared it.

Rivera once more played a second half in place of Mazzola, although the substitution appeared to have less to support it than the same tactic had against Mexico. Then Mazzola's repeated, penetrative running had effectively broken the resolve of the Mexican defence. But this match had not developed in the same way. It was now rising to its peak of

P

combat, and Rivera's first movements looked far too relaxed. Surely no other Italian player, having lived through the first hour of this game, would have been so detached as Rivera was when Riva sent him cleanly into the German penalty area with an exact ground pass. Rivera might have been in a pre-match kickabout, he was so gentle with the ball. Maier, well positioned, was permitted a simple save.

There was nothing remotely associated with patience in Germany's work now. The weight of their attacks, with Libuda and Held brought on to refresh the running, was a far greater challenge than Italy had met before in the tournament. The Italians were back to their familiar pattern of eight defensive and withdrawn midfield men, leaving Riva and Boninsegna to wait for the long ball; but at last a real test had come for their skills and their nerve.

Both proved adequate. Perhaps the Italian nerve was the most influential factor of the match. Few defensive players in the world can better the calm of De Sisti and Facchetti when the pressure is strongest. The Germans were never surprising enough in their attacks, whatever the pace and brave stamina of them, to quite ruin the Italian order.

But West Germany had their misfortune. A tremendous half-volley from Overath hit the bar; Beckenbauer was callously felled by Cera in mid-stride, and denied a penalty when one seemed unavoidable; in one gripping flurry of drama Held's shot beat Albertosi and Rosato kicked off the line, the ball flew to Seeler, who crumpled under a tackle as he tried to shoot, and Schnellinger flicked the ball over the bar.

The orange figures of the Aztec clock said that time had run out for West Germany. Mr Yamasaki had let play run on for well over a minute, to compensate for interruptions, when Schnellinger scored the goal that would ensure this match a place in football's exotica. Held sent a long, high cross from the left. Schnellinger, running frantically from outside the penalty area, had to leap at the ball to reach it. He got both feet to it. Albertosi was helpless.

The remainder of the event was perpetually amazing. When Schnellinger scored, equalising for Germany, the crowd produced a noise that made the eyes shudder. In this uproar Schnellinger collapsed under a mass of German flesh, including that of Maier, who had sprinted the length of the field from his goal-line. The Italians mostly stood with their mouths sagging in dejection, although Bertini fell full length with both hands cupping his tears. Within a few seconds the referee whistled for the end of the ninety minutes. Soon we would have the marvels of the day.

When extra-time began Beckenbauer was seen to be playing with his right arm held in a sling across his chest. Italy had made a substitution, taking off Rosato for Fabrizio Poletti, who immediately made two dramatic contributions. First he hacked down Held alarmingly close to the Italian penalty area, then he intervened between Albertosi and Muller as both were poised for the ball, and managed to help Muller send it rolling into the net. The stadium was again a dancing bedlam. Bertini once more was prostrate on the grass, drumming both fists into it.

There was a lowering sepia gloom over the scene. An exhausted desperation was showing in the yellowing faces of the players. Four minutes after Poletti's calamitous jostle with Muller Italy had drawn level again. At last Rivera's fastidious touch had found its situation. His chip, hit as softly as if he was kicking crystal, dropped the ball at Burgnich's feet at the far post. The German defence wheeled wearily towards him as the shot went in. And five minutes later Italy scored their third: a short, sharp stab forward from Rivera, another diagonally from Domenghini, and Riva was hunching away from Schnellinger to drive low past Maier from an acute angle.

The crowd were seldom in their seats during this half hour; they roared and howled, besotted by the emotion in the melodrama. It was now beyond the players' physical capacities, in their tiredness, for them to make any pretence at midfield build-up or defensive discipline. The grass between the two penalty areas was uncontested. But the thrill of the entertainment never diminished. The game was freakish, and magnificent.

Its culminating astonishment came in the space of ninety seconds during the second period of extra time. While several players were motionless in postures of agonised exhaustion, Albertosi and Poletti engaged in bewildering comedy. The goalkeeper flung the ball against Poletti's back; the defender, trying to retrieve it, slapped it with one hand just outside the penalty area; Overath took the free kick, Seeler's header bounced high in front of Albertosi, who just managed to tip over the bar; Libuda's corner was headed forward by Seeler, but blocked, and Muller forced the ball in. The crowd were still in rapturous voice as Boninsegna, achieving the most courageous acceleration, lifted his cross from the left and Rivera, as sweetly as if posing for the camera, met the ball side-footed to score.

The game's final image was of despair: Beckenbauer surging towards the Italian penalty area, the injured right arm rigid in its sling, then waiting for Muller's return pass and sagging limp as Cera and Burgnich won the ball to destroy the Germans' last hope. In a few seconds the match was over, the crowd still sustaining their dazed ovation as the players lurched away into the tunnel.

Italy, so resolute before in their disregard of excitement in their football, had at last been forced into thrilling us, and then all but suffocated us with entertainment. Yet they had won with the counter-punch. They had not quite been stimulated out of character.

Italy 4   West Germany 3

BRAZIL *v.* URUGUAY

Guadalajara, June 17

The moment it became clear that Brazil's opponents in the semi-final would be Uruguay, and that the match would be played in Guadalajara, the mountain air of Jalisco was heavy with old and new grudges. By the time the Uruguayans arrived at the airport, muttering that they had been victimised but would still win through to the final, the atmosphere was about as pleasant as it was in New York before the second fight between Joe Louis and Max Schmeling. Having seen how ruthless they could be against countries who evoked no special emotions in them, we were alarmed by the thought of what they might do in an embittered mood.

Uruguay's immediate grievance was that they had been shunted exhaustingly around the World Cup centres of Mexico. They claimed they had been promised that, after playing their earlier matches in Puebla and Toluca, they would be allowed to have their semi-final in Mexico City. Instead, they were being made to travel to Guadalajara which was lower and hotter and had been Brazil's home ground since the first kick of the competition. FIFA denied that any promises had been given or that Brazil were being favourably treated and told the Uruguayans brusquely to get on with the game. The party of dark, powerful men looked more forbidding than ever as they headed sullenly for the Camino Real Hotel.

Even without this complication, the match would have been a tense experience for the Brazilians. They always worry far more about the Uruguayans and the Argentines than about European teams and in this case their nervousness was increased by memories of 1950. That was the year when Brazil staged the World Cup, creating the largest stadium ever built to do justice to the event and their passionate enthusiasm. They had beaten Uruguay in earlier meetings that season and when they faced their neighbours in the deciding match needing only a draw to take the Trophy, 200,000 people crowded

Maracana for a national celebration. What they got was a traumatic lesson in anticlimax. After threatening to sweep the opposition off the field in the first half and at last taking the lead at the start of the second, Brazil lost two goals and the World Cup to a spirited counter-attack. It was the kind of wound that never really heals and now, in Guadalajara, it bled freely enough to give the Brazilians an exaggerated sense of mortality as they approached the semi-final. Few were reassured by the knowledge that, of all the matches played between the two countries since 1950, Uruguay had won only three. 'They are different in the World Cup,' we were told. 'They could lose ninety times out of a hundred and still win in the World Cup. There, they are more determined, tougher, more cunning. They are very dangerous.'

The Brazilian neurosis about 1950 was, one felt, even more dangerous, especially when journalists began urging the players that a full, cleansing revenge must be exacted. As Mário Zagalo said later: 'Some of the boys they were talking to were not even born in 1950. Yet they were burdening these players with all that old resentment and frustration. It was the sort of help you can do without.' The Brazil camp took a less impatient attitude to word from a television commentator that the referee appointed for the match, José Ortiz de Mendibil, was on suspiciously cordial terms with the Uruguayans at the Camino Real. When they were told that he had been seen drinking and chatting with the enemy, the Brazilians despatched the imposing Captain Claudio Coutinho and another official to make their feelings known. Coutinho went to the hotel and had a message delivered to Mendibil, telling him that he was being watched closely.

Neutrals, seeing the strongest force in world football so profoundly disconcerted, found themselves once again admiring the qualities that enabled the Uruguayans to earn such respect in spite of having only two-and-a-half million population and only two great clubs. Their achievement is astonishing, for all the strength resides in Nacional and Peñarol of Montevideo,

which invariably provide all but a small minority of the
national squad. It is as if the city of Glasgow, through Rangers
and Celtic, regularly took on the world. Glaswegians may see
nothing outrageous in that but most of us would find it an
unlikely proposition. The dominance of Nacional and
Peñarol is so complete that the game as a whole in Uruguay
stumbles from one economic crisis to the next. Yet no country
can ever take the field confident of beating Uruguay. Certainly
Brazil were conspicuously short of swagger when they came out
at the Jalisco Stadium on an afternoon that was inevitably hot
but held an encouraging threat of rain.

Their apprehension was not lessened by the ferocity of
Uruguay's beginning. It would be unfair to say that the men
in the Uruguayan back line looked as if they had been chosen
according to height and weight; they were, as it happened,
notably well balanced and skilful for their size. Nevertheless
the comparisons made earlier in this book with tag-team wrestlers and night club bouncers require no apology, as Mújica
demonstrated by fouling Jairzinho viciously from the back as
he played the ball to Carlos Alberto. Mújica was formally
cautioned and so was Fontes soon afterwards when he swept
the feet from under Everaldo. At least the referee appeared to
be giving a swift answer to those who doubted his impartiality.

Uruguay's violence was the chilling tip of an iceberg of
defensiveness. Their apparently depthless conservatism demanded that Cortés, nominally a midfield player, reject any
constructive impulse as if it were a fatal contagion. His sole
concern was to smother Gérson and he stayed so close that
occasionally they looked like one man with four legs. Pelé was
similarly attended by Montero Castillo and all Tostão's
subtle drifting and darting seldom took him out of the long
shadow of Ancheta. Nevertheless, Tostão did provide Brazil's
one hopeful moment in the first quarter-of-an-hour with a
short pass just inside the penalty area but Gérson was blocked
as he tried to exploit it.

Having adopted a stance about as fluidly aggressive as

Edinburgh Castle's, Uruguay were presumably content to hope that an opponent's error would give them a chance of a goal. Such a shamelessly barren philosophy hardly deserved the extraordinary vindication it was granted as early as the eighteenth minute when Brazil contributed not one but two unbelievable mistakes. First Brito, without any excuse, pushed the ball straight to Morales, giving him the opening for a sprint along the left wing and a curling pass behind Everaldo and in front of Cubilla beyond the far post. Cubilla controlled the ball on his chest but had to take it too close to the bye-line, so that the shot was struck slackly across the face of the goal. Félix then supplied the second blunder. Moving like a man trying to walk on golf balls, he stumbled and groped across his line as the ball bounced languidly into the far side of the netting.

Félix looked disgusted. Only the Uruguayans did not. Several of the other Brazilians were on the verge of despair, none more obviously than Gérson who held his head as if to staunch a wound. Pelé ran calmly through the shattered ranks of the team and collected the ball to bring it back for the kick-off. All the way to the centre circle he was talking soothingly to those around him. He knew how debilitating mutual recriminations could be and he did not intend to let anything stand between him and the World Cup.

A free kick brought Brazil's first opportunity for retaliation. Rivelino's feint misled the four-man wall but when the ball was slipped wide Carlos Alberto reacted too slowly and was crowded out before he could shoot. Their attacking was still disturbingly tentative, however, and the appeals for a penalty as Pelé went down were self-consciously optimistic. The referee acknowledged the difference when Jairzinho was fouled collecting Pelé's pass but, though the kick was only twenty yards out, within that crescent of space from which Brazilian set-pieces had done such damage in previous matches, it produced nothing. There was more positive menace in a drive by Clodoaldo from Rivelino's pass and a first-time centre by

Gérson that let Pelé in for a diving header. Both flew wide.

Uruguay's assurance increased in direct proportion to Brazil's anxiety. The rear-line defenders, especially the tall, slim Ancheta, used their reach and strength as they converged on the ball with the lunging briskness of swans snatching bread away from nervous ducks. The Brazilians were not shy of physical contact. It was composure, not courage, that they lacked, a fact emphasised by Carlos Alberto when he was given a caution for hooking the feet from under Morales. The full-back returned to more sensible ways with a hard centre which was instantly flicked on by Pelé. Jairzinho narrowly failed to get to the pass in a telling position. When Pelé was fouled following a corner the Uruguayans arranged five men in a wall for the free kick. Rivelino succeeded in curving the ball over the barrier but Mazurkiewicz edged it above his crossbar. Through most of this time of frustration for Brazil Rivelino had been admirably prominent but now he made himself hazardously so by dwelling on the ball long enough to invite a harsh foul by Maneiro. Fortunately, there was no lasting injury, except to Maneiro's reputation. And he was not likely to worry deeply about being the fourth man to be cautioned.

As the interval approached, Brazil at last began to show signs of regaining belief in themselves. Tostão, who gives the impression that he would remain coolly calculating if dropped head-first into a pool of piranha fish, had been working with quiet persistence to smooth the frenetic tendencies out of the team. 'I knew we had to steady ourselves and keep rolling the ball around, to find our rhythm and make our greater skill tell,' he said afterwards. 'We had to remind ourselves and the Uruguayans that this was a football match, that the better footballers should win it'. Late in the first half Tostão exemplified his ideas perfectly with his part in one of the most brilliant and satisfying manoeuvres we were to see in the whole of the World Cup. Jairzinho, deep on the right, began it with a forward pass to Tostão, who leaned back against the challenge of

Ancheta to push the ball crisply outside to Pelé. By the time
the ball was at its second destination, Jairzinho was already
racing past Tostão and as Pelé's measured pass looped towards
the penalty spot Jairzinho was swooping in to meet it. It is
almost an insulting under-statement to say this amalgam of
imagination, economy and highly deliberate precision was
worth a goal. Jairzinho was clear and seemed poised to take
one but as he sought to bring the ball down it leapt treacherously
off his right instep and out of his range.

We could feel Uruguay's relief rising into the stands like a
breeze. Mújica celebrated with a renewal of his earlier viciousness. But Brazil had rediscovered their identity and with the
electronic clock showing zero, confirming that the first half
had gone into injury time, they scored a goal that said as much
for their tactical intelligence as for their unequalled virtuosity.
Gérson played a major part in it without touching the ball. He
had, as he told later, tested the determination of Cortés by
taking the Uruguayan upfield into the attack, out on the left
wing, out on the right wing. 'Still he would not leave me for a
second. I realised there was only one place to take him – back
into our defence. Since they were not interested in attacking,
that would mean that Cortés was out of the match. There
would be one body fewer between us and the goal. So I took
him back and told Clodoaldo to move up and do my job. They
did not expect the change and they did not adjust to it. Cortés
stayed faithfully with me. Clodoaldo had freedom.'

No one could have done more with the freedom than
Clodoaldo did in those last few seconds of the half. After
receiving the ball from Everaldo on the left he sent it along
the wing to Tostão, who had cunningly advanced near the
touchline. Tostão steadied, glanced up to check on the progress
of Clodoaldo's hurtling run from midfield and, with that
delicately powerful left foot, steered the ball in a long horizontal
arc across the unbalanced defence. It fell with delicious accuracy
into the runner's stride ten or twelve yards out and he hit
it unhesitatingly with his right foot to smash it beyond

Mazurkiewicz's left side. 'Some of the best balls you give are by luck,' Tostão said later. 'But that one went just where it was meant to go. I saw Clodoaldo was running through and I aimed the pass where I thought he would want to meet it.'

Clodoaldo had no complaints but if he or the other Brazilians imagined they would be received with congratulations in the dressing room they were soon disillusioned. Mário Zagalo is a small, spare man whose neat, alert features are usually suffused with a healthy but unremarkable colour. He can be sharp but is nearly always calm, seeking words to match the cool, level gaze of eyes that are yellowish brown. One of his middle names, Lobo, means wolf but he has had the reputation in the past of being so unsavage as to seem excessively accommodating, particularly to those in authority. His principal virtues have been seen to be intelligence and unremitting application to his duties, justifying the nickname of his playing days, The Ant. Now in a dressing room of the Jalisco Stadium the ant turned man-eater. The Brazilian players straggled in to find their manager purple in the face, bellowing swear words they had suspected to be beyond his vocabulary. 'They got a great shock,' Zagalo recalled after the World Cup. 'They had never seen me act like that or heard me use that kind of language. I told them their play in the first half was ridiculous. I said I could not recognise them out on the field. Then I did something I thought I would never do. I criticised the opposition. I said the Uruguayans were nothing. "You are the only people who don't seem to know you are much better than they are," I told my players. "Look at their record. They have scored three goals in four matches. You have scored twelve. Yet you are treating them as equals. It is crazy." I sent them out to play like Brazil.'

They did. Jairzinho was the first to indicate the new spirit, accelerating away from Mújica and evading another tackle to drive across a low centre from the bye-line. Even the excellent Mazurkiewicz had a struggle to cut it out. Next, Carlos Alberto nearly curled a pass to Pelé but Ancheta, who stands almost high enough to have an altitude problem at sea level, made an intercepting header. Jairzinho, who had been used all along by Zagalo as a spearhead, breaking as often into the middle as on the right wing, once again charged disruptingly into the thicket of blue shirts in the Uruguayan penalty area and, as he challenged, the ball spun vertically into the air. Pelé, coming in first, tried to put it away with the outside of his right foot but did not make a clean contact and Mazurkiewicz saved.

The match was vibrantly alive now, its tempo rising minute by minute as Brazil's great players emerged from the unnatural meekness of the first half. In those forty-five minutes Pelé had been so restrained that many were persuaded he was craftily lulling the opposition into complacency. Honesty obliged him to refute that complimentary theory and admit that he had been inhibited by the close marking of Montero Castillo and the general psychological sluggishness of the team. Clodoaldo's goal was, he felt, crucial in relieving the pressure. Whatever the effect of that or of Zagalo's revivalist meeting at the interval, Pelé came into the second half as if he had resolved to remind the Uruguayans that they were against the best player in the world. He was not merely at his most vigorous, exploding on unforeseen runs as if in response to a gun that only he could hear, checking and swerving and doubling back, the religious medal around his neck glinting as he spun in the afternoon sunshine. He was also at his most outrageously ambitious, attempting plays that the fantastic heroes of our boyhood comics would have found taxing. At the heart of Pelé's game is a joyful pursuit of the impossible. He has dominated the mythology of world football as no man before him ever did, scoring a thousand goals and creating ten thousand moments of exhilarating beauty. But he is happily dissatisfied. He does not hide the insistent desire to score one goal that will stand apart from all the others, a goal that will be impossible until he makes it possible, one that nobody else can emulate: Pelé's goal. He had sought it against Czechoslovakia, lifting the ball from his own half of the centre circle in an incredibly long and accurate

arc over the goalkeeper and just wide of the posts. We sensed
he was in a mood to reach out for it again. We were right, but
first we had to put up with some less edifying sights. It was
amusing to see Ubiñas play the giant by picking the ball off
the ground with one hand, as casually as someone preparing
to serve on the tennis court. But Uruguayan size and strength
were not always funny. Jairzinho did not laugh when he was
hurled several feet into the air by a body check. Pelé was the
next victim of the opposition's growing uneasiness. He broke
from a melée on the left edge of the halfway line and went past
man after man towards the goal. Virtually the entire Uruguayan
defence, Ubiñas, Ancheta, Fontes and those other intimidating
men, were scrambling and plunging in an effort to stop him.
Finally, as he moved into the penalty area he was dragged
down. To most of us it was undeniably a penalty but the referee
convinced himself that the offence had occurred outside the
area and awarded a free kick. Rivelino dummied as if to take
it, then left it to Pelé. Astonishingly, the shot was spooned all of
fifty feet wide of the goal. Perhaps it was surprise at that
reprieve that caused Mazurkiewicz to mishit his goal-kick so
that it dropped to Pelé about thirty-five yards out. The
goalkeeper received a second surprise of a different kind, for
Pelé chose this moment to bid again for the unique goal.
Where almost any other player would have tried to bring the
ball down and take aim or to close on Mazurkiewicz, he
screwed his body into position for a magnificent volley, hammering it straight back into the middle of the goal. The
reflexes, the athleticism and the technical finesse involved in
achieving such spontaneous exactness were scarcely believable.
It took a marvellous somersaulting save by Mazurkiewicz,
leaping from outside the line of his left-hand post, to transform
it into an unforgettable near-miss.

Soon Pelé was working for a more conventional goal. After
Jairzinho had made a fine run along the right, cut inside and
eased the ball back, Pelé came on to it with the high-stepping
action with which he often moves into his shots. He struck the

ball well but it went low outside the upright. Tostão, penetratively intelligent as ever, then made room for a shot but it was with his weaker right foot. Mazurkiewicz then met a bigger problem. A pass misplaced by Fontes in midfield went to Clodoaldo and when he sent the ball straight forward Pelé, on the right with his back to the distant goal, made a marvellously concealed flick square to Tostão on his inside. Jairzinho had seen the possibilities and was already at a gallop on the right as Tostão guided the ball brilliantly outside Mújica, almost brushing his toes. Showing his habitual courage, Jairzinho went past the defender with a breezy rush, like a train passing a derelict station, resisted further interference and slid the ball decisively across Mazurkiewicz's right side into the net.

Uruguay's retort was bitter. Ancheta fouled Pelé, Clodoaldo was felled by Montero Castillo and while he was still on the ground Jairzinho, too, was brought down. Soon Mújica, who had frequently ill-used Jairzinho, found the Brazilian punching him violently on the back while the ball was out of play. There was some danger that the Uruguayans would give their convincing impersonation of a lynch mob but, fortunately, their anger stopped short of mayhem. Of the wholesome action that infiltrated those rough minutes, the most interesting was a slow, graceful leap by Mazurkiewicz as he clutched Gérson's drive and a deflected shot from Cortés which Félix held. Neither save compared in quality or significance with the next one made by Félix. It can be said to have settled the match. The necessity for it came from neglect of the threat always presented by Cubilla. The winger, round as a panda but elusive as a snake, was unrestricted as he jumped for a long, angled centre from the left. He was just inside the far post and near the six-yard line when he struck his strong, downward header. Félix, so often a caricature of uncertainty, dived left as if the very impact of the header had released a spring, and parried the ball superbly.

The Uruguayans had had enough. But Brazil had not. When many would have been glancing at the changing figures on the clock to see the last minute or so being counted away, they scored a third thrilling goal. Carlos Alberto lifted the ball forward and, though Ancheta reached it before Pelé, the clearance did not go beyond Tostão. Pelé, reading the situation before it had taken shape, was moving left as Tostão clipped the ball to him. The break put him wide of Ancheta and with time to steady and keep the advantage over the defender as he scurried back. Pelé jockeyed Ancheta into confused hesitancy on the edge of the penalty area, then, with stunning simplicity, rolled the ball a few feet back into the path of Rivelino. From twenty-two yards that prodigious left foot skidded it past Mazurkiewicz's left side.

Even then, Pelé had not finished. He was prepared to go yet again for the magical goal. The invitation was a diagonal centre from Clodoaldo on the left wing. Pelé came towards it at furious speed from inside-right but Mazurkiewicz, typically alert, raced off his line. It seemed there must be a save in the form of a collision, for the Brazilian could not expect to carry the ball cleanly round the goalkeeper or hope for space to score by hitting it past him. There was, we soon saw, an alternative, though it was one that only Pelé could have envisaged. As the ball came within two or three feet of him he suddenly shrugged his body and paralysed Mazurkiewicz with a miraculous dummy. The ball ran beyond the goalkeeper and Pelé swerved round the other side of him and swung back, changing direction with a muscular wrench. He was first to the ball but even he could not balance himself for the shot he needed and it trundled wide.

Sheltering from the fierce rain that splashed through our shirts as we left the stadium, we drank beer and talked of how Pelé's failures cheapen the successes of others. 'That last caper – it wasn't a bad trailer for the final,' someone said. 'I wonder what he'll do there.' Whatever it was, we knew we would enjoy it much more than the Italians.

Brazil 3   *Uruguay 1*

30 Wolfgang Overath scores West Germany's goal in the third place play-off as Uruguayan goalkeeper Mazurkiewicz reacts too late. Left is Matosas and right (No. 2) is Ancheta

31 Jairzinho finds Pelé's headed pass so precise that there is time for a miskick before the winger takes Brazil's third goal in the Final

32 Carlos Alberto shoots the last goal of the tournament to beat Italy in the Final 4–1

33 Pelé, with Carlos Alberto at his left shoulder, holds the Jules Rimet Trophy

8 Third Place Play-off

URUGUAY *v.* WEST GERMANY

Aztec Stadium, June 20

The third place match in the World Cup is by nature an
occasion for the connoisseur of anticlimax, a half-hearted
struggle for an honour that is less like a laurel wreath than a
crown of thorns. But this game was rousingly to disown its
tepid predecessors, providing upwards of eighty thousand
spectators with an afternoon of hectic entertainment.

The Germans, drained and dejected as they were by that
surrealist marathon against Italy, announced their determination to remain competitive until the last ball had been kicked.
In some cases, however, the spirit was stronger than the flesh.
Beckenbauer, who had laboured through extra-time against
Italy with his right arm in a sling, like an extra in an American
Civil War film, was unfit, and several others were too jaded
to take the field against Uruguay. The Uruguayans had no
such problems, perhaps because there were few footballers
brave or powerful enough to inflict injury on their array of
heavyweights, and their team read as it had done in the
quarter-final and the semi-final.

In the early minutes the South Americans gave alarming
hints that the triviality of the prize would not discourage them
from seeking it with the physical ruthlessness that is too often a
central theme of their game. Before the surprisingly large
crowd had seen more than a glimpse of legitimate action
Fontes had fouled Overath harshly and Ancheta, unembarrassed
by a difference in height of half a foot, had done the same to
Muller. Cortés, Ubiñas and Morales soon followed the violent

example and for a time it seemed that the Germans would conclude their exhausting World Cup with a painful lesson in unarmed combat. Admirably, they showed themselves intent on meeting force with football, drawing reassurance from the precise subtleties of Overath in midfield. From the start his long passes cut through the thick ranks of the Uruguayan defence with a frequency that encouraged Muller to chase the four goals he needed to better Juste Fontaine's individual scoring record in the competition. But Muller had apparently suffered more than most as a result of the four hours of significant action against England and Italy. Having reacted too slowly to benefit from one inviting pass by Overath, he found himself provided with an even more classic ball. It was released ten yards inside the German half and slid treacherously between the square defenders, Matosas and Ancheta. Muller at his sharpest would certainly have scored with such a clear run in on Mazurkiewicz, but now his solid shot was too predictable and the save was confident.

Germany deserved a goal at this point and when they took it after twenty-six minutes Overath, appropriately, was its beginning and its end. Another long pass to Libuda on the right allowed the winger to beat Mújica and centre beyond the far post for Seeler to steer the inevitable header back across goal. Muller, near the penalty spot and under pressure from Matosas, bravely controlled the ball and rolled it out to Overath on the edge of the penalty area. Overath's left-foot shot was low and fierce and though Mazurkiewicz reached the ball he scarcely interrupted its progress.

Instead of being strengthened by this goal the Germans almost instantly began to struggle. The source of their difficulties was unmistakable: the extraordinary nervousness and incompetence of Wolter, who had apparently been given the game in the interests of his morale, since Maier was on the substitutes' bench. Wolter began by missing a cross by Ubiñas and from the corner that was conceded in the salvage operation Montero Castillo's header easily beat the goalkeeper as he came racing impetuously from between his posts. Patzke kicked off the line but was fortunate to see an immediate rebound fly wide. Two headers by Cortés brought anxious leaping saves from Wolter and he had an even narrower escape after Ubiñas took a throw on the right and Maneiro flicked the ball skilfully across the face of the goal. Schnellinger stretched acrobatically to hook away from Montero Castillo.

Schnellinger appeared to injure himself in making that interception, and in the second half his place in the back four was taken by Lorenz. Uruguay, too, made an immediate substitution and theirs produced a more positive advantage. Espárrago came on at centre-forward, turning Morales into an orthodox left-winger. With the departure of Fontes, a midfield player, this gave Uruguay a more attacking formation in preference to the 5–3–2 with which they had begun. Having already lost the taste for mayhem, they were poised to excite the crowd, and did. Unfortunately, they excited themselves noticeably too. A sudden switch from their traditional defensiveness to uninhibited attack was as disconcerting as walking from a dungeon into bright sunlight. They could not find their bearings. This was another world. Never having developed the techniques involved in applying cumulative pressure, the best they could do was to charge like a Highland regiment going over the top.

Nevertheless it took monstrous ill-luck to prevent them from winning the match clearly. Time and again they played the opposition into breathless tangles but the ball revealed an almost supernatural reluctance to enter Wolter's net – despite the encouragement he offered it. There was an early hint of the frustration to come when the goalkeeper dived out foolishly and missed a low centre from Cubilla without being punished, then pranced in helpless agitation as another cross from the right winger carried within a yard of him. Espárrago lunged in on the second, only to cannon off a post and finish in the net, which is where the ball should have been.

A sudden superb volley from Seeler that travelled twenty-two yards to shake Mazurkiewicz's crossbar and a longer shot from Overath that the goalkeeper saved did not blur the Uruguayans' supremacy. An angled centre from Maneiro on the right was headed down on to the foot of the far post by Cubilla and as the ball rebounded over his falling body the winger nearly scored with a backward bicycle kick. Uruguay's luck was already so bad as to be laughable to everyone but themselves, and it deteriorated before the end. Vogts headed away near the goal line and Weber kicked clear from almost behind it. Shortly afterwards Sandoval replaced Maneiro and with sixteen minutes left Lohr came on for Libuda. But the pattern remained as it had been since Ancheta transferred his vast physical presence and unsuspected adroitness with the ball to the spearhead of the Uruguayan attack. Montero Castillo gave driving support from midfield and Cubilla, his talent easily offsetting his swollen waistline, maintained an abundant service from the right. The Germans defended desperately and still required unbelievable good fortune to stay ahead.

In the midst of their scrambling resistance Lorenz was cautioned by the referee for fouling, but the dirtiest and most surprising blow came from Wolter. So inept for so long, he chose to make an incredible save in the last minutes to keep out a splendid header by Ancheta.

The Germans ran round the field with the Mexican flag at the end. They should have carried a hundredweight of horse-shoes.

Uruguay o   West Germany 1

9 *The Final*

BRAZIL *v.* ITALY

Aztec Stadium, June 21

There is a beautiful self-contained quality about a World Cup Final. All the other matches, whatever their own vivid excitements, can only nourish the expectations of that last collision. Earlier days offer sudden death but this is the only one that offers instant immortality. Now the thousand background noises of the competition, the politicking, the training camp gossip, the accusations and insinuations, the boasts and hard-luck stories, are stilled by the imminence of a pure climax. The thousand complex pressures that shape a World Cup have squeezed out all irrelevance and left the single thrilling reality of a game of football. That process of simplification is not always fair but its drama is to do with irrevocability rather than justice. No matter how many start out, in the Final only two can play, and only one can win.

To those of us whose childhood and adolescence left us permanently impregnated with the mythology of football, it is inevitably a moving occasion. Sprinting through the rain to the bare, hard-seated buses that were to take us from the Maria Isabel Hotel to the Aztec Stadium on the morning of Sunday, June 21, we had that heightened sense of anticipation that invests every trivial preliminary with a tremor of pleasure. Every joke seemed funnier, every face friendlier. You could say that our behaviour was childish or you could say that we were reacting normally to the prospect of one of the last great communal rituals available to our society. You can say what you like. We were just glad to be going to the World Cup Final.

The rain thinned and the exhaust fumes thickened as the bus hurried in a series of lunges through traffic that was even more raucously lively than usual. Brazilians, with vast flags streaming behind tall poles thrust from their car windows, weaved hazardously between lanes, seeking Italian victims for their banter. The Italians, for their part, were a minority but not a meek one. Disembarking in a gentle smirr at the Aztec, we were happy to let them get on with it. We could not lose. And yet it would be dishonest to claim total objectivity. Seeing the Brazilians come to this last obstacle was like watching Arkle gallop into the last fence of a steeplechase. A bad fall, even an ungraceful stumble, would be a painful blow to anyone who loved the sport. No one would begrudge Italy victory so long as they beat Brazil at their best. Indeed, if they rose above the highest standards of Pelé and Gérson and Tostão and the rest, the world would be obliged to acclaim them great champions, a team fully deserving to keep the Jules Rimet Trophy as their own property. What no neutral wanted, however, was to see Brazil undersell themselves. It can happen to the finest teams: the brutal anti-climax of an unworthy performance in the final. We suspected that it would not happen to Brazil, that their thinking players, and above all Pelé, would not let it happen. We had flown up with them from Guadalajara and been impressed by their deep calm. Most of the damaging tension had been drained out of them by the defeat of Uruguay. They would obviously be nervous now as the kick-off approached but theirs would be an alert, stimulated edginess, uncomplicated by neurotic apprehensions. At the technical level they admitted that they would have been far more concerned if set to face England, whose zonal marking presented much greater problems than the man-for-man covering of Italy. But no opposition would have frightened them. They believe Brazilian football is made for World Cup Finals and could not wait to prove the point.

In the Press room beneath the stands, we drank the last cups of coffee and exchanged hopes and speculations about what would happen in the next two hours. The Italians, so patiently defensive in the earlier matches that they sometimes appeared willing to wait for opponents to grow old before striking at them with Riva, Boninsegna, Domenghini and the others, were not short of supporters, a few of whom were interested in taking a shade of odds. For the other side, the most compellingly specific argument was put forward by Armando Noguerra, a Rio columnist. Noguerra is not given to extravagant statements or claims to omniscience but now he shook us by saying there was one simple, technical reason why Brazil would definitely win. 'The Italians cannot mark everyone and the Brazil player they will not mark is Gérson. He will be deep in midfield at the start and they will leave him alone. He will have space, he will move through to shoot, probably score and certainly decide the match.' On our way upstairs to our seats, we were tempted to tap his pockets for the clink of a crystal ball.

Outside the stadium, the three preceding nights of thunderstorms had left a scene that was almost Mancunian in its dripping greyness. But here inside, the colour and spirit of the crowd had splintered the dullness of the day. Dressed defiantly for sunshine, the spectators rippled down in a dazzling mass from the high rim of the arena, like garish wallpaper hung under a dirty ceiling. The field looked as lush as an Irish meadow, greener than the Brazilian flags that easily outnumbered the Italian tricolours. On the rich grass the military band, in full battle order and with rifles slung over their shoulders as they played, looked incongruously warlike. They were equipped exactly as they had been at the opening ceremony, as if to remind us that in a country as politically tense as Mexico a festival like the World Cup must be parenthesised with steel.

When the teams came out the Italians threw flowers to the crowd. Whether as a reward or because they were viewed with morbid fascination as condemned men, they claimed almost the entire attention of the photographers thronging the pitch. The Brazilians were left in comparative peace to limber up and even in this exercise Pelé caught the eye, opening his legs with a peculiar sideways motion that carried him round in jaunty circles. At last Herr Rudi Glockner was in the centre circle with his whistle in his mouth, Gérson was impatiently waving the last straggling photographers on to the sidelines and the match these players had been dreaming about for four years was just a breath from beginning.

The first aggressive gesture had, to Italian eyes, the quality of a portent. With only two minutes played, Mazzola made a square pass from the right and Riva stepped forward un-hurriedly to meet it twenty-two yards from goal. There was that familiar impression of cold anger as he swung the left foot and the next time most people saw the ball clearly it was above Félix's head. The goalkeeper touched it over his cross-bar without attempting to conceal his discomfort. Such a blow might have acted as a slap on the rump to many teams, sending them galloping eagerly into attack. But the habits of genera-tions are not easily forgotten and Italy quickly restrained them-selves in readiness for retaliation. Brazil did not let them down. A foul by Bertini on Pelé thirty yards out brought no worrying consequences and a simple shot by Everaldo was equally negligible but there was real concern when Jairzinho sprinted for goal after intercepting a misplaced pass. Facchetti inter-rupted Jairzinho's progress at the cost of a free kick. We had foreseen that the Italians would concede many such kicks dangerously close to their penalty area and had guessed that Brazil, with their mastery of set-piece manoeuvres, would punish them for it. But, while Tostão and Gérson scuffled distractingly in the defensive wall, Rivelino shot unthreateningly high. Rivelino was blatantly ill at ease in these early minutes and for some time afterwards. He was the worst affected of several Brazilian players who were finding difficulty maintaining balance on the wet surface, in spite of having overcome their traditional reluctance to wear long studs. When Carlos Alberto's dangerous centre pressed Albertosi into punching the ball behind, Rivelino was again unsure of his footing as he prepared to take the corner and the kick spun away on an aimless trajectory.

Jairzinho's wanderings were already dragging Facchetti far from the left-back position and leaving room for Carlos Alberto to move up the wing. This had been a basic element in the strategy laid down by Zagalo before the match but, as he sat on the touchline with his clipboard in his hand, the manager must have been pleasantly astonished by the naïve reaction to his ruses. Above all, he must have been even more gratified than Armando Noguerra to find that Gérson was indeed left unmarked in midfield, that the Italian man-for-man covering stopped short of perhaps the most influential builder in the Brazilian side. For the moment, however, it was Carlos Alberto, tall and powerfully upright, who made most impressive use of the freedom he was given. After careful possession play had trapped the Italians into giving space yet again on their left, the full-back drove a low centre across goal and saw it stay just out of reach of Tostão's lunge.

Albertosi's anxiety was balanced at the other end when Riva took the ball through on the left with Domenghini waiting, free and poised to shoot, on the other side of the goal. Untypically, Riva shot wastefully at Félix and Brazil relaxed. But not for long. Having seen his goalkeeper make an uneasy save that left the defence in confusion, Pelé tried to dribble forcefully upfield but was penalised a dozen yards outside the penalty area. Mazzola's free kick from the left took the ball to Riva but, though the header was struck solidly, it carried slightly too high. Almost as soon as the goal-kick had swept the ball away from Félix, the Italian recoil brought it back. Facchetti sent it out of defence to Domenghini, who beat Clodoaldo and passed to Boninsegna. With his long, thick hair slapping the nape of his neck, Boninsegna began one of the thrusting, tenacious runs that would soon make him, and not Riva, Italy's most dangerous attacker. This time he was smothered in yellow shirts on the edge of the area. His disappointment was instantly doubled by a goal for Brazil. It was a fine example of their gift for transmuting the apparently innocent into something deadly.

Facchetti, hurriedly clearing a cross from the Brazilian left, gave away a throw on that side. Tostão threw to Rivelino and he quickly found room for a crisp, well judged centre high over the six-yard line. Pelé, just short of the far post and facing squarely on to the goal, planted both feet firmly for the jump and rose far above Bertini, his hapless marker. Jerking his head back and then forward like the firing hammer of a pistol, Pelé smashed the ball down past Albertosi's left side. We remembered something else the perceptive Sr Noguerra had said. 'For the first time Pelé and Brazil share the same destiny,' he told us. 'In the past there were always two entities, Pelé and Brazil. Their objectives may have been similar but they moved towards them separately. In the past he was never a leader, not even at Santos. Now Brazil and Pelé are integrated. He is leading this team to their destiny'. That goal, its timing and its uncompromising character, represented the best kind of leadership.

It was a commodity Italy were apparently lacking. Their response to the goal was to acknowledge the obvious: that it had been an error to allot to Bertini, an attacking wing-half, the job of subduing Pelé. Feruccio Valcareggi could perhaps advance the ironic excuse that he had long since lost control of team selection. Whoever had control on the field did not improve dramatically on the original miscasting of Bertini. He was moved to right-back, allowing Burgnich to switch on to Pelé. So instead of being an inept central marker, Bertini became an inept right-back. At least he could console himself with the certainty that Burgnich had the worse of the deal, although it did not look that way when Bertini was bustled into fouling Rivelino, justifying a free kick that nearly brought a goal. Rivelino readily misled the defenders by shaping to take the kick, then darted forward on to Pelé's chip. But his feet were still behaving like a comedy skater's and he had to let the ball run past. A moment before, the alarm had been elsewhere as Carlos Alberto, attempting a fancy pass, gave the ball to Riva. Félix raced out to kick away from the Italian's feet but the goalkeeper could only pray when a high, diagonal centre from Mazzola eluded everyone. The crowd sighed, too, as the ball fell wide.

There was further encouragement for Italy in the sight of Tostão (who was normally to be found far upfield, stroking off his cogent passes under heavy pressure from Rosato) chasing far back to clear off his own penalty line. And if Burgnich was sufficiently troubled to earn a caution for hitting Pelé from the back, Piazza was far from composed when he pushed Riva while both may well have been inside the Brazilian area and not outside, as the referee decided. Bertini's free kick was eased wide to Riva but his shot died in the cushioning barricade of defenders.

Boninsegna, harrying with keen intelligence, tirelessly putting himself in those positions that offered his own players a target and denied the opposition peace of mind, was now clearly the searching point of Italy's attack. This was demonstrated once more when he took a pass from Riva, beat Brito and drove the ball a few feet wide. The one other Italian who equalled and perhaps outshone Boninsegna was Mazzola. Mazzola was, unmistakably, the heart of the team, pumping out spirit and purpose from midfield. He is a strong, resilient, abundantly skilled player but his performance was probably even more a definition of courage than of talent. His family has a proud tradition in the game and he seemed determined that his contribution to the World Cup Final would be worthy of it, that his team would never surrender quietly. None of the 112,000 people who filled the Aztec Stadium is likely to forget how he played.

De Sisti, whose imaginative persistence had been a pleasing motif in earlier matches, was largely submerged and it was almost a surprise when he contrived a graceful series of passes with Mazzola on the left. Mazzola was given the shot but Gérson and Carlos Alberto combined to smother it. Gérson, despite the absence of any shadowing opponent, was still content to operate from deep positions. He, and indeed the whole

Brazilian team, gave an impression of great patience. That quality had been discernible in Italy, too, since the start of the competition and the loss of a goal had not ruffled them excessively. Yet the attitudes of the two sides, and the emanations that came from them, were fundamentally different. Italy had Cera sweeping behind a back line of four, and Mazzola, De Sisti and Domenghini as a middle line that only occasionally released a man to support Riva and Boninsegna at the front. Theirs tends to be the patience of a garrison that has laid in supplies to withstand a siege and hopes to step from the fort eventually and find the attackers dead of starvation. Patience with them was a weapon in itself. With the Brazilians it was a launching pad for more spectacular weapons. We assumed confidently that the period of calculation, of weighing up, would be limited, that Gérson would soon come forward, that Pelé would begin to turn the screw as he had done in previous games, that Carlos Alberto would make more runs along the right wing and that Tostão, who was unsuppressed by the adhesive thoroughness of Rosato, would increase the rate of those passes that run out from him like live fuses. All this was different from assuming a Brazilian victory, though some of us did that too. The point was that we were sure the Italians would have to cope with these problems, that in their attempt to find answers would be the resolution of the match, the climax of the World Cup. We sensed in Brazil's restraint during that first half a promise as palpable as the ticking of a time bomb.

The ticking was temporarily drowned, however, when the Italians, armed by an outrageous error, produced a blast of their own. Jairzinho had just made a splendid run that led to passes between Tostão and Pelé and a shot from Tostão which had to be right-footed, and therefore comparatively weak, when Italy found a surge that pressured Brazil into rough defence. A foul by Pelé on De Sisti was swiftly followed by Brito's on Riva. Before the strain had eased Brito, in a tightening situation in front of goal but perhaps thirty-five yards out, played the ball square towards Clodoaldo on the Brazilian left. It was, blatantly, a time for a simple, forceful clearance but Clodoaldo chose to be clever and attempted a back-heel flick to Everaldo. If Clodoaldo had been unaware that Boninsegna was descending on him, he soon saw the implications of the forward's presence. Boninsegna snatched the ball away and sprinted for the penalty area. He might still have been delayed crucially, for Carlos Alberto and Brito were striving to converge on him. But Félix, fatally miscalculating the percentages, ran from his line. In the muddled collision over the ball on the edge of the area, the bones that crunched most loudly were those of Brito and his goalkeeper. Boninsegna regained his balance long before they did and pursued the ball as it broke out towards the left. When he reached it Riva was also in attendance and might have scored. But, fittingly, the man who had made the chance was permitted to take it. He did so briskly, turning the ball back into goal ahead of the scrambling Brazilian defenders.

The eight minutes that were left of the first half were tense with the knowledge that another loss on either side could be permanently wounding. Bertini hurriedly surrendered a corner when Gérson threatened to dribble through. Then Carlos Alberto and Boninsegna crashed painfully together as Italy broke to take a retaliatory corner. The trainers returned to their benches in time to see a long shot by Domenghini fumblingly saved by Félix. Rivelino, having been aggravatingly fouled, replied by stamping his heel over the ball on to Bertini and was rightly cautioned. The free kick awarded for the original foul was taken by Gérson and brought a much more controversial decision from the referee. Gérson lifted his kick over the entire Italian defence and Pelé, killing the ball with relaxed deliberation, slid it easily past Albertosi. But Herr Glockner's whistle had ended the first half before that last blow was struck. The electronic clock showed a few seconds remaining but, of course, the referee is his own timekeeper. Brazil made a muted, confused protest as they left the field.

A Mexican journalist who seemed inclined to use the interval to put the complaint more aggressively through the wire fence separating the Press seats from the Italian supporters found himself heading away a few small flagpoles. By the time he had been dragged out of range and we had noted that the sun – having won *its* fight – was now shining with a slightly glazed confidence, the teams were out for the second half. Brazil, who had climbed nearly two-and-a-half thousand feet from Guadalajara to face men who were actually reducing their altitude problem by playing in Mexico City, had been urged by Zagalo to be wary with their energies in the first forty-five minutes. Now whatever had been saved must be let loose on Italy. Like a racehorse that has been hard-held into the straight, Carlos Alberto's team must try to quicken and leave the opposition standing. The captain himself took only three minutes to give a firm declaration of intent. Released by Jairzinho's pass, he moved along the right for another of those low centres across goal. Pelé, sliding in with the alarming suddenness of a skidding motor bike, rammed the ball just outside the far post. Burgnich, discomfited by the evidence that Pelé was about to become even more threatening, responded with fouls that could easily have been self-destructive. The first, thirty yards out, gave Rivelino the opening for a swerving shot that Albertosi beat down as he dived to his left. The second, a bicycle kick on Pelé's head as the forward sought to capitalise on a one-two between Gérson and Tostão resulted in an indirect free kick two yards inside the penalty box. Pelé passed to Gérson but his shot was unexpectedly harmless. Gérson's next intervention, another effort at a break into the area with Tostão, also misfired but there was no mistaking the significance of the contribution he was now making. His reticence in the first half had persuaded the Italians that they were justified in leaving him without specific cover. Free to build composure in his side and to scan the enemy at leisure for the principal points of weakness, his play until the interval had been in the nature of a preparation. He was like an arsonist who had been allowed to stoke up with matches and petrol. Now he was ready to set the game alight. Bill Shankly, the manager of Liverpool, has said that nothing in the World Cup impressed him more than the patience with which Gérson stayed his hand. 'He discovered before half-time that he could move up and put Italy in trouble,' said Shankly. 'But he knew if he did too much of it they would see what was happening and try to find a solution at the interval. So he waited until the second half. Then the Italians had no chance to discuss the problem. They were sunk.'

Even judged as a reaction in the heat of battle, however, the Italian dithering over Gérson was lamentable. They should surely have known that to neglect him in the first place was a huge risk, that they might be in need of a quickly arranged compromise. They managed none. The consequences of that failure were briefly concealed by two stirring assaults on Félix's goal. After Facchetti had slipped away on the left and Boninsegna swung the ball out wide for Domenghini to deliver a shot that was deflected for a corner, De Sisti set the splendid Mazzola on a thrilling run. His shot was powerful but he did not keep it low enough. Before they could draw encouragement from these endeavours Italy were swept back as if by a landslide. Amid the debris of their crumbling assurance, Bertini pulled down Rivelino. When the same happened to Jairzinho as he went for Tostão's return pass on the eighteen-yard line the referee charitably placed the ball five yards farther out for the free kick. But it was still nearly disastrous for the Italians, though they crowded every man back into the box. Gérson merely pushed the ball square and Rivelino, swinging the right foot that is supposed to be no more than a crutch for the left, lashed it brutally against the crossbar wide of Albertosi's left shoulder. Rivelino had fully recovered from his early nervousness and soon he was bearing down on Albertosi to shoot again. The ball rose wildly high but Riva, almost as big and bony as Henry Cooper, kept his team in difficulties by backhanding Rivelino on the mouth as the Brazilian followed through. That free kick brought a scramble of shots but none that counted.

Italy, stretched to the limit, retained the elasticity to snap back dangerously. Facchetti passed down the left to the untiring

Boninsegna and when the cross beat a puzzled, scurrying Félix, Riva struck an excellent header from beyond the far post. The goalkeeper was lucky to see the ball bounce off Everaldo, lucky again when a foolish attempt at a punching save produced nothing worse than a moment of hectic confusion. At this point Gérson, persumably worried by the possibility that Félix was about to make some fatuous interpolations in the script, took the sensible precaution of scoring a magnificent goal.

Spinning clockwise in a deep inside-left position, Gérson sent a blind but unerring pass to Everaldo on the wing. Everaldo pushed the ball straight ahead to Jairzinho and the forward, after starting to dribble inside, saw the advantage of rolling it back to Gérson. With that carefully schooled left foot, Gérson first dragged the ball outside a tackle and then cracked it with the clean force of a perfect one-iron aimed under the wind. It flew more than twenty yards in a killing diagonal and was still only waist height when it hit the far side netting. That goal, scored in the sixty-fifth minute, gave formal recognition to the fact that Gérson was the central influence of the match, the hub of the wheel that was grinding Italy down. Within five minutes he was helping to squeeze the last of their resistance into the damp turf. A foul on Pelé was punished with the twelfth free kick given to Brazil in the second half and Everaldo used it to make a short pass to Gérson. The balding head flicked up to take in the sight of Pelé sidling behind Burgnich beyond the far post. No one in the world passes the ball more accurately in the air than Gérson does. Now it was lifted in a precise, elongated arc over the head of Burgnich onto that of Pelé. An immediate strike at goal would have been in order but Pelé, whose mind is quicker than most men's eyes, coolly headed down to Jairzinho. The manoeuvre was so deadly in its simplicity that Jairzinho could afford to miskick and still have time to run the ball into the net.

Italy faced a further twenty minutes on the rack. Bertini, at least, was spared the torture. He collapsed in the centre

circle, with a pulled muscle in his right thigh, and was replaced by Juliano. One of Juliano's first contributions was to
give the ball to Gérson, which is about as profitable as throwing
live grenades against a rubber wall. This time Gérson made a
chance for Rivelino but he did not connect adequately. Brazil,
who might have become drugged with their own brilliance,
instead emphasised the tactical discipline inculcated by Zagalo.
The idea that their football in 1970 was all some kind of
beautiful, primitive dance is charmingly absurd. Of course,
there is an elemental rhythm about their play, a natural
gymnastic grace and flexibility, but their game is as rational
as it is instinctive. Can anyone seriously argue that the stunning
subtleties of Gérson, Tostão and Pelé do not represent the
highest form of the games-player's intelligence? It is questionable if any team in the World Cup other than England equalled
the tactical sophistication shown, individually and collectively,
by Brazil. The recurring weaknesses in their defence were
flaws of temperament and technique, not errors of innocence.
In this last quarter of the match the strong personalities in the
side organised the total manpower to make sure that any
kamikaze inclinations among the Italians would not bring late
embarrassment. At one moment every Brazilian was working
in his own half. Thus when a mistake by Piazza let Boninsegna
through there was an extra man, Brito, to fill the gap with a
superb tackle.

That moment marked the exhaustion of Italy's spirit and
Brazil were free to finish with the sort of rich flourish that suits
their natures and the dramatic range of their talents. Those
last minutes contained a distillation of their football, its beauty
and *élan* and undiluted joy. Other teams thrill us and make us
respect them. The Brazilians at their finest give us pleasure so
natural and deep as to be a vivid physical experience. This was
what we had hoped for, the ritual we had come to share. The
qualities that make football the most graceful and electric and
moving of team sports were being laid before us. Brazil are
proud of their own unique abilities but it was not hard to

R

believe that they were anxious to say something about the game
as well as about themselves. You cannot be the best in the world
at a game without loving it and all of us who sat, flushed with
excitement, in the stands of the Aztec sensed that what we
were seeing was a kind of tribute.

No player's statement was more eloquent that Gérson's.
One marvellous run on the left produced a cross that was just
too high for Tostão, then a great pass to Everaldo sent the full-
back careering in on goal to be denied by Albertosi's brave save
at his feet. The sympathy that was due Italy was tempered by
continuing disappointment at their folly. It was almost unbelievable that a country with a neurotic obsession about
tactical theory should reveal such an elementary lack of fore-
sight and imagination. With less than seven minutes left they
again betrayed their masochistic eccentricity. Despite being
two goals behind and glaringly short of firepower, they withdrew their one consistently effective forward, Boninsegna, and
substituted the delicate midfield player, Rivera. To have any
relevance Rivera would have needed much longer on the field.
Bringing him on at this point simply meant that an angry man
(and Boninsegna had a right to his show of disgust) was replaced by a sulky one. The only benefit Rivera earned from
his promotion to active service was that he had a closer view
of one of the best goals scored in the World Cup. Naturally
enough, it was scored by Brazil. Barely four minutes remained
when Clodoaldo, whose donation of a goal to Italy had been
isolated in an otherwise excellent performance, began the
attack with a dribble that was as brilliant as it was untypical.
Normally he is happy to apply his skills with firm economy but
here, wriggling and feinting in the manner of Rivelino, he
mesmerised five challengers and from the left-half position
passed the ball forward to Jairzinho. Moving inside from the
left wing, Jairzinho sent it on to Pelé, who was twenty yards
out in front of goal. Yet again Jairzinho had drawn Facchetti
far out of position and Carlos Alberto was coming through
on an angled run with the intimidating directness of a torpedo.

Pelé, seeing him come, turned unhurriedly and rolled the ball into his path with the relaxed precision of a lawn bowler. Without having to check, deviate or adjust his stride, Carlos Alberto smashed the ball with his right foot low into the side net behind Albertosi's right-hand post. It was an unforgettable goal and its seeming inevitability increased rather than diminished its excitement.

Dozens of photographers and supporters were sufficiently overcome to invade the pitch while the match was still going on. They were made to retreat but stayed near enough to lead the massed charge that came when the referee did signal the end. Pelé and Tostão ran to hug one another but were soon in the more hazardous embrace of their admirers. Tostão was stripped boot by boot, sock by sock and had a struggle to keep his shorts. Vast flags, acres of green and yellow, swam above the delirious mob. Men with banners danced until they collapsed exhausted on the grass. There were now thousands on the field and in the middle of this South American celebration was the marching, bowing figure of Ken Bailey, the English cheerleader. As usual, he was dressed in a tail coat of hunting pink and black top hat. He was carrying his toy bulldog and waving a tiny Union Jack. But for those unreal happenings in León, some less outlandish Englishmen would have been entertaining the crowd at the Aztec.

There was no discrimination about the laps of honour. Anyone could join in and it was not easy to pick out the players in the swarms of supporters. One local patriot made himself prominent with a placard reading 'Mexico – World Champions of Friendship.' Sir Alf Ramsey would have savoured that one.

Zagalo was still carrying his clipboard as he rode round the arena on an uncomfortable platform of shoulders. The presentation by the Mexican president, Gustavo Díaz Ordaz, which was loud with the music of naval and civilian bands and bright with the flags of all the FIFA members, was a moment of profound satisfaction for Zagalo. He had been accused of a defensive approach to the challenge in Mexico but in the event

his team scored nineteen goals, more than Brazil had taken in
1958 or 1962, and an average of better than three a match. In
the process they beat three former champions, Uruguay, Italy
and England, and proved they could match the tactical
discipline and physical condition of the Europeans. Stamina
and composure helped them to score important goals in the last
twenty minutes of their games.

The manager could claim another more personal achievement. He overcame at last the resentment that had persisted
among the men, notably Pelé, who had played with him in 1958
and 1962. No one questioned the value of his contribution in
those years ('Zagalo was the one who showed the world 4–3–3,'
says one Brazilian, 'who made it clear to all of us that a footballer must have two shirts – a defender's and an attacker's.')
But his team-mates felt that his luck, which is legendary, had
kept better players out. In 1958 and 1962 Pepe, the great
goal-scoring winger of Santos, was removed by injury and
Germano was similarly unfortunate in 1962. Pelé was one of
those who believed the Zagalo luck had put a jinx on his rivals.
It was an intriguing scene, therefore, when Pelé and Zagalo
came face to face in a momentarily quiet corner of the dressing
rooms after the final. Pelé put down the glass of water he was
drinking and, without a word, they ran to each other for a long,
tearful embrace. Later Pelé gave the manager his shirt. (Tostão
gave his, along with his winner's medal, to the doctor who
operated on his eye in Houston, Texas.)

At roughly the same time as Pelé and Zagalo were burying
past differences the President of Brazil, General Garrastazú
Médici, was draping a national flag round his shoulders and
going out of his palace to play informal football with the
crowds in Praça dos Tres Poderes, the main square of Brasilia.
The one player President Médici strenuously advocated, Dario,
a Negro centre-forward, did not help directly in the winning of
the World Cup but he was of some assistance in keeping it.
Carlos Alberto, while being buffeted around on his lap of
honour, failed to notice that the gold top of the World Cup had

slipped on to the ground at his feet. Dario, following on behind, saw a small boy pick it up and after a brief chase was able to retrieve it.

Paulo Cézar had to survive a chase to hold on to another prize, the match ball, which he snatched on behalf of a friend who is a fanatical follower of Brazil. When he was pursued by an Italian player, Paulo Cézar had an unanswerable advantage. He had been resting on the substitutes' bench throughout the match.

Long after the Final was over some of the Brazilians still found difficulty in absorbing what had happened. Pelé says that when he woke next morning he seriously wondered if he had been dreaming. The sight of his medal at the bedside only partially reassured him and he telephoned his wife Rose at home in Brazil to ask: 'Are we really the champions?'. Rose, who was seven months pregnant with their second child, told him she had felt a severe pain when he scored the first goal. She must have been one of the few people in Brazil who did. Even the Italians in the Aztec Stadium could not have found the experience of this final too hurtful. Football, and all of us who regard it as something worthwhile, can only gain from such occasions. As tons of coloured confetti were spilled from the roof of the stands to drift down upon us in a dry, bright rain we realised that the mood of schoolboy expectancy with which we had come to the match had been sustained. The afternoon had become cool and mild once more but we had enough Brazilian friends to make us suspect that a long, hot night of revelry lay ahead.

Outside the ground we were met by vendors offering pennants commemorating Brazil's World Cup victories in 1958, 1962 – and 1970. They had mass-produced the mementoes well in advance. It was not much of a risk.

Brazil 4   Italy 1

10 Summing-Up

To urge the mind back through that shimmering haze of confetti, back beyond the handsome final match and the considerable bravura of the football that led to it is to rediscover with a jolt that this World Cup began in predictions of gloom and general human collapse, at best, and of ruinous violence at worst. What is more strange to recall is that before May 31 there seemed plenty of justification for viewing this tournament as something the game might be better without. We were not wrong to worry. It is highly gratifying to have seen our fears invalidated.

The proliferating popular literature on the sport ensured that the 1970 World Cup was the most previewed, most anticipated, most promoted event in international football there had ever been. Much of the pre-discussion was of a head-shaking, ominous kind, heavy with relish for a spectacular catastrophe on the way. The altitude and heat of the stadiums in Mexico would cripple the sea-level sides, rendering the competition into a bizarre, slow-motion, sick comedy, as if the world's great players were suspended just above the turf like those wooden figures on the old-fashioned table-soccer games, lunging to the tug of the hand. But that was the lesser of the two promises of doom for this tournament. The other was that the very real hostility which had been gathering in recent years between the football codes of North Europe and of the Latin countries would find its inevitable combustibility in Mexico, and the football would be submerged in an escalating brawl.

In the event, Mexico's climate proved a handicap which the best teams could nurse, even when it was as intimidating a

factor as Toluca's 8,800 feet. But the importance of these
climatic influences must not be minimised just because the
good footballers refused to be suppressed by them. The pace
and industry and sustained concentration of players like
Moore, Cooper, Pelé and Tostão in Guadalajara's heat, and of
Mazzola, Domenghini and De Sisti at Toluca's height were
evidence of the players' quality, not of the conditions' in-
nocuousness. This World Cup stays the brighter in the memory
for the degree of courage that was needed to bring about its
excitements. The tendency for some observers to dismiss the
climate as having been of no consequence, after all, was
thoughtless ingratitude: rather like shrugging off the fact of a
boxer's broken jaw on the grounds that it didn't stop him
going the distance. Unquestionably the altitude of the Aztec
Stadium was as influential in the amassing of seven goals in the
Italy–West Germany semi-final as were the skills of the scorers.
Exhaustion and individual players' will to break clear of it
produced that improbable last half-hour. Mexico never let us
forget where the football was being played.

The overall respectability of the conduct of the tournament
was similarly attributable to the excellence of some people more
than a vindication of the system which deployed them. The
teams were largely well behaved on the field; most of the
matches were efficiently refereed – or, at least, handled without
obtrusive dispute. The FIFA Referees' Committee could
properly claim some credit for this. The innovation of bringing
all the referees together for a week of talks and physical training
was born out of the special need to acclimatise these thirty men
to rapid movement in unaccustomed conditions. But the
opportunity was imaginatively taken. The matter of treating
them like the tournament's 17th team proved of real psychological value, both to the referees and to the playing squads.
Footballers have never taken to the pompous institution of the
aloof referee, supposedly outside the sweat and anxiety of the
game. For FIFA to let it be known that the referees were
lapping, skipping and kicking footballs in properly designed

group training sessions every morning brought the officials a lot nearer the action in other people's minds. The fact that the referees were arguing out the interpretations of the ruling on foul tackling and its punishment was an enormous advance on the stubborn pretence that referees don't have doubts. This kind of preparation of the referees, even if it was belated and skimpy when compared against the low standard in the game, was vital if FIFA were to command any respect for their repeated assertions that the matches would be sternly controlled and violent play ruthlessly punished.

It was still impossible for FIFA to escape derision over their selection of the referees. (Perhaps the qualified success of the Mexico exercise will encourage FIFA to think how much more rewarding it may be to train the world's *best* thirty referees for a week, instead of assorted ones chosen by committee diplomacy.) The miscastings were all too obvious. Kandil, the 50-year-old Egyptian, had looked alarmingly unsuitable in the training sessions, and he duly contributed some provocative confusion (along with a never-explained orange ball) to the game between Mexico and El Salvador. The innocence of the Ethiopian, Tarekegn, in the Sweden–Israel match, led him to provide a model example of how a referee can encourage footballers in their dangerous wilfulness by misapplying the advantage rule. It was hard to exonerate the Argentine, Coerezza, from a charge of malleability when he gave Mexico their penalty against Belgium amid the ferocious persuasion of the Aztec crowd. The decision by Van Ravens, of the Netherlands, which permitted Uruguay to score against Russia in the quarter-finals with a ball dragged back from out of play, looked like an excess of self-conviction over objectivity.

There were other moments when one could have wished for a sharper eye from a referee, for less recourse to compromise over harsh tackles inside the penalty area, for instance. But in these officials' defence it is fair to recall again that they were working in extraordinary conditions. One of them explained part of the problem tersely: 'We are twice the age of some of these players. At high altitude we just can't keep up with the play as we normally do. So it's a mistake to try to apply the advantage rule at all, really. If you're running the line you can use your chewing gum and your salt tablets. But when you're on the field blowing your whistle it's a lot harder. You get this tightness and dryness in the throat and chest.'

The refereeing was well short of exemplary; but it was also of high enough quality to allow the tournament to retain its self-respect. Perhaps one of the most valuable aspects of this World Cup was that it showed inarguably that increasing indiscipline on the football field is *not* inevitable as the intensity of the competition increases. It also showed that imperfect refereeing is more acceptable to players when authority admits the imperfection and is seen to be trying to remove it. Foot-ballers understand the business of fitness and form and variable skill; they are not impressed by claims of infallibility. For West Germany in 1974 perhaps FIFA will be even more daring? Perhaps they could gather their referees together for several pre-tournament sessions, paying them full compensation for absence from normal wage-earning? The growing sense of 'team', of collective accountability was a significant help in Mexico, and it ought to be fostered.

There are, of course, legitimate objections to the staging of a World Cup in an under-developed country which have nothing to do with Mexico's complications of climate and topography or with any supposed exposure of Northern Europeans to the dangers of assault by swarthy natives in a frenzy of resentment. Whatever the wealth and worldly panache of Mexico City, and the promise (for the tourist) of limitless fun in Acapulco, Mexico has enough visible wretchedness to keep it on the 'under-developed' list, even if mention of the fact gives bitter offence to its politicians. Is it not a moral affront to transport such a costly, frivolous show as the World Cup to such a place of need? Should football and its best people be exploited to bolster the prestige of a party dictatorship? Mexico had no claim, after all, to major talent in the game. The questions can have only opinions for answers. Certainly there were Europeans who hated being in Mexico; who never lost a sense of personal menace in the tension that always exists where privilege and poverty live so close; who were appalled also by the passion of those Mexican crowds, convinced that the next outbreak of chanting would signal a massacre of the pale foreigners from bar to bed. One heard solemn assertions in various forms of English that we were all 'poised on a knife edge' or 'sitting on top of a volcano'. Sometimes we were in both situations in the same sentence, which must surely be the ultimate peril. But except for having 'Me-hee-co' bawled into one's face often, there was little animosity towards the foreigner in evidence, at least individually. The hostility was mostly for distant England, the faceless arrogance; or for Sir Alf Ramsey, the embodiment of all English haughtiness, to be hissed by the Mexican Press. The English half of this authorship has felt more threatened in Glasgow.

When everything else has been considered a World Cup can be finally justified or not only by its football, and well before the confetti came drifting on to our eyelids on June 21 this tournament was an emphatic success. Brazil's performance against Italy had a completeness that derived from logical progression. It was no sudden flowering of previously concealed talents. Brazil had been required to use all their strengths before, against England and against Uruguay, who both troubled them far more than Italy could. The final was a splendid ceremonial for Brazil, an opportunity for a restatement of all they had done before, and they took it with a swagger. The tournament merited it. The predictions had been of three weeks of grim defensiveness and few goals. Instead there were 95 goals, and the champions scored four in the climax. They were sweet figures to roll in the mouth.

This is not to pretend that the competition was all adventurousness unalloyed. It began sombrely, with Herr Tschenscher doing the work of a querulous sheepdog among the blundering tussles of the Mexico–Russia match; and in

Puebla and Toluca the six matches of Group Two yielded the dismal harvest of six goals. Italy and Uruguay, with so much talent available to them, tested one's capacity for forgiveness to its limit with that disgracefully non-contested 0–0 draw which was the key to both countries' entry to the quarter-final. And there were disappointments in teams and in individual players. Belgium's appearance of lean ease before the tournament shrivelled to one of pallid diffidence on the field, little of consequence coming from Devrindt or Van Himst. Sweden never managed to find eleven players out of a squad of able ones to reflect the skill in the camp, and not until his last game did Ove Kindvall persistently produce the dash and shooting that make him so dangerous a forward for his Dutch club, Feyenoord.

Mexico benefited from the Belgians' unexpected frailty – a failure of spirit rather than talent, and connected with resentment over disproportionate earnings inside the squad. But the host country were also better footballers than they were expected to be, with a notably astute midfield man in Munguía and a general coherence which repaid the austere months of studious coaching by Raul Cárdenas. As football grows in Mexico, with more facilities in the state schools and more boys ambitious for the game's rewards, the country can reasonably hope to claim a place among the world's leading soccer nations. The sport will develop there as industry does, with its accompanying crammed, working communities. It will develop, one feels, the pragmatic European way, not with the natural exuberance of the Brazilian game.

To reflect on the latter stages of the tournament is, for the British observer, to taste again some of the bitter disconsolation that followed England's calamity at the hands of West Germany. Even at a distance of 5,000 miles and several weeks the sense of cruelty in misfortune is little diminished. It has been enough for some people to say that a team which is two goals ahead deserves no sympathy if it fades to a 3–2 defeat. Others have seized, with regrettable enthusiasm, on the 'discrediting' of

Ramsey's whole approach to football. To praise the Germans' optimistic enterprise is entirely acceptable; but it is the most dubious proposition to say that it beat England. The blow that did the damage was the one that Gordon Banks took in the stomach on the morning of the game, giving Peter Bonetti the chance to keep goal as if he had never heard a spectator shout in his life. Few players or team officials one spoke to in Mexico said other than that England were the second best team in the tournament – and that opinion was still firm in the Italian camp the day after the quarter-finals. Giacinto Facchetti, the Italian captain, was speaking for many when he said: 'England should not have lost. It was not real.' Equally for many in Mexico the match between England and Brazil remained the best of the tournament. It produced the extreme tension of unrelenting contest; every player's skills and stamina were under constant stress. No other game in the competition had its vital demand on exactness. In such a context Banks's miraculous save from Pelé's header was something *expected*, and Astle's failure directly in front of the goal was preposterously out of place. It is this game which should be remembered by those people who so glibly repeat that Ramsey's, and the whole of English, football has got to be re-thought because of what happened to England in Mexico. The World Cup did reinforce the case for making more consistent and specialised use of the wings than Ramsey's teams do and for avoiding situations when one forward, such as the unbreakable Hurst, is left in painful isolation among swarms of hostile defenders. But it is as absurd to think of Englishmen trying to impersonate the Brazilian verve in football as it is maddening to hear people asking questions like: 'If George Best was English would Ramsey pick him?' (The reply, in kind, to that question should be something like: 'Yes, as long as George was willing.')

The record shows that England failed in Mexico, but it does not deny some particular English brilliance. Banks's goalkeeping was of such a quality as to put him in a separate dimension in the tournament; Moore was generally agreed to be the greatest defensive player and Cooper was the equal of any full-back; Hurst had one match that lifted him among the world's half-dozen best forwards; Ball lived up to his reputation and Mullery, stimulated by the scope of the challenge, superbly transcended his; if Bobby Charlton had a modest tournament by the standards of his greatest games he still commanded favourable comparison with, say, Seeler, of West Germany, Mazzola or Rivera, of Italy, or Asatiani of Russia. England, in fact, had as much to offer as any side except Brazil, who have to be considered as an altogether different case from the instant one begins to list their names: Pelé, Tostão, Rivelino, Gérson, Jairzinho, Clodoaldo. . . . It was a grouping of talents outside any other country's reach. To talk of 'learning from them', as numerous Englishmen were on their return from Mexico, is simply slogan-mouthing. Perhaps one's government might acquire them for stud.

If one looks forward to 1974, it is plain that both England and Brazil will have to find largely new teams. The Charlton brothers will be too old, and so probably will Moore, Banks, Mullery, Newton and Hurst. But Cooper should still be strong, and may then be partnered by the other Leeds back, Paul Reaney, denied Mexico by a broken leg; there will not be a remorseless heat to overburden the stocky Lee; Peters may re-establish himself; Ball should then be in full maturity as a midfield player, and the names of Peter Shilton, Brian Kidd, Alan Hudson, Ralph Coates, Emlyn Hughes, Joe Royle, Peter Osgood come insistently to mind. Others, as yet vague on the fringe of our minds, may glow with possibilities by then. One thing is certain, and that is that England's team in Munich will not be any kind of counterfeit Brazilian one.

There is no reason to expect anything compromising from Brazil either. In addition to the irreplaceable Pelé, they are almost certain to lose Gérson and Carlos Alberto as well as one or two others of lesser importance. But with luck they will still have Rivelino, Jairzinho, Clodoaldo and, above all, Tostão. Watching him play, marvelling at the intelligence and subtlety that inform everything he does, the impregnability of his composure under the heaviest pressure, it is hard to realise that he is only twenty-four years old. When Pelé departs Tostão is likely to switch back again from being the advanced pivot of the attack to performing a more central role in the team. With his deep understanding of the game, his high skills and his willingness to run endlessly, Tostão could easily emerge four years from now as a player of the capacity and stature of Di Stefano. Almost inevitably, he will be the driving spirit of Brazil in Munich. He could be much more. Embodying as he does the best of the European and the South American footballer, the best of the old arts and the new sciences of the game, he could be the perfect symbol of a great World Cup in 1974. The thought of it is enough to quicken the pulse.

Appendices

I THE QUALIFYING COMPETITION

(Countries in bold type qualified in each group)

GROUP 1

Switzerland	1	Greece	0
Rumania	2	Switzerland	0
Portugal	0	Switzerland	2
Switzerland	0	**Rumania**	1
Greece	4	Switzerland	1
Switzerland	1	Portugal	1
Greece	2	**Rumania**	2
Greece	4	Portugal	2
Portugal	2	Greece	2
Rumania	1	Portugal	0
Portugal	3	**Rumania**	0
Rumania	1	Greece	1

	P	W	D	L	F	A	Pts.
Rumania	6	3	2	1	7	6	8
Greece	6	2	3	1	13	9	7
Switzerland	6	2	1	3	5	8	5
Portugal	6	1	2	3	8	10	4

GROUP 2

Hungary	2	**Czechoslovakia**	0
Czechoslovakia	3	Hungary	3
Ireland	1	Hungary	2
Hungary	3	Denmark	0
Denmark	3	Hungary	2
Czechoslovakia	3	Ireland	0
Ireland	1	**Czechoslovakia**	2
Czechoslovakia	1	Denmark	0
Denmark	0	**Czechoslovakia**	3
Ireland	1	Denmark	1
Denmark	2	Ireland	0
Hungary	4	Ireland	0

	P	W	D	L	F	A	Pts
Czechoslovakia	6	4	1	1	12	6	9
Hungary	6	4	1	1	16	7	9
Denmark	6	2	1	3	6	10	5
Rep. of Ireland	6	0	1	5	3	14	1

Play-off in Marseilles:
Czechoslovakia 4, Hungary 1

GROUP 3

Wales	0	**Italy**	1
East Germany	2	**Italy**	2
East Germany	2	Wales	1
Wales	1	East Germany	3
Italy	4	Wales	1
Italy	3	East Germany	0

	P	W	D	L	F	A	Pts
Italy	4	3	1	0	10	3	7
E. Germany	4	2	1	1	7	7	5
Wales	4	0	0	4	3	10	0

GROUP 4

N. Ireland	4	Turkey	1
Turkey	0	N. Ireland	3
N. Ireland	0	**U.S.S.R.**	0
U.S.S.R.	3	Turkey	0
U.S.S.R.	2	N. Ireland	0
Turkey	1	**U.S.S.R.**	3

	P	W	D	L	F	A	Pts
U.S.S.R.	4	3	1	0	8	1	7
N. Ireland	4	2	1	1	7	3	5
Turkey	4	0	0	4	2	13	0

GROUP 5

Sweden	5	Norway	0
France	0	Norway	1
Norway	2	**Sweden**	5
Norway	1	Franc	3
Sweden	2	Francee	0
France	3	**Sweden**	0

					GOALS		
	P	W	D	L	F	A	Pts
Sweden	4	3	0	1	12	5	6
France	4	2	0	2	6	4	4
Norway	4	1	0	3	4	13	2

GROUP 6

Finland	1	**Belgium**	2
Yugoslavia	9	Finland	1
Belgium	6	Finland	1
Belgium	3	Yugoslavia	0
Yugoslavia	0	Spain	0
Spain	1	**Belgium**	1
Belgium	2	Spain	1
Spain	2	Yugoslavia	1
Finland	1	Yugoslavia	5
Finland	2	Spain	0
Spain	6	Finland	0
Yugoslavia	4	**Belgium**	0

					GOALS		
	P	W	D	L	F	A	Pts
Belgium	6	4	1	1	14	8	9
Yugoslavia	6	3	1	2	19	7	7
Spain	6	2	2	2	10	6	6
Finland	6	1	0	5	6	28	2

GROUP 7

Austria	7	Cyprus	1
Austria	0	**W. Germany**	2
Scotland	2	Austria	1
Cyprus	0	**W. Germany**	1
Cyprus	0	Scotland	5
Scotland	1	**W. Germany**	1
Cyprus	1	Austria	2
W. Germany	1	Austria	0
Scotland	8	Cyprus	0
W. Germany	12	Cyprus	0
W. Germany	3	Scotland	2
Austria	2	Scotland	0

					GOALS		
	P	W	D	L	F	A	
W. Germany	6	5	1	0	20	3	
Scotland	6	3	1	2	18	7	
Austria	6	3	0	3	12	7	
Cyprus	6	0	0	6	2	35	

GROUP 8

Luxembourg	0	Holland	
Bulgaria	2	Holland	
Holland	4	Luxembourg	
Poland	8	Luxembourg	
Bulgaria	2	Luxembourg	
Holland	1	Poland	
Bulgaria	4	Poland	
Poland	2	Holland	
Luxembourg	1	Poland	
Holland	1	**Bulgaria**	
Poland	3	**Bulgaria**	
Luxembourg	1	**Bulgaria**	

					GOALS		
	P	W	D	L	F	A	
Bulgaria	6	4	1	1	12	7	
Poland	6	4	0	2	19	8	
Holland	6	3	1	2	9	5	
Luxembourg	6	0	0	6	4	24	

GROUP 9

England qualified automatically
World Cup holders.

GROUP 10

Bolivia	3	Argentina	
Peru	1	Argentina	
Bolivia	2	**Peru**	
Peru	3	Bolivia	
Argentina	1	Bolivia	
Argentina	2	**Peru**	

					GOALS		
	P	W	D	L	F	A	
Peru	4	2	1	1	7	4	
Bolivia	4	2	0	2	5	6	
Argentina	4	1	1	2	4	6	

GROUP 11

›lombia	3	Venezuela	0
ʼnezuela	1	Colombia	1
›lombia	0	**Brazil**	2
ʼnezuela	0	Paraguay	2
›lombia	0	Paraguay	1
ʼnezuela	0	**Brazil**	5
ʼraguay	0	**Brazil**	3
ʼazil	6	Colombia	2
ʼraguay	1	Venezuela	0
ʼazil	6	Venezuela	0
ʼraguay	2	Colombia	1
ʼazil	1	Paraguay	0

	P	W	D	L	GOALS F	A	Pts
ʼazil	6	6	0	0	23	2	12
ʼraguay	6	4	0	2	6	5	8
›lombia	6	1	1	4	7	12	3
ʼnezuela	6	0	1	5	1	18	1

GROUP 12

uador	0	**Uruguay**	2
ʼile	0	**Uruguay**	0
ʼuguay	1	Ecuador	0
ʼile	4	Ecuador	1
uador	1	Chile	1
ʼuguay	2	Chile	0

	P	W	D	L	GOALS F	A	Pts
uguay	4	3	1	0	5	0	7
ʼile	4	1	2	1	5	4	4
uador	4	0	1	3	2	8	1

GROUP 13

ni-finals:

iti	2	U.S.A.	0
5.A.	0	Haiti	1
Salvador	3	Honduras	0
nduras	1	**El Salvador**	0

ʼy-off: **El Salvador** 3, Honduras 2

ʼal:

Salvador	0	Haiti	3
iti	1	**El Salvador**	2

ʼy-off: **El Salvador** 1, Haiti 0
(after extra time)

GROUP 14

Mexico qualified automatically as host country.

GROUP 15

15.1

Japan	1	**Australia**	3
S. Korea	2	Japan	2
Australia	2	S. Korea	1
Australia	1	Japan	1
Japan	0	S. Korea	2
S. Korea	1	**Australia**	1

	P	W	D	L	GOALS F	A	Pts
Australia	4	2	2	0	7	4	6
S. Korea	4	1	2	1	6	5	4
Japan	4	0	2	2	4	8	2

15.2

	P	W	D	L	GOALS F	A	Pts
Israel	2	2	0	0	6	0	4
New Zealand	2	0	0	2	0	6	0

North Korea withdrew

Second phase play-off:

Australia	0	Rhodesia	0
Rhodesia	1	Australia	3

Final:

Israel	1	Australia	0
Australia	1	**Israel**	1

GROUP 16

First round group winners: Tunisia, Morocco (after play-off with Senegal), Ethiopia, Sudan, Cameroons, Ghana.

Second round:

Tunisia	0	**Morocco**	0
Morocco	2	Tunisia	2

(after extra time: Morocco go through to group final by drawing of lots)

Ethiopia	1	Sudan	1
Sudan	3	Ethiopia	1
Nigeria	2	Ghana	1
Ghana	1	Nigeria	1

Final Group:

							P	W	D	L	GOALS F	A	P
Nigeria	2	Sudan	2										
Morocco	2	Nigeria	1	Morocco			4	2	1	1	5	3	5
Sudan	3	Nigeria	3	Nigeria			4	1	2	1	8	7	4
Sudan	0	**Morocco**	0	Sudan			4	0	3	1	5	8	3
Morocco	3	Sudan	0										
Nigeria	2	**Morocco**	0										

The listing of teams in the championship varied considerably, some appearing in the traditional style and some being set out to indicate how the players actually lined up on the field. It is easy to tell one from the other but, in fact, neither is a comprehensive indication of how the teams operated. The only guide to this is to be found in the reports, which make the relevant points about tactics.

Group One

U.S.S.R. 0, MEXICO 0 (0–0) *Mexico City, May 31*
U.S.S.R.
Kavazashvili; Kaplichni, Lovchev, Logofet, Shesternev, Asatiani, Muntian, Serebrianikov, Bishovets, Evriuzhikhin, Nodia. Subs: Puzach for Serebrianikov (45 mins), Khmelnitski for Nodia (66 mins)
MEXICO
Calderón; Peña, Pérez, Hernández, López, Vantolra, Guzmán, Pulido, Velarde, Valdivia, Fragoso. Sub: Munguía for Velarde (67 mins)
Referee: K. Tschenscher (West Germany)
Attendance: 112,000

BELGIUM 3, EL SALVADOR 0 (1–0) *Mexico City, June 3*
BELGIUM
Piot; Heylens, Thissen, Dewalque, Dockx, Semmeling, Van Moer, Devrindt, Van Himst, Puis, Lambert. Sub: Polleunis for Lambert (79 mins)
EL SALVADOR
Magaña; Rivas, Mariona, Osorio, Manzano, Quintanilla, Vásquez, Cabezas, Rodríguez, Martinez, Aparicio. Subs: Cortes Méndez for Manzano (63 mins), Sermeño for Rodríguez (79 mins)
Referee: A. Radulescu (Rumania). *Scorers:* Van Moer (2), Lambert (pen.)
Attendance: 30,000

U.S.S.R. 4, BELGIUM 1 (1–0) *Mexico City, June 6*
U.S.S.R.
Kavazashvili; Shesternev, Khurtsilava, Kaplichni, Afonin, Dzodzuashvili, Asatiani, Muntian, Evriuzhikhin, Bishovets, Khmelnitski. Subs: Lovchev for Kaplichni (34 mins), Kiselev for Dzodzuashvili (74 mins)
BELGIUM
Piot; Heylens, Dewalque, Jeck, Thissen, Van Moer, Dockx, Puis, Semmeling, Van Himst, Lambert
Referee: R. Scheurer (Switzerland). *Scorers:* Bishovets (2), Asatiani, Khmelnitski (Russia)
Lambert (Belgium)
Attendance: 90,000

279

MEXICO 4, EL SALVADOR 0 (1–0)   *Mexico City, June 7*
MEXICO
Calderón; Peña, Pérez, Munguía, Borja, Padilla, Vantolra, Guzmán, González, Valdivia, Fragoso. Subs: López for Borja (45 mins), Basaguren for López (75 mins)
EL SALVADOR
Magaña; Rivas, Mariona, Cortes Méndez, Osorio, Quintanilla, Rodríguez, Vásquez, Martinez, Cabezas, Aparicio. Subs: Mendez for Aparicio (56 mins), Monge for Cortes Méndez (66 mins)
Referee: A. Kandil (United Arab Republic). *Scorers:* Valdivia (2), Fragoso,
Attendance: 107,000   Basaguren

U.S.S.R. 2, EL SALVADOR 0 (0–0)   *Mexico City, June 10*
U.S.S.R.
Kavazashvili; Shesternev, Dzodzuashvili, Khurtsilava, Afonin, Serebrianikov, Kiselev, Muntian, Puzach, Bishovets, Khmelnitski. Subs: Evriuzhikhin for Puzach (45 mins), Asatiani for Kiselev (79 mins)
EL SALVADOR
Magaña; Rivas, Osorio, Cabezas, Mariona, Vásquez, Monge, Portillo, Rodríguez, Castro, Méndez. Sub: Aparicio for Cabezas (79 mins)
Referee: R. Díaz Hormazabal (Chile). *Scorers:* Bishovets (2)
Attendance: 15,000

MEXICO 1, BELGIUM 0 (1–0)   *Mexico City, June 11*
MEXICO
Calderón; Vantolra, Peña, Guzmán, Pérez, Pulido, González, Munguía, Valdivia, Fragoso, Padilla. Sub: Basaguren for Valdivia (45 mins)
BELGIUM
Piot; Heylens, Jeck, Dewalque, Thissen, Van Moer, Dockx, Polleunis, Semmeling, Van Himst, Puis. Sub: Devrindt for Polleunis (63 mins)
Referee: N. A. Coerezza (Argentina). *Scorer:* Peña (pen.)
Attendance: 107,000

Group Two

URUGUAY 2, ISRAEL 0 (1–0)   *Puebla, June 2*
URUGUAY
Mazurkiewicz; Ancheta, Matosas, Ubiñas, Montero Castillo, Mújica, Cubilla, Rocha, Espárrago, Maneiro, Losada. Sub: Cortés for Rocha (13 mins)
ISRAEL
Wissoker; Primo, Rosenthal, Shoum, Shpiegel, Faigenbaum, Shpiegler, Schweger, Rom, Talbi, Rosen. Subs: Wallach for Talbi (46 mins), Bar for Rom (57 mins)
Referee: R. Davidson (Scotland). *Scorers:* Maneiro, Mújica
Attendance: 22,000

SWEDEN 0, ITALY 1 (0–1)   *Toluca, June 3*
SWEDEN
Hellström; Axelsson, Nordqvist, Grip, Svensson, Larsson, Eriksson, Kindvall, Grahn, Cronqvist, Olsson. Subs: Ejderstedt for Eriksson (57 mins), Nicklasson for Larsson (79 mins)

ITALY
   Albertosi; Burgnich, Facchetti, Cera, Niccolai, Bertini, De Sisti, Domen-
   ghini, Mazzola, Riva, Boninsegna. Sub: Rosato for Niccolai (37 mins)
Referee: J. Taylor (England). *Scorer:* Domenghini
Attendance: 18,000

URUGUAY 0, ITALY 0   (0–0)   *Puebla, June 6*
URUGUAY
   Mazurkiewicz; Matosas, Ancheta, Ubiñas, Mújica, Cortés, Maneiro,
   Montero Castillo, Cubilla, Espárrago, Bareño. Sub: Zubía for Bareño
   (70 mins)
ITALY
   Albertosi; Cera, Burgnich, Rosato, Facchetti, Bertini, Domenghini,
   Mazzola, De Sisti, Boninsegna, Riva. Sub: Furino for Domenghini
   (46 mins)
Referee: R. Glockner (East Germany)
Attendance: 35,000

ISRAEL 1, SWEDEN 1   (0–0)   *Toluca, June 7*
ISRAEL
   Wissoker; Bar, Primo, Rosen, Rosenthal, Shoum, Shpiegel, Faigenbaum,
   Shpiegler, Schweger, Wallach. Sub: Shuruk for Wallach (55 mins)
SWEDEN
   S.-G. Larsson; Selander, Axelsson, Grip, Svensson, B. Larsson, Kindvall,
   Persson, Nordahl, Turesson, Olsson. Sub: Palsson for Persson (31 mins)
Referee: S. Tarekegn (Ethiopia). *Scorers:* Turesson (Sweden)
                                               Shpiegler (Israel)
Attendance: 5,000

SWEDEN 1, URUGUAY 0   (0–0)   *Puebla, June 10*
SWEDEN
   S.-G. Larsson; Axelsson, Selander, Nordqvist, Grip, Svensson, B. Larsson,
   Nicklasson, Eriksson, Kindvall, Persson. Subs: Turesson for Kindvall
   (58 mins), Grahn for Nicklasson (83 mins)
URUGUAY
   Mazurkiewicz; Matosas, Ubiñas, Ancheta, Mújica, Montero Castillo,
   Cortés, Maneiro, Zubía, Espárrago, Losada. Sub: Fontes for Espárrago
   (60 mins)
Referee: H. Landauer (U.S.A.). *Scorer:* Grahn
Attendance: 15,000

ITALY 0, ISRAEL 0   (0–0)   *Toluca, June 11*
ITALY
   Albertosi; Burgnich, Cera, Rosato, Facchetti, Bertini, De Sisti, Domen-
   ghini, Mazzola, Boninsegna, Riva. Sub: Rivera for Domenghini (45 mins)
ISRAEL
   Wissoker; Bellow, Shpiegler, Rosen, Bar, Primo, Shoum, Rosenthal,
   Schweger, Faigenbaum, Shpiegel. Sub: Rom for Faigenbaum (45 mins)
Referee: A. de Moraes (Brazil)
Attendance: 7,000

Group Three

ENGLAND 1, RUMANIA 0 (0–0)   *Guadalajara, June 2*
ENGLAND
Banks; Newton, Cooper, Mullery, Labone, Moore, Lee, Ball, R. Charlton, Hurst, Peters. Subs: Wright for Newton (52 mins), Osgood for Lee (77 mins)
RUMANIA
Adamache; Satmareanu, Lupescu, Dinu, Mocanu, Dumitru, Nunweiller, Dembrowski, Tataru, Dumitrache, Lucescu. Sub: Neagu for Tataru (74 mins)

Referee: V. Loraux (Belgium). *Scorer:* Hurst
Attendance: 40,000

BRAZIL 4, CZECHOSLOVAKIA 1 (1–1)   *Guadalajara, June 3*
BRAZIL
Félix; Brito, Piazza, Carlos Alberto, Clodoaldo, Jairzinho, Gérson, Tostão, Pelé, Rivelino, Everaldo. Sub: Paulo Cézar for Gérson (73 mins)
CZECHOSLOVAKIA
Viktor; Dobias, Horvath, Migas, Hagara, Hrdlicka, Kuna, F. Vesely, Petras, Adamec, Jokl. Subs: Kvasnak for Hrdlicka (45 mins), B. Vesely for F. Vesely (77 mins)
Referee: R. Barreto (Uruguay). *Scorers:* Petras (Czechoslovakia)
                                                           Rivelino, Pelé, Jairzinho (2)
                                                           (Brazil)
Attendance: 50,000

RUMANIA 2, CZECHOSLOVAKIA 1 (0–1)   *Guadalajara, June 6*
RUMANIA
Adamache; Satmareanu, Dinu, Lupescu, Mocanu, Dumitru, Neagu, Dembrowski, Nunweiller, Dumitrache, Lucescu. Subs: Tataru for Lucescu (69 mins), Gergely for Dumitru (81 mins)
CZECHOSLOVAKIA
Vencel; Dobias, Horvath, Migas, Zlocha, Kuna, Kvasnak, B. Vesely, Jurkanin, Petras, Jokl. Sub: Adamec for Jurkanin (45 mins). F. Vesely for Jokl (69 mins)
Referee: D. de Leo (Mexico). *Scorers:* Dumitrache, Neagu (Rumania)
                                                           Petras (Czechoslovakia)
Attendance: 53,000

BRAZIL 1, ENGLAND 0 (0–0)   *Guadalajara, June 7*
BRAZIL
Félix; Carlos Alberto, Brito, Piazza, Everaldo, Paulo Cézar, Clodoaldo, Rivelino, Jairzinho, Tostão, Pelé. Sub: Lopes for Tostão (68 mins)
ENGLAND
Banks; Wright, Cooper, Moore, Labone, Mullery, Ball, R. Charlton, Peters, Hurst, Lee. Subs: Astle for Lee (64 mins), Bell for Charlton (64 mins)
Referee: A. Klein (Israel). *Scorer:* Jairzinho
Attendance: 72,000

BRAZIL 3, RUMANIA 2 (2-1) *Guadalajara, June 10*
BRAZIL
Félix; Carlos Alberto, Brito, Piazza, Everaldo, Paulo Cézar, Clodoaldo, Fontana, Jairzinho, Tostão, Pelé. Subs: Marco Antonio for Everaldo (56 mins), Edu for Clodoaldo (73 mins)
RUMANIA
Adamache; Satmareanu, Dumitrache, Dumitru, Lupescu, Dembrowski, Dinu, Mocanu, Nunweiller, Neagu, Lucescu. Subs: Raducanu for Adamache (28 mins), Tataru for Dumitrache (71 mins)
Referee: F. Marschall (Austria). *Scorers:* Jairzinho, Pelé (2) (Brazil)
Dumitrache, Dembrowski
(Rumania)
Attendance: 43,000

ENGLAND 1, CZECHOSLOVAKIA 0 (1-0) *Guadalajara, June 11*
ENGLAND
Banks; Newton, Cooper, Moore, J. Charlton, Mullery, Bell, R. Charlton, Peters, Clarke, Astle. Subs: Osgood for Astle (60 mins), Ball for R. Charlton (65 mins)
CZECHOSLOVAKIA
Viktor; Dobias, Migas, Hagara, Hrivnak, Pollak, Kuna, Capkovic, Petras, Adamec, F. Vesely. Sub: Jokl for Capkovic (70 mins)
Referee: R. Machin (France). *Scorer:* Clarke (pen.)
Attendance: 35,000

Group Four

PERU 3, BULGARIA 2 (0-1) *León, June 2*
PERU
Rubiños; Baylon, Gallardo, Chumpitaz, Cubillas, Campos, De la Torre, Fuentes, Mifflin, Challe, León. Subs: González for Campos (27 mins), Sotil for Baylon (50 mins)
BULGARIA
Simeonov; Bonev, Dermendjiev, Chalamanov, Dimitrov, Penev, Aladjov, Davidov, Yakimov, Popov, Jekov. Subs: Marachliev for Popov (59 mins), Asparoukhov for Bonev (83 mins)
Referee: A. Sbardella (Italy). *Scorers:* Gallardo, Chumpitaz, Cubillas (Peru)
Dermendjiev, Bonev (Bulgaria)
Attendance: 18,000

WEST GERMANY 2, MOROCCO 1 (0-1) *León, June 3*
WEST GERMANY
Maier; Vogts, Schulz, Fichtel, Hottges, Beckenbauer, Overath, Seeler, Haller, Muller, Held. Subs: Grabowski for Haller (46 mins), Lohr for Hottges (74 mins)
MOROCCO
Allal; Lamrani, Benkhrif, Slimani, Moulay, Driss, Maaroufi, Ghazouani, Bamous, Jarir, Filali. Subs: Elkhiatti for Ghazouani (55 mins), Faras for Bamous (70 mins)
Referee: L. van Ravens (Holland). *Scorers:* Jarir (Morocco)
Seeler, Muller (West Germany)
Attendance: 8,000

PERU 3, MOROCCO 0 (0–0) *León, June 6*

PERU
Rubiños; González, De la Torre, Chumpitaz, Fuentes, Mifflin, Challe, Sotil, León, Cubillas, Gallardo. Subs: Cruzado for Mifflin (55 mins), Ramírez for Gallardo (75 mins)

MOROCCO
Allal; Lamrani, Benkhrif, Moulay, Driss, Slimani, Maaroufi, Filali, Said, Bamous, Ghazouani, Jarir. Subs: Fadili for Benkhrif (65 mins), Allaoui for Said (80 mins)

Referee: T. Bakhramov (Russia). *Scorers:* Cubillas (2), Challe
Attendance: 7,000

WEST GERMANY 5, BULGARIA 2 (2–1) *León, June 7*

WEST GERMANY
Maier; Vogts, Schnellinger, Fichtel, Hottges, Beckenbauer, Overath, Libuda, Seeler, Muller, Lohr. Subs: Grabowski for Lohr (58 mins), Weber for Beckenbauer (71 mins)

BULGARIA
Simeonov; Gaydarski, Jetchev, Penev, Gaganelov, Kolev, Bonev, Nikodimov, Dermendjiev, Asparoukhov, Marachliev. Subs: Mitkov for Dermendjiev (45 mins), Chalamanov for Gaganelov (57 mins)

Referee: J. M. de Mendibil (Spain). *Scorers:* Nikodimov, Kolev (Bulgaria)
Libuda, Muller (3), Seeler
(West Germany)

Attendance: 8,000

WEST GERMANY 3, PERU 1 (3–1) *León, June 10*

WEST GERMANY
Maier; Vogts, Schnellinger, Fichtel, Hottges, Beckenbauer, Overath, Libuda, Seeler, Muller, Lohr. Subs: Patzke for Hottges (45 mins), Grabowski for Libuda (74 mins)

PERU
Rubiños; González, De la Torre, Chumpitaz, Fuentes, Challe, Mifflin, Sotil, León, Cubillas, Gallardo. Subs: Ramírez for León (56 mins), Cruzado for Challe (70 mins)

Referee: A. Aguilar (Mexico). *Scorers:* Muller (3) (West Germany)
Cubillas (Peru)
Attendance: 16,000

MOROCCO 1, BULGARIA 1 (0–1) *León, June 11*

MOROCCO
Hazzaz; Ghazouani, Fadili, Moulay Driss, Slimani, Benkhrif, Maaroufi, Bamous, Said, Allaoui, Filali. Subs: Choukri for Bamous (45 mins), Faras for Allaoui (73 mins)

BULGARIA
Yordanov; Jetchev, Chalamanov, Penev, Gaydarski, Nikodimov, Kolev, Yakimov, Popov, Asparoukhov, Mitkov. Subs: Dimitrov for Penev (42 mins), Bonev for Yakimov (62 mins)

Referee: A. Saldanha Ribeiro (Portugal). *Scorers:* Ghazouani (Morocco)
Jetchev (Bulgaria)
Attendance: 5,000

GROUP ONE

	P	W	D	L	F	A	Pts
Russia	3	2	1	0	6	1	5
Mexico	3	2	1	0	5	0	5
Belgium	3	1	0	2	4	5	2
El Salvador	3	0	0	3	0	9	0

GROUP TWO

	P	W	D	L	F	A	Pts
Italy	3	1	2	0	1	0	4
Uruguay	3	1	1	1	2	1	3
Sweden	3	1	1	1	2	2	3
Israel	3	0	2	1	1	3	2

GROUP THREE

	P	W	D	L	F	A	Pts
Brazil	3	3	0	0	8	3	6
England	3	2	0	1	2	1	4
Rumania	3	1	0	2	4	5	2
Czechoslovakia	3	0	0	3	2	7	0

GROUP FOUR

	P	W	D	L	F	A	Pts
West Germany	3	3	0	0	10	4	6
Peru	3	2	0	1	7	5	4
Bulgaria	3	0	1	2	5	9	1
Morocco	3	0	1	2	2	6	1

Quarter-Finals – June 14

U.S.S.R. 0, URUGUAY 1 (after extra time)   (0–0)   *Mexico City*

U.S.S.R.
 Kavazashvili; Afonin, Dzodzuashvili, Kaplichni, Shesternev, Khurt-silava, Asatiani, Muntian, Bishovets, Evriuzhikhin, Khmelnitski. Subs: Kiselev for Asatiani (71 mins), Logofet for Khurtsilava (83 mins)

URUGUAY
 Mazurkiewicz; Ancheta, Matosas, Ubiñas, Montero Castillo, Mújica, Maneiro, Morales, Cortés, Cubilla, Fontes. Subs: Gómez for Morales (90 mins), Espárrago for Fontes (103 mins)

Referee: L. Van Ravens (Holland). *Scorer:* Espárrago

Attendance: 75,000

ITALY 4, MEXICO 1   (1–1)   *Toluca*

ITALY
 Albertosi; Burgnich, Facchetti, Cera, Rosato, Bertini, De Sisti, Domen-ghini, Mazzola, Riva, Boninsegna. Subs: Rivera for Mazzola (45 mins), Gori for Domenghini (86 mins)

MEXICO
 Calderón; Peña, Pérez, Munguía, Padilla, Vantolra, Guzmán, Pulido, González, Valdivia, Fragoso. Subs: Díaz for Munguía (59 mins), Borja for González (67 mins)

Referee: R. Scheurer (Switzerland). *Scorers:* González (Mexico)
                                   Domenghini, Riva (2), Rivera
                                   (Italy)

Attendance: 30,000

BRAZIL 4, PERU 2   (2–1)   *Guadalajara*

BRAZIL
 Félix; Carlos Alberto, Brito, Piazza, Marco Antonio, Gérson, Clodo-aldo, Rivelino, Jairzinho, Tostão, Pelé. Subs: Paulo Cêzar for Gérson (67 mins), Lopes for Jairzinho (80 mins)

PERU
 Rubiños; Campos, Fernández, Chumpitaz, Fuentes, Mifflin, Challe, Baylon, León, Cubillas, Gallardo. Subs: Sotil for Baylon (53 mins), Reyes for León (61 mins)

Referee: V. Loraux (Belgium). *Scorers:* Tostão (2), Jairzinho, Rivelino (Brazil)
                                   Gallardo, Cubillas (Peru)

Attendance: 50,000

WEST GERMANY 3, ENGLAND 2 (after extra time)   (0–1)   *León*

WEST GERMANY
 Maier; Hottges, Schnellinger, Fichtel, Vogts, Beckenbauer, Overath, Libuda, Seeler, Muller, Lohr. Subs: Schulz for Hottges (45 mins), Grabowski for Libuda (57 mins)

ENGLAND
Bonetti; Newton, Labone, Moore, Cooper, Mullery, R. Charlton, Ball, Peters, Lee, Hurst. Subs: Bell for Charlton (69 mins), Hunter for Peters (80 mins)
Referee: N. A. Coerezza (Argentina). *Scorers:* Mullery, Peters (England)
                                        Seeler, Beckenbauer, Muller
Attendance: 30,000   (West Germany)

Semi-Finals

BRAZIL 3, URUGUAY 1 (1-1)   *Guadalajara, June 17*
BRAZIL
Félix; Carlos Alberto, Brito, Piazza, Everaldo, Gérson, Clodoaldo, Rivelino, Jairzinho, Tostão, Pelé
URUGUAY
Mazurkiewicz; Ubiñas, Ancheta, Matosas, Mújica, Montero Castillo, Maneiro, Cortés, Cubilla, Fontes, Morales. Sub: Espárrago for Maneiro (74 mins)
Referee: J. M. de Mendibil (Spain). *Scorers:* Cubilla (Uruguay)
                                  Clodoaldo, Jairzinho, Rivelino
Attendance: 65,000   (Brazil)

ITALY 4, WEST GERMANY 3 (after extra time) (1-0)
                                        Mexico City, June 17
ITALY
Albertosi; Burgnich, Facchetti, Cera, Rosato, Bertini, De Sisti, Domenghini, Mazzola, Riva, Boninsegna. Subs: Rivera for Mazzola (45 mins), Poletti for Rosato (90 mins)
WEST GERMANY
Maier; Schnellinger, Beckenbauer, Schulz, Vogts, Overath, Seeler, Muller, Patzke, Lohr, Grabowski. Subs: Libuda for Lohr (51 mins), Held for Patzke (65 mins)
Referee: A. Yamasaki (Mexico). *Scorers:* Boninsegna, Burgnich, Riva, Rivera (Italy)
                                  Schnellinger, Muller (2) (West
Attendance: 95,000   Germany)

3rd Place Play-Off

WEST GERMANY 1, URUGUAY 0 (1-0)   *Mexico City, June 20*
WEST GERMANY
Wolter; Vogts, Schnellinger, Fichtel, Weber, Patzke, Overath, Libuda, Seeler, Muller, Held. Subs: Lorenz for Schnellinger (45 mins), Lohr for Libuda (73 mins)
URUGUAY
Mazurkiewicz; Ubiñas, Ancheta, Matosas, Mújica, Montero Castillo, Maneiro, Cortés, Cubilla, Morales, Fontes. Subs: Espárrago for Fontes (45 mins), Sandoval for Maneiro (67 mins)
Referee: A. Sbardella (Italy). *Scorer:* Overath
Attendance: 60,000

Final

BRAZIL 4, ITALY 1 (1-1)   *Mexico City, June 21*

BRAZIL
Félix; Carlos Alberto, Brito, Piazza, Everaldo, Gérson, Clodoaldo, Rivelino, Jairzinho, Tostão, Pelé

ITALY
Albertosi; Burgnich, Facchetti, Cera, Rosato, Bertini, Domenghini, De Sisti, Mazzola, Riva, Boninsegna. Subs: Juliano for Bertini (74 mins), Rivera for Boninsegna (83 mins)

Referee: R. Glockner (East Germany). *Scorers:* Boninsegna (Italy)
Pelé, Gérson, Jairzinho, Carlos Alberto, (Brazil)

Attendance: 112,000